APIL Guide to Costs and Funding

APIL Guide to Costs and Funding

Gary Barker, Mark Harvey & David Marshall

JORDANS

Published by
Jordan Publishing Limited
21 St Thomas Street
Bristol BS1 6JS

Whilst the publishers and the author have taken every care in preparing the material included in this work, any statements made as to the legal or other implications of particular transactions are made in good faith purely for general guidance and cannot be regarded as a substitute for professional advice. Consequently, no liability can be accepted for loss or expense incurred as a result of relying in particular circumstances on statements made in this work.

© Jordan Publishing Limited 2014

All rights reserved. No part of this publication may be reproduced, stored in a retrieval system, or transmitted in any way or by any means, including photocopying or recording, without the written permission of the copyright holder, application for which should be addressed to the publisher.

Crown Copyright material is reproduced with kind permission of the Controller of Her Majesty's Stationery Office.

British Library Cataloguing-in-Publication Data

A catalogue record for this book is available from the British Library.

ISBN 978 1 84661 784 3

Typeset by Letterpart Limited, Caterham on the Hill, Surrey CR3 5XL

Printed in Great Britain by CPI Antony Rowe, Chippenham and Eastbourne

ASSOCIATION OF PERSONAL INJURY LAWYERS (APIL)

APIL is the UK's leading association of claimant personal injury lawyers, dedicated to protecting the rights of injured people.

Formed in 1990, APIL now represents around 5,000 solicitors, barristers, academics and students in the UK, Republic of Ireland and overseas.

APIL's objectives are:

- to promote full and just compensation for all types of personal injury;
- to promote and develop expertise in the practice of personal injury law;
- to promote wider redress for personal injury in the legal system;
- to campaign for improvements in personal injury law;
- to promote safety and alert the public to hazards;
- to provide a communication network for members.

APIL is a growing and influential forum pushing for law reform, and improvements, which will benefit injured people.

APIL has been running CPD training events, accredited by the Solicitors Regulation Authority and Bar Standards Board, for nearly 20 years and has a wealth of experience in developing the most practical up-to-date courses, delivered by eminent leading speakers, either publicly or in-house.

APIL training now runs almost 200 personal injury training events nationally each year, plus up to a further 100 meetings of our regional and special interest groups. Topics cover a wide range of subjects and are geared towards giving personal injury lawyers a thorough grounding in the core areas of personal injury law, whilst keeping lawyers thoroughly up to date in all subjects.

APIL is also an authoritative information source for personal injury lawyers, providing up-to-the-minute PI bulletins, regular newsletters and publications, information databases and online services.

For further information contact:

APIL
3 Alder Court
Rennie Hogg Road
Nottingham NG2 1RX
DX 716208 Nottingham 42
Tel 0115 9580585
Email mail@apil.org.uk
Website www.apil.org.uk

PREFACE

April 2013 saw a fundamental change in civil litigation which went further than just the so-called 'Jackson reforms'. Out went 'loser pays' in personal injury litigation and recoverable additional liabilities, whilst in came qualified one-way costs shifting, a new definition to proportionality, budgeting and provisional assessment.

The early uncertainty of how the courts would tackle these changes (not helped when almost before the ink was dry on the revised rules the senior judges decided to exempt the commercial courts from budgeting when this was supposed to apply to all litigation) was soon replaced by a feeling of shock, some anger and then closely followed by bewilderment. The Court of Appeal's first clarion call in the *Mitchell* case sent a shudder through practitioners. Realising there was going to be a much harsher regime in which they would be practising was one thing; the somewhat mixed way in which the judges applied it was another. Some appeared to ignore the Court's phrase de minimis and set about applying a scorched earth policy to every application for relief. Shortly after that and as a result of this mood parties began to stop agreeing even routine extensions of time for fear they may be doing their client a disservice by eschewing a potential windfall result of a debarring or even striking out order. The Royal Courts of Justice Masters then sought to calm the mood with the unusual step of issuing their draft direction in clinical negligence cases in the RCJ only by which the parties were given a limited disposition to agree extensions of time, to be followed in other cases. And so the new climate has arrived and although the *Mitchell* decision arose out of budgeting and the filing of the fearsome Precedent H, we still await guidance on what budgets will be allowed and how the court will determine what is proportionality in each case.

Against this background APIL and its authors hope this book is both timely and of some comfort. The authors, whilst having a specific interest in the subject of costs and funding, are also practitioners. Hence they have attempted to help the practitioner with background, detail and guidance to all of the elements of the new world of costs and funding. The busy practitioner will need to become familiar with the new funding alternatives and the greater scope for the claimant to be charged for the work they benefit from. Then they will need to be well informed as to both the value of the claim and the costs involved in winning it so that they can produce a reasonable budget that anticipates the court's view on proportionality. Finally, they will need to be ready to support their costs claims in one of the three ways of having their costs determined by the court: summary and detailed assessment and the new provisional assessment.

The authors hope that this book will go some way to helping the busy practitioner navigate their way through the new and challenging reforms that run through the litigation. They wish to thank Tony Hawitt their editor for his guidance and significant involvement in the book, particularly the sensitive way he tells a lawyer how to write!

Grateful thanks are also offered to Victoria Walne, solicitor, for her assistance with the chapter on qualified one-way costs shifting and to our partners and colleagues for their help and support whilst this book was written. All and any errors are our own and we apologise for them!

February 2014

CONTENTS

Association of Personal Injury Lawyers (APIL)   v
Preface   vii
Table of Cases   xv
Table of Statutes   xix
Table of Statutory Instruments   xxi

Chapter 1
Code of Conduct and Funding Options   1
1.1   Solicitors Regulation Authority (SRA)   1
       Ten Principles   1
       Risk management and compliance   2
       Alternative business structures (ABS)   3
1.2   Client care and costs   3
1.3   Outcomes   5
1.4   Indicative behaviours   7
       Funding information to client   8
1.5   Referral arrangements   10
1.6   Retainer   13
1.7   The Cancellation of Contracts Made in a Consumer's Home or Place of Work etc Regulations 2008   14
1.8   Consumer Protection (Distance Selling) Regulations 2000   16
1.9   Solicitor and own client costs   18
1.10   Counsel   19

Chapter 2
Conditional Fee Agreements   21
2.1   The development of conditional fees   21
2.2   CFAs – 1 November 2005 to 31 March 2013   23
2.3   1 April 2013 CFAs   24
       Personal injury exceptions   25
       Qualifying date for the post-April regime   26
       Appeals   26
       Counsel   26
       Form   27
       Legal expenses insurance   28
       Satisfactory BTE insurance   29
       Freedom of choice   30
       Appointment by the BTE firm concerned   31

		What retainer?	31
		Terms and conditions of business	32
		Discounted CFA	32
		Satisfactory BTE but where the insurers will not appoint the firm	32
		Self insurance	33
		Advising on insurance	34
		Disbursements	34
		Completing the agreement	35
		Calculating the success fee	37
2.4		Exceptional cases	37
		Assignments of CFAs	37
		Personal Contracts	38
		The burden (as opposed to the benefit) of a contract cannot be assigned.	39
		Specific issues	40
2.5		Defective CFAs	46
		Rectification	47
		Deed of variation	47
		Equitable rectification by the court	48
		Terminate the existing CFA and start again	48
		Retrospectivity	49
		Recoverability of ATE	52
		Price increase clause	52
		Notice	53

Chapter 3
Damages-based Agreements 55
3.1	Introduction	55
	Contingency fees in the United Kingdom	55
	Overseas experience	56
	The Civil Justice Council	58
	The Jackson review	58
	Civil Justice Council Working Party	60
3.2	Damages-based agreements: statutory requirements	61
	Legal Aid, Sentencing and Punishment of Offenders Act 2012 (LASPO)	61
	A compliant DBA is 'not unenforceable'	61
	What is a DBA?	62
	Requirements prescribed by statute	66
	Further requirements prescribed by regulations	66
	Additional requirements for personal injury claims	69
	The indemnity principle applies	71
3.3	Liability for adverse costs	71
3.4	DBAs in practice	73
3.5	CFA v DBA	74
3.6	Content of a DBA	76
3.7	The future	79

Chapter 4
Qualified One-Way Costs Shifting — 81
4.1	Introduction	81
4.2	Jackson report	82
4.3	QOCS in practice	83
4.4	QOCS and Part 36 offers	86
4.5	Strike out applications	88
4.6	'Fundamental dishonesty'	89
4.7	Mixed claims	91
4.8	QOCS and ATE insurance	93
4.9	Discontinued claims	94
4.10	Appeals	94

Chapter 5
Fixed Recoverable Costs — 97
5.1	Introduction	97
	Solicitor and client costs, fixed costs and fixed recoverable costs	97
	Lord Woolf and beyond	98
	Swings and roundabouts?	99
	CPR format	100
	Budgets	100
5.2	Fixed recoverable cost regimes implemented prior to 2013	100
	Small claims track	100
	Fixed trial costs in the fast track	102
	'Predictive costs' regime: accidents 6 October 2003–31 July 2013	102
	The first portal (road accident cases only, claim notifications 30 April 2010–29 April 2013)	104
	MIB schemes	105
	Uninsured drivers	105
	Untraced drivers	106
5.3	The second portal (the 2013 amendments)	107
	Road traffic cases	108
	The portal for accidents after 31 July 2013	108
	Offers within the portal	109
	Settlements for children	110
	Failure to follow the protocol	111
	Cases that fall out of the protocol	111
5.4	Fixed recoverable costs in the fast track	111
	Fast track fixed recoverable costs	112
	The stages	113
	Disbursements	113
	Children	114
	Escape	114
	Defendant's costs	115
	Costs of interim applications	116

	Offers	116
	Defendant's offers	117
	Claimant's offer	117
5.5	London weighting	118
5.6	Multiple claimants	119
5.7	Counsel	119
5.8	Working with fixed recoverable costs	119
5.9	Fixed recoverable costs: the future	120
5.10	Summary of applicable fixed recoverable costs schemes	120

Chapter 6
Cost Orders 123
6.1	Proportionality	123
	Post 1 April 2013	125
	Transitional provisions	126
6.2	Budgeting	129
	Planning – the firm	130
	The case	132
	Teamwork	134
	Post issue	135
	Completing the form	137
	Failure to file a budget	140
	Cost management orders	141
	Cost management conferences	142
	Preparation for the budgeting hearing	142
6.3	Costs capping	146
6.4	Costs process	148
6.5	Variations	152
6.6	Court's discretion as to costs	155
6.7	Summary assessment	156

Chapter 7
Part 36 and Offers to Settle 157
7.1	History	157
7.2	Jackson reforms	158
7.3	How to deal with an offer	159
7.4	The law	160
7.5	Non-portal offers	160
	Formalities	160
	Timing and clarification of an offer	161
	Acceptance of an offer	162
	When permission is needed to accept an offer	162
	Amount as single sum, periodic payment, etc	164
	Interest on amount offered	165
	Deductible benefits	165
	Costs consequences of accepting an offer within the period for acceptance	166
	Late acceptance of an offer outside the period for acceptance	167

		Procedure following acceptance of offer	171
		Costs consequences following trial	171
		Costs following a trial on liability or a preliminary issue	174
		Withdrawal of an offer	174
		Tactical Part 36 offer	175
		Defendant failing to make a Part 36 offer	176
	7.6	Portal offers	176

Chapter 8
Trial — 179
8.1	Introduction	179
8.2	Summary assessment	180
8.3	Final hearing summary assessment	180
8.4	Multitrack	182

Chapter 9
Detailed Assessment — 185
9.1	General	185
9.2	Time for detailed assessment of costs	185
9.3	Effect of an appeal	186
9.4	Authorised court officer	186
9.5	Costs disclosure	187
9.6	Venue for assessment	188
9.7	Time for assessment procedure	189
9.8	Assessment procedure – party and party costs	190
9.9	Form of bill of costs	191
9.10	Points of dispute	193
9.11	Costs agreed	194
9.12	Default costs certificate	194
9.13	Requesting an assessment hearing	195
9.14	Provisional costs assessment	196
9.15	Detailed assessment hearing	199
9.16	Detailed assessment – tactics	201
9.17	Conditional fee agreements signed before 1 April 2013	203
	Costs disclosure	203

Appendix 1
The Damages-Based Agreements Regulations 2013, SI 2013/609 — 207

Appendix 2
Law Society Model Agreement (For Use in Cases after 1 April 2013) — 215

Appendix 3
Precedent H – Costs Budgets — 231

Appendix 4
Andrew Mitchell MP v News Group Newspapers Limited [2013]
EWCA Civ 1537   241

Index   261

TABLE OF CASES

References are to paragraph numbers.

AB v CD [2011] EWHC 602	7.5.12
Acre 1127 Ltd (In Liquidation) (formerly Castle Galleries Ltd) v De Monford Fine Art Ltd [2011] EWCA Civ 130	7.5.11
Ahmed v The Bread Roll Company Ltd [2009] EWHC 90141, Costs	1.4.1
Arkin v Borchard Lines Ltd [2005] EWCA Civ 655, [2005] 1 WLR 3055, [2005] 3 All ER 613, [2005] 2 Lloyd's Rep 187, [2005] CP Rep 39, [2005] 4 Costs LR 643, (2005) 155 NLJ 902, (2005) *Times*, 3 June, (2005) *Independent*, 7 June	3.3
Awwad v Geraghty & Co (a firm) Awwad v Geraghty & Co (a firm) [2001] QB 570, [2000] 3 WLR 1041, [2000] 1 All ER 608, [2000] 1 Costs LR 105, [1999] NPC 148, (1999) *Independent*, 1 December	3.1.1
Bailey v IBC Vehicles Limited [1998] 3 All ER 570, [1998] 2 Costs LR 46, (1998) 142 SJLB 126, (1998) *Times*, 9 April	9.5
Baldwyn v Smith [1900] 1 Ch 588	2.4.1.3
Beasley v Alexander [2012] EWHC 2715 (QB), [2013] 1 WLR 762, [2012] 6 Costs LR 1137, [2013] RTR 7, (2012) *Times*, 2 November	7.5.12
Brennon v Associated Asphalt [2006] EWHC 90052 (Costs) 18 May 2006	2.5.1
C v D [2011] EWCA Civ 646, [2012] 1 WLR 1962, [2012] 1 All ER 302, [2011] CP Rep 38, 136 Con LR 109, [2011] 5 Costs LR 773, [2011] 2 EGLR 95, [2011] 23 EG 86 (CS), (2011) 161 NLJ 780	7.5.1
Carver v BAA plc [2008] EWCA Civ 412, [2009] 1 WLR 113, [2008] 3 All ER 911, [2008] CP Rep 30, [2008] 5 Costs LR 779, [2008] PIQR P15, [2008] LS Law Medical 351, (2008) 152(17) SJLB 28, *Times*, June 4, 2008	4.4
Cawdery Kaye Fireman & Taylor v Minkin [2012] EWCA Civ 546, [2012] 3 All ER 1117, [2012] 4 Costs LR 650, [2013] 2 FCR 125, [2012] PNLR 26, [2012] 19 EG 94 (CS), (2012) 162 NLJ 681, (2012) 156(18) SJLB 31	1.6
Cook v Graham (unreported) 2005 Liverpool CC	5.2.3
Crane v Cannons Leisure [2007] EWCA Civ 1352, [2008] 1 WLR 2549, [2008] 2 All ER 931, [2008] CP Rep 15, [2008] 1 Costs LR 132, (2008) 105(1) LSG 23, (2008) 158 NLJ 103, (2008) *Times*, 10 January	2.4.1.3
Crook v Birmingham City Council (unreported) 21 August 2006, SCCO	2.5.5
David Truex Solicitor (a firm) v Kitchen [2007] EWCA Civ 618, [2007] 4 Costs LR 587, [2007] 2 FLR 1203, [2007] PNLR 33, [2007] Fam Law 903, (2007) 157 NLJ 1011, (2007) 151 SJLB 926, [2007] NPC 87, (2007) *Times*, 29 August	1.4.1
Davies v Jones [2009] EWCA Civ 1164	2.4.1.2
Drew v Nunn (1879) 4 QBD 661	2.4.1.3
Durrant v Chief Constable of Avon & Somerset Constabulary [2013] EWCA Civ 1624	9.17.1
Dyson v Hoover [2003] EWHC 624 (Pat), [2004] 1 WLR 1264, [2003] 2 All ER 1042, [2003] CP Rep 45, (2003) 100(15) LSG 25, *Times*, March 18, 2003	8.4
Elvanite Full Circle Ltd v AMEC Earth and Environmental (UK) Ltd [2013] EWHC 1643 (TCC), [2013] 4 All ER 765, [2013] BLR 473, [2013] TCLR 7, [2013] 4 Costs LR 612, [2013] CILL 3385	6.5

Excelsior Commercial and Industrial Holdings Ltd v Salisbury Hamer Aspden and
 Johnson, a firm [2002] EWCA Civ 879, [2002] CP Rep 67, [2002] CPLR 693,
 (2002) *Independent*, 18 June   7.5.11

F & C Alternative Investments (Holdings) Ltd v Barthelemy [2012] EWCA Civ 843,
 [2013] 1 WLR 548, [2012] 4 All ER 1096, [2013] Bus LR 186, [2013] 1 Costs LR
 35   7.5.1
Findley v Jones (1) and MIB (2) (unreported) SCCO Master Hurst, 13 January 2009   2.4.1.3
Fitzpatrick Contractors Ltd v Tyco Fire & Integrated Solutions (UK) Ltd [2009] EWHC
 274 (TCC), [2009] BLR 144, 123 Con LR 69, [2010] 2 Costs LR 115, [2009] CILL
 2700   7.5.9, 7.5.11
Flatman v Germany [2013] EWCA Civ 278, [2013] 1 WLR 2676, [2013] 4 All ER 349,
 [2013] CP Rep 31, (2013) 163(7556) NLJ 16, (2013) 157(15) SJLB 31   2.3.16, 3.3
Floods of Queensferry Ltd v Shand Construction Ltd [2002] EWCA Civ 918, [2003]
 Lloyd's Rep IR 181   2.3.16
Forde v Birmingham City Council [2009] EWHC 12 (QB), [2009] 1 WLR 2732, [2010] 1
 All ER 802, [2009] 2 Costs LR 206, [2009] NPC 7   2.4.1.3, 2.5.5
Forstater v Python (Monty) Pictures Ltd [2013] EWHC 3759   9.17.1
Fox v Foundation Piling Ltd [2011] EWCA Civ 790, [2011] CP Rep 41, [2011] 6 Costs
 LR 961   7.5.11, 7.5.15

Garbett v Edwards [2005] EWCA Civ 1206, [2006] 1 WLR 2907, [2006] 1 All ER 553,
 [2006] CP Rep 8, [2006] 1 Costs LR 143, (2005) 102(43) LSG 30, [2005] NPC 122,
 (2005) *Times*, 3 November   2.2
Garrett v Halton BC, Myatt and others v NCB [2006] EWCA Civ 1017, [2007] 1 WLR
 554, [2007] 1 All ER 147, [2006] 5 Costs LR 798, (2006) 103(31) LSG 26, (2006)
 150 SJLB 1190, (2006) *Times*, 25 July, (2006) *Independent*, 26 July   3.2.1.1, 3.6
Gibbon v Manchester City Council: LG Blower Specialist Bricklayer Ltd v Reeves [2010]
 EWCA Civ 726, [2010] 1 WLR 2081, [2011] 2 All ER 258, [2010] CP Rep 40,
 [2010] 5 Costs LR 828, [2010] PIQR P16, [2010] 3 EGLR 85, [2010] 36 EG 120,
 [2010] 27 EG 84 (CS)   7.5.3, 7.5.13
Gloucester CC v Evans [2008] EWCA Civ 21, [2008] 1 WLR 1883, [2008] 2 Costs LR
 308, (2008) 158 NLJ 219   2.3.12
Gundry v Sainsbury [1910] 1 KB 645, [1997] Costs LR (Core Vol) 1   9.1

Hemming (t/a Simply Pleasure Ltd) v Westminster City Council [2012] EWHC 1582
 (Admin)   7.5.11
Henry v News Group Newspapers Limited [2013] EWCA Civ 19, [2013] 2 All ER 840,
 [2013] CP Rep 20, [2013] 2 Costs LR 334, (2013) 163 NLJ 140, (2013) 157(5) SJLB
 31   6.5
Hodgson v Imperial Tobacco Ltd [1998] 1 WLR 1056, [1998] 2 All ER 673, [1998] 1
 Costs LR 14, [1999] PIQR Q1, (1998) 41 BMLR 1, (1998) 95(15) LSG 31, (1998)
 148 NLJ 241, (1998) 142 SJLB 93, (1998) *Times*, 13 February, (1998) *Independent*,
 17 February   3.3
Hollins v Russell [2003] EWCA Civ 718, [2003] 1 WLR 2487, [2003] 4 All ER 590,
 [2003] 3 Costs LR 423, (2003) 100(28) LSG 30, (2003) 153 NLJ 920, (2003) 147
 SJLB 662, (2003) *Times*, 10 June, (2003) *Independent*, 3 June   2.5, 3.2.1.1
Holmes v Alfred McAlpine [2006] EWHC 110 (QB), [2006] 3 Costs LR 466, (2006) 150
 SJLB 263   2.5.5
Home Office v Lownds [2002] EWCA Civ 365, [2002] 1 WLR 2450, [2002] 4 All ER
 775, [2002] CP Rep 43, [2002] CPLR 328, [2002] 2 Costs LR 279, (2002) 99(19)
 LSG 28, (2002) 146 SJLB 86, (2002) *Times*, 5 April   6.1
Hutchings v British Transport Police [2006] EWHC 900064, Costs   9.17.1

Jefferson v National Freight [2001] EWCA Civ 2082, [2001] 2 Costs LR 313   6.1.2
Jenkins v Young Bros [2006] EWHC 151 (QB), [2006] 1 WLR 3189, [2006] 2 All ER
 798, [2006] 3 Costs LR 495   2.4.1.2

Table of Cases

Kellar v Williams [2004] UKPC 30, 148 Sol Jo LB 821, [2005] 1 LRC 582, [2004] All ER (D) 286, Jun — 2.5.5

King v Telegraph Group Ltd [2004] EWCA Civ 613, [2005] 1 WLR 2282, [2004] CP Rep 35, [2004] 3 Costs LR 449, [2004] EMLR 23, (2004) 101(25) LSG 27, (2004) 154 NLJ 823, (2004) 148 SJLB 664, (2004) *Times*, 21 May — 2.3.16

KU v Liverpool City Council [2005] EWCA Civ 475, [2005] 1 WLR 2657, [2005] 4 Costs LR 600, (2005) *Times*, 16 May — 2.3.18

Kunaka v Barclays Bank plc [2010] EWCA Civ 1035, [2011] 2 Costs LR 179 — 7.5.9

Kyriakides & Braier (A Firm) v Klamer [2005] EWHC 90013, Costs — 1.6

Little v George Little Sebire & Co [2001] EWCA Civ 894, [2001] STC 1065, [2001] BTC 292 — 7.5.11

Long v Value Properties Ltd & Another [2014] EWHC SCCO JR130605713 January — 9.17.1

Lumb v Hampsey [2011] EWHC 2808, QB — 7.5.9

Mars UK Ltd v Teknowledge Ltd (No 2) [2000] ECDR 99, [1998-99] Info TLR 331, [1999] Masons CLR 322, (1999) 22(8) IPD 22076, (1999) *Times*, 23 June, (1999) *Independent*, 1 July — 8.4

McGinty v Pipe [2012] EWHC 506, QB — 7.5.11

McPhilemy v Times Newspapers Ltd [2001] EWCA Civ 933, [2002] 1 WLR 934, [2001] 4 All ER 861, [2002] CP Rep 9, [2001] 2 Costs LR 295, [2001] EMLR 35, (2001) *Times*, 3 July — 7.5.11

Mitchell v News Group Newspapers Limited [2013] EWCA Civ 1537; [2013] 6 Costs LR 1008; (2013) 163(7587) NLJ 20 — 6.2.6, 9.17.1

Morrish & Co v No-one APIL Focus vol 13, issue 1, February 2003, Leeds County Court) — 2.5.3

Morrison v Buckinghamshire County Council SCCO 20 January 2011, HQ09D05424 — 6.4

Motto v Trafigura Limited [2011] EWCA Civ 1150, [2012] 1 WLR 657, [2012] 2 All ER 181, [2011] 6 Costs LR 1028, (2011) *Times*, 22 November — 2.3.7

Musa King v Telegraph [2004] EWCA Civ 613, [2005] 1 WLR 2282, [2004] CP Rep 35, [2004] 3 Costs LR 449, [2004] EMLR 23, (2004) 101(25) LSG 27, (2004) 154 NLJ 823, (2004) 148 SJLB 664, (2004) *Times*, 21 May — 2.5.5

Myatt v National Coal Board (No 2) [2007] EWCA Civ 307, [2007] 1 WLR 1559, [2007] 4 All ER 1094, [2007] 4 Costs LR 564, [2007] PNLR 25, *Times*, March 27, 2007 — 3.3

Myatt v National Coal Board and Garrett v Halton Borough Council [2006] EWCA Civ 1017, [2007] 1 WLR 554, [2007] 1 All ER 147, [2006] 5 Costs LR 798, (2006) 103(31) LSG 26, (2006) 150 SJLB 1190, (2006) *Times*, 25 July, (2006) *Independent*, 26 July — 2.1

Nizami v Butt [2006] EWHC 159 (QB), [2006] 1 WLR 3307, [2006] 2 All ER 140, [2006] 3 Costs LR 483, [2006] RTR 25, (2006) 103(9) LSG 30, (2006) 156 NLJ 272 — 5.1.1

Oyston v RBS [2006] EWHC 90053 (Costs) 16 May 2006 — 2.5.2

Patel v Fortis Insurance Ltd [2011] EWCC Leicester 23 December LTL 11 January 2012 — 5.3.5

Pearless De Rougemont & Co v Pilbrow [1999] 3 All ER 355, [1999] 2 Costs LR 109, [1999] 2 FLR 139, (1999) 149 NLJ 441, (1999) 143 SJLB 114, (1999) *Times*, 25 March, (1999) *Independent*, 10 May — 1.6

Petrotrade Inc v Texaco Ltd [2002] 1 WLR 947 (Note), [2001] 4 All ER 853, [2001] CP Rep 29, [2000] CLC 1341, [2002] 1 Costs LR 60, (2000) *Times*, 14 June, (2000) *Independent*, 10 July — 7.5.11

Proform Sports Management Ltd v (1) Proactive Sports Management Ltd (2) Paul Stretford [2006] EWHC 2903 (Ch), [2007] 1 All ER 542, [2007] 1 All ER (Comm) 356, [2007] Bus LR 93, (2006) 156 NLJ 1723, (2006) *Times*, 13 November — 2.4.1.3

Ryan Beach v Dimitri Smirnov (1) and Service Point (UK) Limited [2007] EWHC 3499 (QB) — 8.4

Safetynet Security Limited v Coppage [2013] EWCA Civ 1176, [2013] IRLR 970	6.2.9
Sarwa v Alam [2001] EWCA Civ 1401, [2002] 1 WLR 125, [2001] 4 All ER 541, [2002] 1 Costs LR 37, [2002] RTR 12, [2002] Lloyd's Rep IR 126, [2002] PIQR P15, (2001) 151 NLJ 1492, (2001) *Times*, 11 October, (2001) *Daily Telegraph*, 25 September	2.3.6
SG v Hewitt [2012] EWCA Civ 1053, [2013] 1 All ER 1118, [2012] 5 Costs LR 937	4.4, 7.5.9, 7.5.11
Sharratt v London Central Bus Co Ltd and Other Appeals (The Accident Group Test Cases), Hollins v Russell and Other Appeals [2003] EWCA Civ 718, [2003] 1 WLR 2487, [2003] 4 All ER 590, [2003] 3 Costs LR 423, (2003) 100(28) LSG 30, (2003) 153 NLJ 920, (2003) 147 SJLB 662, (2003) *Times*, 10 June, (2003) *Independent*, 3 June	2.1
Sibthorpe v Southwark [2011] EWCA Civ 25, [2011] 1 WLR 2111, [2011] 2 All ER 240, [2011] CP Rep 21, [2011] 3 Costs LR 427, [2011] HLR 19, (2011) 108(6) LSG 18, (2011) 161 NLJ 173, [2011] NPC 11, (2011) *Times*, 14 February	2.3.14, 3.3
Simpson's Motor Sales (London) Limited v Hendon Corporation (No 2) (1965) [1965] 1 WLR 112, [1964] 3 All ER 833, (1965) 109 SJ 32	9.5
Soliman v London Borough of Islington 2001 LTL16/10/01	8.4
Solomon v Cromwell Group and Oliver v Doughty [2011] EWCA Civ 1584, [2012] 1 WLR 1048, [2012] 2 All ER 825, [2012] CP Rep 14, [2012] 2 Costs LR 314, [2012] RTR 24, [2012] PIQR P9	7.5.8
Southway v Wolff 57 BLR 33, 28 Con LR 109, [1991] EG 82 (CS), (1991) *Independent*, 30 August	2.4.1.2
Stevens v Watts [2000] LTL July 14	6.1.2
Sullivan v Co-operative Insurance Society [1999] CPLR 487, [1999] 2 Costs LR 158, *Times*, May 19, 1999, Independent, May 18, 1999	9.16
Summers v Fairclough Homes Limited [2012] UKSC 26, [2012] 1 WLR 2004, [2012] 4 All ER 317, [2012] 4 Costs LR 760, [2013] Lloyd's Rep IR 159, (2012) 162 NLJ 910, (2012) 156(26) SJLB 31, (2012) *Times*, 18 July	4.5
Swatton v Smithurst (unreported) 3 February 2005 (unreported) Liverpool CC	5.2.3
Thewlis v Groupama [2012] EWHC 3 (TCC), [2012] BLR 259, [2012] TCLR 3, 142 Con LR 85, [2012] 5 Costs LO 560	7.5.1
Thompson & Thompson (By Their Father & Litigation Friend Christopher Thompson & Maureen Williams (Administrators of the Estate of Tracy Ann Williams, Deceased)) v Bruce [2011] EWHC 2228 (QB)	7.5.8
Tinseltime Ltd v Roberts & Ors [2012] EWHC 2628 (TCC), [2012] TCLR 9, [2012] 6 Costs LR 1094, [2013] PNLR 4, (2012) 162 NLJ 1290, (2012) 156(38) SJLB 31	2.3.16
Tito v Wadell [1977] Ch 106, [1977] 2 WLR 496, [1977] 3 All ER 129, (1976) 121 SJ 10, *Times*, December 6, 1976	2.4.1.2
Tolhurst v Portland Cement [1902] 2 KB 660, [1903] AC 414	2.4.1.2
Truscott v Truscott, Wraith v Sheffield Forgemasters Ltd [1998] 1 WLR 132, [1998] 1 All ER 82, [1997] 2 Costs LR 74, [1998] 1 FLR 265, [1998] 1 FCR 270, [1998] Fam Law 74, (1997) *Times*, 15 October	9.16
United Airlines Inc v United Airways Limited [2011] EWHC 2411 (Ch)	8.4
Vinayak v Lovegrove and Eliot [2007] EWHC 10 July SCCO	9.5
Walsh v Singh [2011] EWCA Civ 87	7.5.7
Wharton v Bancroft [2012] EWHC 91 (Ch), [2012] WTLR 727	7.5.14
Willis v MRJ Rundell [2013] EWHC 2923 (TCC), [2013] 6 Costs LR 924, [2013] CILL 3428	6.4
Yonge v Toynbee [1910] 1 KB 215, [1908-10] All ER Rep 204, 79 LJKB 208, CA	2.4.1.3

TABLE OF STATUTES

References are to paragraph numbers.

Access to Justice Act 1999	2.1, 2.2, 2.4.1.3, 4.2
s 27	2.2
s 29	2.1, 2.3.6, 4.2
s 30	9.17.1
Compensation Act 2006	
s 4(2)	3.2.1.2
Courts and Legal Services Act 1990	2.1, 2.2, 2.3.1, 3.1.1, 3.2.1, 3.2.1.1, 3.2.1.4
s 1	2.3.1
s 58	2.2, 3.1.1, 3.2.1.1
s 58(4)	2.1
s 58A(1)	3.2.1.3
s 58AA	3.2.1, 3.2.1.1, 3.2.1.2
s 58AA(4)(c)	3.2.1.4
s 58AA(7A)	3.2.1.2
s 58C(2)	2.3.1
s 58C(3)	2.3.1
s 58C(4)	2.3.1
s 119	3.2.1.2
Criminal Injuries Compensation Act 1995	3.2.1.2
Defective Premises Act 1972	3.2.1.2
s 4	3.2.1.2
Environmental Protection Act 1990	3.2.1.2
s 82	2.3, 3.2.1.2
Fatal Accidents Act 1976	4.3, 4.7, 7.5.4
s 1(3)	4.7
Financial Services and Markets Act 2000	2.3.14

Landlord and Tenant Act 1985	3.2.1.2
s 11	3.2.1.2
Law Reform (Miscellaneous Provisions) Act 1934	4.3, 7.5.4
s 1(1)	4.3
Legal Aid, Sentencing and Punishment of Offenders Act 2012	2.3, 2.5.5.1, 4.1
s 44	2.3
s 44(2)	3.6
s 45	2.3, 3.2.1
s 46	2.3, 4.8
s 47	2.3, 4.8
s 56	1.5
s 57	1.5
s 58	1.5
s 59	1.5
s 60	1.5
Limitation Act 1980	
s 11	6.2.3
Mental Capacity Act 2005	2.4.1.3
s 7	2.4.1.3
Senior Courts Act 1981	5.1.1
s 51	5.1.1
Solicitors Act 1974	1.6, 1.9, 2.5.5, 3.1.1, 3.2.1.2
s 57	3.2.1.2
s 59	2.5.5
s 68	1.9
s 70	1.9
Unsolicited Goods and Services Act 1971	1.8
s 1	1.8
s 2	1.8

TABLE OF STATUTORY INSTRUMENTS

References are to paragraph numbers.

Cancellation of Contracts made in a Consumer's Home or Place of Work etc Regulations 2008,
SI 2008/1816   2.3.17, 9.17.1
reg 16   2.3.17
Civil Procedure Rules 1998,
SI 1998/3132   2.1, 3.2.1.2, 3.3, 5.1.1, 5.1.2, 7.1
    r 1.1   9.1
    r 2.2   6.4
    r 2.3   3.2.1.5, 4.3, 4.10
    r 2.4   6.4
    r 2.11   9.7
    Pt 3   5.1.5
    r 3.1(2)(a)   9.7
    r 3.3   6.2.4
    r 3.4(2)   4.5
    r 3.4(2)(a)   4.5
    r 3.4(2)(b)   4.5
    r 3.4(2)(c)   4.5
    r 3.13   6.2.4, 6.2.5
    r 3.14   6.2.6
    r 3.15   6.2.7, 6.4
    r 3.16   6.2.8
    r 3.17   6.2.9
    r 3.18.   6.2.9
    r 3.19(5)   6.3
    r 3.20(2)(b)   6.3
    r 3.21   6.3
    PD 3E   6.2.9
      para 1   6.2.4
      para 2.2   6.4
      para 2.3   6.4
    Pt 7   5.3.5
    r 16.3   5.4.6
    Pt 23   1.9, 7.4, 9.4, 9.9, 9.11
    Pt 26   6.2.4
    r 26.1   5.2.1
    r 26.3(1)   6.2.4
    r 27.14   5.2.1
    r 27.14(h)   5.2.1
    PD 27   5.2.1
    Pt 31   6.4
    Pt 32   6.4
    r 32.1   6.2.9
    r 35.4(2)   6.2.3
    Pt 36   2.1, 4.1, 4.3, 4.5, 4.6, 4.8, 5.3.3, 5.4.8, 5.4.8.1, 5.4.8.2, 7.1, 7.2, 7.3, 7.4, 7.5.7, 7.5.11, 7.5.13, 7.5.14, 7.5.15, 8.4, 9.7

Civil Procedure Rules 1998,
SI 1998/3132—*continued*
    r 36.1   7.4
    r 36.2   7.4, 7.5.1
    r 36.2(2)(b)   7.5.1
    r 36.2(2)(c)   4.4
    r 36.3   7.4, 7.5.3, 7.5.6, 7.5.13
    r 36.3(2)(a)   7.5.8
    r 36.3(7)   7.5.13
    r 36.4   7.4, 7.5.5
    r 36.5   7.4, 7.5.5, 7.5.10
    r 36.6   7.4, 7.5.5, 7.5.10
    r 36.7   7.4, 7.5.2
    r 36.8   7.4, 7.5.2
    r 36.9   7.4, 7.5.3, 7.5.7
    r 36.10   7.4, 7.5.8, 7.5.9
    r 36.10(1)   7.5.8
    r 36.10(4)(b)   4.4
    r 36.10(5)   4.4
    r 36.11   7.4, 7.5.10
    r 36.12   7.4, 7.5.4
    r 36.13   7.4, 7.5.4
    r 36.14   5.4.8.2, 7.4, 7.5.7, 7.5.9, 7.5.11, 7.5.15
    r 36.14(1A)   7.5.11
    r 36.14(2)   4.4
    r 36.14(4)   7.5.11
    r 36.14A   4.4, 5.4.8.1, 5.4.8.2
    r 36.15   7.4, 7.5.4
    r 36.16   7.4, 7.6
    r 36.17   7.4, 7.6
    r 36.18   7.4, 7.6
    r 36.19   7.4, 7.6
    r 36.20   7.4, 7.6
    r 36.21   7.4, 7.6
    r 36.22   7.4, 7.6
    PD 36   7.5.3
    Pt 38   4.1, 9.7
    r 38.4   4.6, 9.7
    r 38.6   4.9
    r 41.3A   7.5.4
    r 43.2(1)(a)   8.1
    r 43.2(1)(k)   8.1
    r 43.2(1)(l)   8.1
    r 43.2(1)(m)   8.1
    r 43.2(1)(n)   8.1
    r 43.2(1)(o)   8.1
    r 43.2(2)   8.1
    r 43.2(3)   8.1
    r 43.2(4)   8.1
    r 43.3   8.3

Civil Procedure Rules 1998, SI 1998/3132—continued		Civil Procedure Rules 1998, SI 1998/3132—continued	
Pt 44	5.4.6, 7.3, 7.5.1, 9.13	r 45.20	8.1
r 44.2(4)	6.6	r 45.21	5.3.4, 8.1
r 44.2(6)	6.6	r 45.22	5.3.4, 8.1
r 44.2(8)	6.6, 8.4	r 45.23	5.3.4, 8.1
r 44.3	3.2.1.6, 6.1.2, 7.5.9, 7.5.11, 7.5.15	r 45.23B	5.3.2
		r 45.24	5.3.5, 8.1
r 44.3(2)	6.6, 7.5.15	r 45.25	8.1
r 44.3(2)(a)	6.1.2, 6.2	r 45.26	8.1
r 44.3(3)	6.6	r 45.28	5.3.6, 8.1
r 44.3A	8.1, 8.4	r 45.29C	5.4.2
r 44.3B	8.1	r 45.29E	5.4.2
r 44.5	8.4	r 45.29F(8)	5.4.6
r 44.5(3)	6.1.2	r 45.29F(9)	5.4.6
r 44.6	6.7	r 45.29F(10)	5.4.6
r 44.11	9.7	r 45.29H	5.4.7
r 44.12B	8.1	r 45.29I	5.4.3
r 44.13	4.3	r 45.29J	5.4.5
r 44.13(2)	4.3	r 45.29K	5.4.5
r 44.14	4.3, 4.4, 5.4.8.1	r 45.29L	5.4.5
r 44.14(1)	4.4	r 45.31	8.1
r 44.14(2)	4.4	r 45.32	8.1
r 44.14(3)	4.4	r 45.33	8.1
r 44.15	2.5.5, 4.3, 4.4, 4.5, 5.4.6, 5.4.8.1, 8.1	r 45.34	8.1
		r 45.35	8.1
r 44.15(b)	4.5	r 45.36	8.1
r 44.16	4.3, 4.4, 5.4.6, 5.4.8.1, 8.1	r 45.37	8.1
r 44.16(1)	4.5, 4.6	r 45.38	8.1
r 44.16(2)	4.7	r 45.39	8.1
r 44.16(2)(b)	4.7	r 45.40	8.1
r 44.16(2)(c)	4.7	PD 45	5.2.5.1
r 44.16(3)	4.7	Pt 46	5.1.2
r 44.17	4.3	r 46.3	8.1
r 44.18	3.2.1.6, 3.4	r 46.8	8.1
PD 44		Pt 47	9.9, 9.10
para 2.1	8.3	r 47.1	9.2
para 6	8.3	r 47.2	9.3
para 9.1	6.7	r 47.3	9.4
para 9.2	6.7	r 47.4(1)	9.6
para 9.5(4)	8.3	r 47.4(2)	9.6
para 12.2	4.7	r 47.4(3)	9.6
para 12.3	4.7	r 47.6	9.8
para 12.4(a)	4.6	r 47.7	9.7
para 12.4(c)	4.6	r 47.8(1)	9.7
para 12.4(d)	4.6	r 47.8(2)	9.7
para 12.5	4.7	r 47.9	9.9
para 12.6	4.6, 4.7	r 47.12	9.12
para 13.2	8.3	r 47.13	9.9
para 14.9	8.3	r 47.14(1)	9.13
para 20.3(1)	8.3	r 47.14(2)	9.13
Pt 45	5.1.4, 9.17.1	r 47.14(3)	9.13
r 45.2F	5.4.6	r 47.14(4)	9.13
r 45.8	8.1	r 47.14(5)	9.15
r 45.9	5.2.3	r 47.14(6)	9.15
r 45.10	5.2.3, 8.1	r 47.14(7)	9.15
r 45.11	5.2.3	r 47.15(1)	9.14
r 45.12	8.1	r 47.15(2)	9.14
r 45.13	8.1	r 47.15(3)	9.14
r 45.15	8.1	r 47.15(4)	9.14
r 45.16	8.1	r 47.15(5)	9.14
r 45.17	8.1	r 47.15(6)	9.14
r 45.18	5.2.1, 5.3.5, 8.1	r 47.15(7)	9.14
r 45.19	5.3.2, 8.1	r 47.15(8)	9.14

Table of Statutory Instruments

Civil Procedure Rules 1998,
SI 1998/3132—continued
r 47.15(9)	9.14
r 47.15(10)	9.14
PD 47	
para 1.1	9.2
para 1.2	9.2
para 1.3	9.2
para 1.4	9.2
para 2	9.3
para 3	9.4
para 3.1	9.4
para 3.2	9.4
para 3.3	9.4
para 4.1	9.6
para 4.2(1)	9.6
para 4.2(2)(B)	9.6
para 5.2	9.8
para 5.5(1)	9.8
para 5.5(2)	9.8
para 5.5(3)	9.8
para 5.6	9.8
para 5.7	9.9
para 5.8	9.9
para 5.10	9.9
para 5.11	9.9
para 5.12	9.9
para 5.13	9.9
para 5.14	9.9
para 5.15	9.9
para 5.16	9.9
para 5.18	9.9
para 5.19	9.9
para 5.22(3)	9.9
para 5.22(4)	9.9
para 5.22(5)	9.9
para 5.22(6)	9.9
para 8.2	9.10
para 8.3	9.10, 9.14
para 9	9.11
para 10.1	9.12
para 10.2	9.12
para 10.3	9.12
para 10.4	9.12
para 10.5	9.12
para 10.6	9.12
para 10.7	9.12
para 11	9.12
para 13.2	9.14, 9.15
para 13.4	9.15
para 13.5	9.15
para 13.6	9.15
para 13.13	9.5
para 14.1	9.14
para 14.2	9.14
para 14.4	9.14
para 14.15(1)	9.14
para 14.15(2)	9.14
para 14.15(3)	9.14
Sch	9.10
r 48.2	4.3
PD 48	
para 1.3	8.1
para 1.4	8.1

Civil Procedure Rules 1998,
SI 1998/3132—continued
PD 51G	6.4
r 52.9A	4.10
Collective Conditional Fee Agreements Regulations 2000, SI 2000/2988	
reg 5(1)(c)	9.17.1
Compensation (Specification of Benefits) Order 2006, SI 2006/3321	
art 3	3.2.1.2
Conditional Fee Agreement Order 2000, SI 2000/823	2.2
Conditional Fee Agreement Regulations 2000, SI 2000/692	3.6
Conditional Fee Agreements Order 1995, SI 1995/1674	2.1
Conditional Fee Agreements Order 2000, SI 2000/823	2.3
Conditional Fee Agreements Order 2013, SI 2013/689	2.3, 2.3.1
art 3	2.3.18
art 4	2.3.1
art 5	2.3.1
art 5(1)(b)	2.3.3
art 6(1)(a)	2.3.2
art 6(1)(b)	2.3.2
art 6(2)(a)	2.3.1
Conditional Fee Agreements Regulations 1995, SI 1995/1675	2.1
Conditional Fee Agreements Regulations 2000, SI 2000/692	3.2.1.4
reg 1(2)	3.2.1.4
reg 3(1)(a)	9.17.1
reg 3(c)	3.2.1.5
reg 5	3.2.1.5
reg 6	3.2.1.5
reg 7	3.2.1.5
Conditional Fee Agreements (Revocation) Regulations 2005, SI 2005/2305	9.17.1
Consumer Contracts (Information, Cancellation and Additional Charges) Regulations 2013, SI 2013/3134	1.7, 1.8
Consumer Protection (Distance Selling) Regulations 2000, SI 2000/2334	9.17.1
reg 3	1.8
reg 4	1.8
reg 8(3)	1.8
reg 10	1.8
reg 14	1.8
reg 15	1.8
reg 19	1.8
reg 24	1.8
reg 25	1.8
Sch 1	1.8

Damages-Based Agreements Regulations 2010/1206, SI 2010/1206	3.1.1, 3.6
reg 2	3.6
Damages-Based Agreements Regulations 2013, SI 2013/609	3.2.1.2, 3.4
reg 4	3.2.1.2
reg 5	3.2.1.2
reg 6	3.2.1.2
reg 7	3.2.1.2
reg 8	3.2.1.2
Insurance Companies (Legal Expense Insurance) Regulation 1990, SI 1990/1159	2.3.6
Legal Aid, Sentencing and Punishment of Offenders Act 2012 (Commencement No 6) Order 2013, SI 2013/453	2.3
Recovery of Costs Insurance Premiums in Clinical Negligence Proceedings (No 2) Regulations 2013, SI 2013/92	2.3.1
Unfair Terms in Consumer Contracts Regulations 1999, SI 1999/2083	2.5.6
Sch 2	2.5.6

CHAPTER 1

CODE OF CONDUCT AND FUNDING OPTIONS

1.1 SOLICITORS REGULATION AUTHORITY (SRA)

The SRA's approach to professional conduct and funding issues is set out in their current Handbook in force since 6 October 2011. It aims to achieve a common standard of protection for clients, regardless of the type of organisation providing legal services to them.

The SRA has moved away from investigating breaches of the rules as an end in itself towards a more risk-based approach that concentrates on the issues that are critical to public confidence in legal services and the well-being of clients, and identifying potential risks at an earlier stage. The SRA Handbook heralded a new approach to regulation by 'outcomes-focused regulation' (OFR).

OFR involves assessing whether a firm can act, or is acting, in an ethical and principled manner, and secure the outcomes or results to which its clients are entitled. A significant point for those regulated by the SRA is that OFR aims at what is achieved and not what steps have been taken.

For solicitors and other regulated individuals, OFR means less box-ticking and should engender a much more collaborative and less confrontational relationship with the regulator. Firms have greater freedom to decide how to achieve the best results for their clients, taking account of their individual needs.

OFR means that the regulator will be concentrating more on the things that matter most to clients: delivery of the service and outcomes they are entitled to rather than the technical rules.

1.1.1 Ten Principles

At the heart of the regime are ten mandatory Principles. These apply to all solicitors and to all firms that are regulated by the SRA and everybody who works in them – including non-lawyers.

They state:

> 'you must:
> 1. uphold the rule of law and the proper administration of justice,
> 2. act with integrity,
> 3. not allow your independence to be compromised,
> 4. act in the best interests of each client,
> 5. provide a proper standard of service to your clients,
> 6. behave in a way that maintains the trust the public places in you and in the provision of legal services,
> 7. comply with your legal and regulatory obligations and deal with your regulators and ombudsmen in an open, timely and co-operative manner,
> 8. run your business or carry out your role in the business effectively and in accordance with proper governance and sound financial and risk management principles,
> 9. run your business or carry out your role in the business in a way that encourages equality of opportunity and respect for diversity, and
> 10. protect client money and assets.'

The Handbook advises:

> 'You should always have regard to the Principles and use them as your starting point when faced with an ethical dilemma. Where two or more Principles come into conflict, the Principle which takes precedence is the one which best serves the public interest in the particular circumstances, especially the public interest in the proper administration of justice.'

These are supported by non-mandatory 'indicative behaviours' (IBs), which are indications or symptoms of whether or not an outcome is being achieved. The IBs in the Handbook are not exhaustive and there may be other and more appropriate ways of achieving the outcomes, depending on the type of firm and the needs of the clients. IBs can be both positive (to be achieved) and negative (to be avoided).

The SRA's enforcement focuses on breach of Principles and failure to achieve defined outcomes rather than failure to comply with detailed rules. The stated primary concern is to work with firms to improve standards. Only when failures are serious or a firm does not show the will to improve does SRA intend to take formal action. Powers to reduce penalties for early admissions and to order suspended penalties exist.

1.1.2 Risk management and compliance

All firms – including sole practitioners – are required to have a Compliance Officer for Legal Practice (COLP) and a Compliance

Officer for Finance and Administration (COFA). Their role is to enhance risk management and compliance. They could be managers or employees, but need to have sufficient authority.

All managers, owners, COLPs and COFAs are subject to a Suitability Test to assess whether they are fit and proper people. This reflects the criteria that solicitors have to meet on admission and declare they continue to meet annually.

Through greater information requirements, the SRA will assess the degree of risk a firm poses and how much supervision they require. The relationships of larger and higher-risk firms with the SRA is managed by specialist staff.

1.1.3 Alternative business structures (ABS)

The powers and rules for disciplining traditional law firms and ABS have been harmonised and their clients and the funds in their custody will enjoy the same level of protection.

All those with a 'material interest' in an ABS, ie those who propose to acquire a 10 per cent share in an ABS (taking into account the cumulative ownership of associates) will be subject to the test for disqualifying an individual or entity from working in an ABS. An ABS has to disclose the ultimate beneficial owners of the firm.

1.2 CLIENT CARE AND COSTS

Client care issues are dealt with in Chapter 1 of the SRA Code. Apart from information about complaints, the outcomes in Chapter 1 do not specify the information that must be given to clients, or the form that it should take. This is because OFR requires you to focus on the Principles and achieving the right outcomes for your clients, and gives you flexibility in how you meet these outcomes.

The IBs provide some examples of the information you may provide in order to meet the outcomes, but these are not mandatory and you will need to work out what is appropriate for your clients, taking into account their particular needs and circumstances.

You will also need to consider whether other rules etc require you to give particular information to clients, eg, in relation to financial services and the interest provisions in the Accounts Rules.

The most relevant Principles in the context of client care are:

- providing a proper standard of service (Principle 5); and
- acting in the best interests of each client (Principle 4).

The outcomes you need to achieve include:
- clients are treated fairly;
- clients are in a position to make informed decisions about the services they need, how their matter will be handled and the options available to them;
- clients receive the best possible information, both at the time of engagement, and when appropriate as their matter progresses, about the likely overall cost of their matter; and
- clients are informed whether and how the services you provide are regulated, and how this affects the protections available to the client.

You must consider the needs and circumstances of your clients when deciding the best way to meet these outcomes.

The IBs include:
- agreeing an appropriate level of service with the client; and
- clearly explaining your fees and if and when they are likely to change, and explaining your responsibilities and those of the client.

These are not mandatory and you may develop your own ways of meeting the outcomes, which are suited to the needs of your clients and the type of work you do. The requirements for a person doing low value RTA claims are different from that of a person doing high value clinical negligence claims. Also these are not an exhaustive list, there may be other information you need to give the client. You know your clients best.

This gives you the freedom to decide what information you give to your clients to ensure they understand the basis on which they are instructing you. Factors you should consider are as follows:
- Whether your client is used to dealing with law firms – the way you deal with a sophisticated client will be very different from the way you deal with a first-time claimant. Your systems and procedures need to consider the firm's client base and areas of work. You may need to adopt a different approach for different types of work and different types of client.
- Whether standard letters are appropriate for all clients and all types of work – if you provide a client with so much, or such complex,

information that they are unable to understand the basis on which they are instructing you, you may not have met the outcomes that clients are in a position to make an informed decision.
- Whether the client is vulnerable, eg if the client has a learning difficulty or other disability that may affect their ability to understand the information you are providing, or if English is not the client's first language. You will also need to bear in mind your duties under the Equalities Act, in particular the need to make reasonable adjustments in relation to clients with disabilities (SRA Code Chapter 2 Equality and diversity).

Providing clear information at the outset and as the matter progresses is of benefit not only to clients but also to your firm. Some of the most common causes of complaints are lack of clear information about costs, failure to follow instructions, delay and failure to keep clients informed. It is important to monitor complaints to your firm, as these can indicate failure to provide good client care as well as other problems within the firm.

Individual client files will often provide the best evidence of good client care. Well maintained files will contain copies of letters to the client, attendance notes or some other record of the information and explanations to the client and the steps you have taken to protect the client's interests. For example:

- In a case where you were concerned about the client's mental capacity the file should clearly document the steps you took to establish that the client had the necessary capacity to instruct you on the matter.
- In a case where you were concerned about the client's ability to speak and/or understand English, the file should indicate whether an independent interpreter was used.
- In a matter involving significant delays, there should be evidence that you have explained the reasons for these delays to the client.
- Where you have acted for a large organisation (eg trade union) on a number of matters under a general retainer, it should be clear that the matter is being dealt with on terms previously agreed.

1.3 OUTCOMES

You must achieve these outcomes:

'O(1.1) you treat your clients fairly;

O(1.2) you provide services to your clients in a manner which protects their interests in their matter, subject to the proper administration of justice;

O(1.3) when deciding whether to act, or terminate your instructions, you comply with the law and the Code;

O(1.4) you have the resources, skills and procedures to carry out your clients' instructions;

O(1.5) the service you provide to clients is competent, delivered in a timely manner and takes account of your clients' needs and circumstances;

O(1.6) you only enter into fee agreements with your clients that are legal, and which you consider are suitable for the client's needs and take account of the client's best interests;

O(1.7) you inform clients whether and how the services you provide are regulated and how this affects the protections available to the client;

O(1.8) clients have the benefit of your compulsory professional indemnity insurance and you do not exclude or attempt to exclude liability below the minimum level of cover required by the SRA Indemnity Insurance Rules;

O(1.9) clients are informed in writing at the outset of their matter of their right to complain and how complaints can be made;

O(1.10) clients are informed in writing, both at the time of engagement and at the conclusion of your complaints procedure, of their right to complain to the Legal Ombudsman, the time frame for doing so and full details of how to contact the Legal Ombudsman;

O(1.11) clients' complaints are dealt with promptly, fairly, openly and effectively;

O(1.12) clients are in a position to make informed decisions about the services they need, how their matter will be handled and the options available to them;

O(1.13) clients receive the best possible information, both at the time of engagement and when appropriate as their matter progresses, about the likely overall cost of their matter;

O(1.14) clients are informed of their right to challenge or complain about your bill and the circumstances in which they may be liable to pay interest on an unpaid bill;

O(1.15) you properly account to clients for any financial benefit you receive as a result of your instructions;

O(1.16) you inform clients if you discover any act or omission which could give rise to a claim by them against you.'

1.4 INDICATIVE BEHAVIOURS

Acting in the following way(s) may tend to show that you have achieved these outcomes and therefore complied with the Principles:

'DEALING WITH THE CLIENT'S MATTER

IB(1.1) agreeing an appropriate level of service with your client, for example the type and frequency of communications;

IB(1.2) explaining your responsibilities and those of the client;

IB(1.3) ensuring that the client is told, in writing, the name and status of the person(s) dealing with the matter and the name and status of the person responsible for its overall supervision;

IB(1.4) explaining any arrangements, such as fee sharing or referral arrangements, which are relevant to the client's instructions;

IB(1.5) explaining any limitations or conditions on what you can do for the client, for example, because of the way the client's matter is funded;

IB(1.6) in taking instructions and during the course of the retainer, having proper regard to your client's mental capacity or other vulnerability, such as incapacity or duress;

IB(1.7) considering whether you should decline to act or cease to act because you cannot act in the client's best interests;

IB(1.8) if you seek to limit your liability to your client to a level above the minimum required by the SRA Indemnity Insurance Rules, ensuring that this limitation is in writing and is brought to the client's attention;

IB(1.9) refusing to act where your client proposes to make a gift of significant value to you or a member of your family, or a member of your firm or their family, unless the client takes independent legal advice;

IB(1.10) if you have to cease acting for a client, explaining to the client their possible options for pursuing their matter;

IB(1.11) you inform clients if they are not entitled to the protections of the SRA Compensation Fund;

IB(1.12) considering whether a conflict of interests has arisen or whether the client should be advised to obtain independent advice where the client notifies you of their intention to make a claim or if you discover an act or omission which might give rise to a claim;

FEE ARRANGEMENTS WITH YOUR CLIENT

IB(1.13) discussing whether the potential outcomes of the client's matter are likely to justify the expense or risk involved, including any risk of having to pay someone else's legal fees;

IB(1.14) clearly explaining your fees and if and when they are likely to change;

IB(1.15) warning about any other payments for which the client may be responsible;

IB(1.16) discussing how the client will pay, including whether public funding may be available, whether the client has insurance that might cover the fees, and whether the fees may be paid by someone else such as a trade union;

IB(1.17) where you are acting for a client under a fee arrangement governed by statute, such as a conditional fee agreement, giving the client all relevant information relating to that arrangement;

IB(1.18) where you are acting for a publicly funded client, explaining how their publicly funded status affects the costs;

IB(1.19) providing the information in a clear and accessible form which is appropriate to the needs and circumstances of the client;

IB(1.20) where you receive a financial benefit as a result of acting for a client, either:
- paying it to the client;
- offsetting it against your fees; or
- keeping it only where you can justify keeping it, you have told the client the amount of the benefit (or an approximation if you do not know the exact amount) and the client has agreed that you can keep it;

IB(1.21) ensuring that disbursements included in your bill reflect the actual amount spent or to be spent on behalf of the client.'

1.4.1 Funding information to client

The Court of Appeal considered the issue of a solicitor's duty to advise a client about funding options in the case of *David Truex Solicitor (a firm) v Kitchen*.[1] This was a family case where following a letter before action on behalf of the client, her husband's solicitor explained that they were seeking Legal Aid for their client. The wife asked whether she qualified for Legal Aid and was told that the firm did not undertake such work but could refer her to another firm. She did not take up this offer until significant further costs had been incurred. She then transferred instructions and obtained Legal Aid. She then objected to paying the first solicitor's costs and they sued her. The Court of Appeal said that a solicitor was bound at the outset to consider the question whether a client might be eligible for Legal Aid.

First, it would be quite wrong to incur substantial expenditure chargeable privately to the client if public funding was available. Secondly, a client was in more difficulties changing firms of solicitors if work has been done and a relationship built up, before advice was given that a different firm could become involved.

It is therefore important that you discuss with the client not just the types of funding that you can offer but also explain that there are other types of funding that may be available elsewhere. This conversation must take place before any funding arrangement is entered into. How much information you give to the client about other methods of funding is a matter for you to decide in the light of your knowledge of the client, their case and the instructions. What is important is that the client knows that they have other options and can find out about them before any commitment is made.

However, you are not required to act as a cost comparison site and you do not have to give information about the different charges of different firms etc, thus in the case of *Ahmed v The Bread Roll Company Ltd*[2] Senior Costs Judge Peter Hurst considered the effect of the then CFA Regulations and stated that 'solicitors were required to point out to the client other ways of funding legal costs, for example, by way of legal aid, or via a trade union, or with the benefit of any available before the event insurance cover. They were not required to inform the client that other firms of solicitors might undertake the work on less onerous CFA terms'. Although those Regulations no longer apply the statement is an accurate explanation of the duty of a solicitor towards the client on costs information.

---

[1] [2007] EWCA Civ 618.
[2] [2009] EWHC 90141 (Costs).

1.5 REFERRAL ARRANGEMENTS

The Legal Aid, Sentencing and Punishment of Offenders Act 2012 introduced a ban on referral fees from 1 April 2013. The ban is created in the Act but it is up to the various regulatory bodies (in our case the SRA) to impose and monitor the ban. Personal injury work is singled out for special treatment as it is only that work where referral fees are banned.

Sections 56 to 60 of the Legal Aid, Sentencing and Punishment of Offenders Act 2012 (LASPO) implement the referral fee ban.

The good news is that the ban does not create an offence or a claim for breach of statutory duty when a referral fee is paid. Also the payment of a referral fee does not affect the validity or enforceability of the retainer with the client. But the contract to pay the referral fee is unenforceable.

The ban covers the payment (or receipt) of a fee for a case to be referred to 'a regulated person' (which includes a lawyer). It also covers the receipt of a payment for referring a client in the course of a case.

A referral occurs where you receive, other than from the potential client, information needed to make an offer to the client. This definition is widely drawn in an effort to limit our ability to get round the ban. Also the definition of payment includes any benefit received by anybody (whether or not the person providing the information) but it excludes reasonable hospitality.

Where it seems to the SRA that a referral fee has been paid they have to investigate. Also they have a rule that it is for the regulated person to show that the payment is for a service rather than for a referral. Finally the Lord Chancellor can specify a maximum amount that can be paid for a specified service. No such maxima have been set so far but clearly if they are then to pay more than that figure will give rise to a suspicion of a referral fee and it will be for the solicitor to prove that is not the case.

Therefore the important point is how the SRA will implement the ban. However, the SRA rules may not be much help in deciding whether an arrangement is valid or not. They say:

> 'Regulated persons should be able to determine from LASPO itself the arrangements which will be prohibited and the risks associated with entering into referral arrangements. The SRA does not intend to provide regulated persons with "pre-approval of business models".'

Also:

> 'Ultimately, in an outcomes-focused regulatory landscape, it will be for practitioners themselves to ensure their own compliance with their legal and regulatory requirements and we expect firms to make their own decisions on whether their arrangements are compliant. LASPO specifically puts the burden of proof to evidence this on the individual firm.'

In other words it is for solicitors to work out for whether a particular arrangement is acceptable or not.

The SRA also say:

> 'We believe that our outcomes-focused approach will allow us to look at the substance of an arrangement, rather than just its form and focus on those arrangements that pose a real risk to the public interest. We will assess arrangements which have been "dressed up" to appear compliant, when the underlying purpose of the arrangement is something different as high risk. In this regard we would remind those we regulate of the Principles that underpin our regulatory regime, in particular the need to act with integrity and to behave in way that maintains the trust the public places in them and in the provision of legal services.'

The SRA is also interested in potential referral arrangements in ABS and it says:

> 'We will look closely at applicants' proposed referral arrangements. Where, for example, a firm and a CMC apply to become an ABS, we will carefully scrutinise the application and the proposed business model. Models which suggest an intention to continue as more than one business, with referrals being made between them, may not be licensed, if we believe the referral arrangements will be unlawful. Applicants will need to demonstrate that they are truly operating as one entity and if referrals are made to another part of the business within a group structure that these comply with LASPO and our regulatory requirements.'

The result of all this is that the only change to the outcomes in the SRA Handbook is:

> 'O(9.8) you do not pay a prohibited referral fee.'

Together with IBs:

> 'IB(9.7) having effective systems in place for assessing whether any arrangement complies with statutory and regulatory requirements;

IB(9.8) ensuring that any payments you make for services, such as marketing, do not amount to the payment of prohibited referral fees;

IB(9.9) retaining records and management information to enable you to demonstrate that any payments you make are not prohibited referral fees.'

If a breach of the referral fee ban is found then the sanctions that the SRA can apply include:
- findings but no sanction;
- rebukes;
- fines of up to £2,000 for a firm or up to £20m for an ABS;
- conditions on a certificate or licence;
- revocation of an authorisation or licence;
- referral of the individual or entity to the SDT which has the power to issue an unlimited fine or suspend or strike from the roll;
- intervention; and
- in most cases a direction to pay our costs of the investigation.

The following factors will indicate more serious misconduct:
- significant detriment to the interests of the client;
- a failure to take steps to assess whether payments made in respect of a referral arrangement are prohibited by LASPO;
- a failure to remedy the breach once identified;
- the passing of unnecessary costs, such as artificially inflated charges or referral fees, to clients or third parties such as defendants;
- repeated contraventions of the ban;
- taking steps to disguise or hide payments in an attempt to pay or receive referral fees contrary to LASPO, which may be evidence of dishonesty; or
- an intentional or reckless contravention of the provisions set out in LASPO.

One of the major areas of lack of clarity is in respect of joint or shared marketing. At what point does a shared marketing arrangement become a referral arrangement? Again the SRA have indicated that they will look at the substance of the arrangement not what it is called.

Only the SRA can make the decision about whether a scheme is compliant but It seems that the following joint marketing arrangements are probably acceptable where:

- a website offers to find a suitable firm of solicitors for members of the public. The potential client is required to input their postcode and the area of law in which they need help. They then receive an email providing contact details of a suitable firm in their area; and
- a scheme where a not-for-profit joint body allocates clients on a rota basis.

The first is acceptable because the client contacts the firm if they wish. The second is acceptable because a not-for-profit organisation cannot charge more than cost so no referral fee can be involved.

In any event it is important that the marketing scheme costs are no more than reasonable given market rates.

1.6 RETAINER

A solicitor acting for a client in a contentious matter must have a valid and enforceable agreement with their client in order to be able to claim costs from a losing opponent. This is a result of the Indemnity Principle and the SRA Code of Conduct.

The retainer is regulated by the Solicitors Act 1974 but also by standard contract law.

Types of retainer with client include:
- private;
- BTE (before the event legal expenses insurance);
- DBA (Damages Based Agreement);
- CBA (contentious business agreement);
- CFA (no win, no fee);
- discounted CFA (no win, lower fee);
- CFA Lite (no money from client);
- CCFA (collective CFA);
- ATE (after the event legal expenses insurance);
- public funding (legal aid where still available); and
- third party funding, including funding by a membership organisation such as a trade union.

The retainer must specify the terms of the relationship between solicitor and client. One aspect of this is the question of costs. However, the retainer has to deal with all aspects, such as who is dealing with the matter and the extent of the instructions. It is not part of this book to deal with the retainer save as it relates to the issue of costs.

The non-costs parts of the retainer may have a knock-on effect on costs. Thus the courts have decided that a client who had work done for him by an unqualified person, did not have to pay for that work when he had requested that the work be done by a solicitor (*Pearless De Rougemont & Co v Pilbrow*[3]). There is a risk that unless the solicitor gives a considerable amount of information, he will simply not be paid.

However, the costs part of the retainer is the most important in this respect because of the Indemnity Principle.

The retainer is the entirety of the contract between the solicitor and client, including the basis for termination, see *Kyriakides & Braier (A Firm) v Klamer*[4] below.

The issue of when a retainer is terminated came to the courts in the case of *Cawdery Kaye Fireman & Taylor v Minkin*.[5] In that case a family solicitor who would only continue to act subject to his client making interim fee payments had merely suspended the retainer, not terminated it, appeal judges ruled. In overturning earlier findings, the Court of Appeal said the lawyer's repeated statements that he would only issue court proceedings for his client subject to funds being made available did not amount to termination. As a result it was the client who terminated the agreement by failing to continue to instruct the solicitor. Therefore Ward LJ said:

> 'The client's termination of the contract absolves the solicitor from any further performance of the contract but it does not absolve the client from paying the costs properly incurred to that date.'

1.7 THE CANCELLATION OF CONTRACTS MADE IN A CONSUMER'S HOME OR PLACE OF WORK ETC REGULATIONS 2008

These Regulations came into effect on 1 October 2008.

These Regulations apply to a contract between a consumer and a trader which is for the supply of goods or services to the consumer by a trader. The general nature of this definition means that a solicitor's retainer will be caught and is subject to the Regulations.

---

[3] (1999) *The Times*, March 25.
[4] [2005] EWHC 90013 (Costs).
[5] [2012] EWCA Civ 546.

The Regulations cover any contract which is made:

(a) during a visit by the trader to the consumer's home or place of work, or to the home of another individual;
(b) during an excursion organised by the trader away from his business premises; or
(c) after an offer made by the consumer during such a visit or excursion.

If a retainer is made in the above circumstances then the trader must give the consumer a written notice of his right to cancel the contract and such notice must be given at the time the contract is made except in the case of a contract which is made as in (c) above, in which case the notice must be given at the time the offer is made by the consumer.

The 'cancellation period' means the period of 7 days starting with the date of receipt by the consumer of a notice of the right to cancel.

The cancellation notice must:

(a) be dated;
(b) indicate the right of the consumer to cancel the contract within the cancellation period;
(c) be easily legible;
(d) contain:
 (i) the information set out in Part I of Sch 4; and
 (ii) a cancellation form in the form set out in Part II of that Schedule provided as a detachable slip and completed by or on behalf of the trader in accordance with the notes; and
(e) indicate if applicable:
 (i) that the consumer may be required to pay for the goods or services supplied if the performance of the contract has begun with his written agreement before the end of the cancellation period;
 (ii) that a related credit agreement will be automatically cancelled if the contract for goods or services is cancelled.

Where the contract is written the notice must be incorporated in the same document and the notice of the right to cancel must:

(a) be set out in a separate box with the heading 'Notice of the Right to Cancel'; and

(b) have as much prominence as any other information in the contract or document apart from the heading and the names of the parties to the contract and any information inserted in handwriting.

The crucial part of the Regulations is that a contract to which the Regulations apply shall not be enforceable against the consumer unless the trader has given the consumer a notice of the right to cancel and the information required in accordance with this regulation. In other words, the solicitor will not be entitled to any costs in these circumstances.

The parties cannot contract out of the Regulations or remedy any defects retrospectively.

For contracts entered into from 13 June 2014 the Consumer Contracts (Information, Cancellation and Additional Charges) Regulations 2013[6] which implement the EU Consumer Rights Directive 2011/83/EU replace the Consumer Protection (Distance Selling) Regulations 2000 and the Cancellation of Contracts made in a Consumer's Home or Place of Work etc Regulations 2008.

1.8 CONSUMER PROTECTION (DISTANCE SELLING) REGULATIONS 2000

These Regulations implement Directive 97/7/EC of the European Parliament and the Council of 20 May 1997 on the protection of consumers in relation to distance contracts, with the exception of Article 10. They came into force on 31 October 2000.

The Regulations apply to contracts for goods or services to be supplied to a consumer where the contract is made exclusively by means of distance communication that is any means used without the simultaneous physical presence of the consumer and the supplier (regs 3 and 4).

Schedule 1 contains an indicative list of means of distance communication:

'1. Unaddressed printed matter.
2. Addressed printed matter.
3. Letter.
4. Press advertising with order form.
5. Catalogue.
6. Telephone with human intervention.

---

[6] SI 2013/3134.

7. Telephone without human intervention (automatic calling machine, audiotext).
8. Radio.
9. Videophone (telephone with screen).
10. Videotext (microcomputer and television screen) with keyboard or touch screen.
11. Electronic mail.
12. Facsimile machine (fax).
13. Television (teleshopping).'

The Regulations require the supplier to provide the consumer with the information referred to in reg 7 prior to the conclusion of the contract. This includes information on the right to cancel the distance contract, the main characteristics of the goods or services, and delivery costs.

Regulation 8 requires the supplier to confirm in writing, or another durable medium which is available and accessible to the consumer, information already given and to give some additional information, including information on the conditions and procedures relating to the exercise of the right to cancel the contract. Regulation 8(3) requires the supplier to inform the consumer prior to conclusion of a contract for services that he will not be able to cancel once performance of the service has begun with his agreement.

Where the Regulations apply, they provide a 'cooling off period' to enable the consumer to cancel the contract by giving notice of cancellation to the supplier. The effect of giving notice of cancellation under the Regulations is that the contract is treated as if it had not been made.

Where the supplier supplies the information to the consumer on time, the cooling-off period is 7 working days from the day after the date of the contract, in the case of services, or from the day after the date of delivery of the goods.

Where the supplier fails to comply with the information requirement at all, the cooling-off period is extended by 3 months.

Where the supplier complies with the information requirement later than he should have done but within 3 months the cooling-off begins from the date he provided the information (regs 10–12).

If the consumer cancels, the consumer must be reimbursed within a maximum period of 30 days (reg 14). Where the consumer cancels the contract, any related credit agreement is automatically cancelled (reg 15).

The Regulations provide that the contract must be performed within 30 days subject to agreement between the parties (reg 19).

The Regulations prohibit the supply of unsolicited goods and services to consumers. Regulation 24 replaces with amendments s 1 of the Unsolicited Goods and Services Act 1971. It also creates an offence in similar terms to s 2 of the 1971 Act but extended to the supply of unsolicited services and limited to supply to consumers.

A term contained in a contract to which the Regulations apply is void if, and to the extent that, it is inconsistent with a provision for the protection of the consumer contained in the Regulations (reg 25).

For contracts entered into from 13 June 2014 the Consumer Contracts (Information, Cancellation and Additional Charges) Regulations 2013[7] which implement the EU Consumer Rights Directive 2011/83/EU replace the Consumer Protection (Distance Selling) Regulations 2000 and the Cancellation of Contracts made in a Consumer's Home or Place of Work etc Regulations 2008.

1.9 SOLICITOR AND OWN CLIENT COSTS

The Solicitors Act 1974 allows the court to order a solicitor to deliver a bill.[8] The High Court has jurisdiction for this purpose even if it did not have jurisdiction for the main action. This may happen when a solicitor tries to retain money on account without delivering a bill or where the client believes that a demand for a payment on account is excessive.

Within 3 months of the solicitors delivering a gross sum bill the client may demand a detailed bill. However, that right is lost if the solicitor starts proceedings to recover the costs in the gross sum bill.

Clients can:
- seek assessment of the bill;
- sue for negligence; or

---

[7] SI 2013/3134.
[8] Section 68.

- complain to the Legal Ombudsman. Remedies available through the Legal Ombudsman are to require the solicitor to:
  - apologise;
  - do more work if this can correct what went wrong;
  - refund or reduce the legal fees; or
  - pay compensation up to £50,000 (most awards are less than £1,000).

A solicitor should consider carefully a request from the client to have their costs assessed. The reason for this is that if the solicitor makes the application then there may well be no order for the costs of the assessment and the assessment order cannot include an order for payment by the client. The best approach is for the solicitor to propose that the client makes the application which will overcome these difficulties.

The application is under CPR Part 23 in the original proceedings or Part 8 if there are no existing proceedings.

Where the application by the client for assessment of the bill is made within one month of the bill being delivered then the court must unconditionally order an assessment. If the application is not made until after one month of delivery of the bill then the order for assessment can be made on whatever conditions the court deems fit.[9] The ordered assessment will be carried out under the normal detailed assessment procedure (see Chapter 9).

1.10 COUNSEL

Counsel are frequently used in various parts of a personal injury claim ranging from drafting particulars of claim to advocacy at the trial. This means that solicitors have to consider at the stage that they take on a case how they are going to build counsel's fees into the costs either recoverable from the other side or from the client. There are two important points to remember in this regard. First, in several forms of funding (such as damages-based agreements or the success fee element of a conditional fee agreement) counsel shares the amount claimable from the client. Secondly, the arrangement is between solicitor and counsel rather than client and counsel. This means that the responsibility for the payment of counsel's fees lies with the solicitor whether or not he/she is able to recover the cost from the client.

---

[9] Solicitors Act 1974, s 70.

The Bar Council's standard arrangement between the solicitor and counsel is in the Standard Contractual Terms for the Supply of Legal Services by Barristers to Authorised Persons 2012. This creates a formal legal contract between the solicitor and the counsel which allows counsel to sue the solicitor for their fees. But those contractual terms do not apply to a conditional fee agreement (CFA) unless it specifically includes them. APIL has agreed with the Personal Injury Bar Association (PIBA) a form of conditional fee agreement for use with counsel. This model CFA incorporates limited parts of the standard terms in relation to the duties of counsel but not the remainder of the terms.

However, if counsel is not instructed on a CFA basis and then the standard terms will apply unless they are specifically excluded or varied.

Counsel will want to be involved in some stages of fixing the costs, for example in relation to costs budgeting where overall costs including counsel's fees will be considered and approved by the court. Not surprisingly counsel will be keen to ensure that their costs are adequately covered. In many cases, of course, counsel will be presenting the costs budget, but even where the solicitor is presenting the budget they need to ensure that counsel's fees are adequately covered given that the solicitor is ultimately responsible for paying them. In practice this means that parts at least of the budget should be agreed with counsel before submitting it to the court. (For more information on costs budgeting see Chapter 6.)

Solicitors are not under a duty to agree a fee for counsel in advance of any work, but, given that the solicitor is personally liable for the fee it is wise to ensure that a reasonable fee is agreed for the proposed work. Notify the client of the counsel to be instructed and the proposed fee. Preferably get the client to agree the fee or get counsel to agree to take whatever fee is assessed as recoverable from the other party. In this way the solicitor will be able to ensure that they do not have to subsidise counsel from their own fees.

One area of potential difficulty is that of the last minute settlement. Where a brief has been delivered to counsel they are entitled to their fee. However, that fee may not be recoverable from the other side and the client may not be prepared to pay it and it may not be allowed, or allowed in full, on a solicitor and own client assessment.

CHAPTER 2

CONDITIONAL FEE AGREEMENTS

2.1 THE DEVELOPMENT OF CONDITIONAL FEES

In July 1995 conditional fee agreements (CFA) were introduced in England and Wales by the Conditional Fee Agreements Regulations 1995[1] and Conditional Fee Agreements Order 1995[2] which were made pursuant to the Courts and Legal Services Act 1990 and designed to sit alongside the legal aid regime. They allowed legal representation on the so-called 'no win no fee' basis in proceedings involving personal injury and insolvency cases, and applications to the European Court of Human Rights.

The Regulations set out the required contents of the conditional fee agreement; and the Order specified the proceedings to which s 58(4) of the Courts and Legal Services Act 1990 applied. It legitimised a practice quite common in personal injury cases in those days but which it was found were, in fact, in breach of the indemnity principle, namely the ability to agree not to charge the client if the case lost but if it won then to seek its normal costs.

A legitimisation of the arrangement also provided for the lawyer to be able to charge a 'success fee'. The success fee would be charged to the client's damages whilst the basic charges were recovered from the defendant. The success fee was described as a charge based on the costs, and not as a percentage of the damages. The limit of the success fee was 100% of the base costs. The Law Society which pioneered the scheme recommended that solicitors should consider imposing a voluntary cap on the charge by reference to the damages recovered to give additional protection to claimants. It suggested that success fees should in no circumstances reduce their damages by more than 25%, irrespective of the actual amount of the success fee, and this would also include counsel's success fee.

---

[1] SI 1995/1675.
[2] SI 1995/1674.

A new breed of insurance known as after the event (ATE) underpinned the scheme. The original product administered by Abbey Legal Protection and backed by Lexington produced a policy of £85 and protected the claimant against any claim made against them for the defendant's costs if the case was lost or abandoned and their disbursements were insured as well. In general the scheme operated successfully and ran alongside legal aid which was still available in personal injury cases. However, cherry picking of cases occurred amongst the legal profession and, inevitably, the insurance received an unfair loading of risky and unsuccessful cases; and some of the largest claims were also made by solicitors who had advised clients to reject Part 36 offers.

The government's plans to restructure legal aid, including the abolition of it for most types of personal injury action, led to a revolution in CFA's in 1999. Section 29 of the Access to Justice Act 1999 (AJA 1999) introduced the concept of 'recoverability' so that both the successful claimant's solicitors' success fee and the ATE premium could be recovered from the defendants in addition to the base charges and disbursements. Recoverability became law on 1 April 2000, one year after the civil justice system reforms and the introduction of the Civil Procedure Rules 1998.[3] There followed many years of what became known colloquially as a 'costs war'. The insurance industry understandably baulked at the concept of recoverability, and its rapid introduction without notice produced a myriad of so-called technical challenges which, when successful, led to lawyers losing all of their costs and not just additional liabilities. The Court of Appeal in *Hollins v Russell*[4] gave what at the time was considered much needed guidance on what sort of technical challenge would be fatal to a CFA resulting in nil recovery of costs and which would not. The phenomenon of the 'material breach' was born and whilst some of the challenges died away, newer ones began to appear.

Against this background, the Department of Constitutional Affairs, a successor to the Lord Chancellor's Department (and forerunner to the Ministry of Justice) produced a new CFA regime in November 2005. This new non-regulation based regime took the client care elements of CFA's out of regulation and placed them into the area of solicitors' professional conduct and was designed to reduce the prospect of

---

[3] SI 1998/3132.
[4] [2003] EWCA Civ 718.

technical challenge. By that time a differently configured Court of Appeal in the joint appears of *Myatt and Garrett*[5] reduced the effect of the material breach argument:

> 'It is unnecessary to determine whether the test stated at paragraph 107 [of Hollins] ie materially adverse effect on the protection afforded to the client or the administrator of justice), was no more than an application of a principle that the law is not concerned with very small things.'

2.2 CFAS – 1 NOVEMBER 2005 TO 31 MARCH 2013

The Department of Constitutional Affairs introduced the Conditional Fee Agreement Regulations 2005 which revoked all of the then existing CFA regulations in relation to CFAs entered into after 1 November 2005. The effect of these regulations was to simplify the CFA by removing the client care elements from regulatory control and placing them into the solicitor's code of conduct. The effect of the new system was to take the CFAs back to the original statutory description as set out in s 58 of the Courts and Legal Services Act 1990 following its amendment by s 27 of the AJA 1999. That required three simple strictures to be an enforceable CFA:

(1) it has to be in writing;
(2) it must relate only to the specified proceedings permitted by law, (in other words they cannot be used in criminal and family proceedings); and
(3) it must state the percentage by which the amount of the fees which would be payable if it were not a conditional fee agreement is to be increased.

The Conditional Fee Agreement Order 2000 continued to apply under which the maximum success fee payable was 100%. The Solicitors Practice (Client Care) Amendment Rule 2005 provided that:

> 'where a client is represented under a conditional fee agreement, the solicitor should explain: (i) the circumstances in which the client may be liable for their own costs and for the other party's costs; (ii) the client's right to assessment of costs, wherever the solicitor intends to seek payment of any or all of their costs from the client; (iii) any interest a solicitor may have in recommending a particular policy or other funding.'

As a result, aside from a fundamental breach of the design of the CFA (eg not in writing or with a success fee in excess of 100% etc) the

---

[5] *Myatt v National Coal Board and Garrett v Halton Borough Council* [2006] EWCA Civ 1017, [2006] All ER(D) 239 (Jul).

remedy lay not with the paying party but the client. In *Garbett v Edwards*[6] the Court of Appeal considered whether or not a breach of the Solicitors Practice Rules was equivalent to a breach of secondary legislation and thereby rendering the CFA unenforceable. The court held that the Solicitor's Costs Information and Client Care Code operated between solicitor and client and the paying party did not benefit from this and so the indemnity principle was not affected.

2.3 1 APRIL 2013 CFAS

The most immediate effect of the review of the costs and funding of the civil justice system by Sir Rupert Jackson was the decision by the government to remove recoverability of additional liabilities accompanied by the introduction of qualified one way costs shifting to remove the need for ATE insurance. It transferred the payment of success fees to the client subject to a cap made by reference to the damages. Part 2 of the Legal Aid, Sentencing and Punishment of Offenders Act 2012 (LASPO) deals with CFA success fees,[7] damage based agreements,[8] recovery of insurance premiums by way of costs[9] and recoverability of insurance premium by membership organisations.[10] These provisions were brought into force on 1 April 2013[11] and in turn the Conditional Fee Agreements Order 2013[12] revoked the Conditional Fee Agreements Order 2000. Nevertheless, the scope of work which was provided for by the 2000 Order remains unchanged save that criminal proceedings under s 82 of the Environmental Protection Act 1990 may be the subject of a CFA but without a success fee.

Neither the order nor the regulations appear to require a risk assessment in the way that pre-April CFAs did, but that is because the risk assessment provided for in the earlier CFA regimes was actually to support recoverability from the paying party. It is submitted that risk assessment of a case still remains an important safeguard to a solicitor in ensuring that they take on cases that can win. In multi-track cases they should be fed into a broader assessment of the value of the case and the appropriate budget that can be spent having regard to fixed costs, proportionality and budgeting. The maximum success fee is 100%[13] on

---

[6] [2005] EWCA Civ 1206.
[7] Section 44.
[8] Section 45.
[9] Section 46.
[10] Section 47.
[11] Article 3 of LASPO (Commencement No 6) Order 2013, SI 2013/453.
[12] SI 2013/689.
[13] Article 3.

base costs but in personal injury cases that sum should be limited to a deduction on the claimant's damages of 25% of:

- the pain, suffering and loss of amenity damages; and
- past financial losses,

net of any sums recovered by the Compensation Recovery Unit of the Department for Work and Pensions.

All other heads of damage are excluded from having the success fee applied to them.

As both the 25% cap and 100% limit on damages include VAT, in real terms the profit costs percentage for the lawyer is 20.83% and 83.33% respectively. In both cases the maximum success fee is fixed by reference to damages must include the fees of all barristers instructed in the case.

2.3.1 Personal injury exceptions

Articles 4 and 5 of the Conditional Fees Order 2013[14] do not apply to any CFA entered into in relation to proceedings relating to a claim for damages in respect of diffuse mesothelioma.[15] Consequently in that respect both the success fee and after the event insurance premium remain recoverable and to all intent and purposes will continue as per the pre-April CFAs.

In personal injury related litigation the only other relevant exemption relates to clinical negligence where a limited recoverability of ATE was retained. Section 58C(2)–(4) of the Courts and Legal Services Act 1990 gave the Lord Chancellor these powers and in turn he introduced the Recovery of Costs Insurance Premiums in Clinical Negligence Proceedings (No 2) Regulations 2013.[16] These provided for recovery of an ATE premium where:

- the financial value of the claim for damages in respect of clinical negligence is more than £1,000; and
- the risk insured is of incurring liability to pay for an expert relating to liability or causation; and

---

[14] SI 2013/689.
[15] Article 6(2)(a).
[16] SI 2013/92.

- recoverability is limited to that part of the premium relating to the 'risk of incurring liability to pay for an expert or reports relating to liability or causation in respect of clinical negligence in connection with the proceedings.'[17]

This is analagous to the way in which some lawyers used public funding in clinical negligence cases, eg establishing through expert opinion that there is a case to answer and then switching to a CFA. The limitations mean that there will be no cover available for work the expert does outside of the report, such as answering letters of clarification or attending conferences and indeed trial. This has meant that many insurers are offering staged policies with a recoverable and non-recoverable premium.

2.3.2 Qualifying date for the post-April regime

To take advantage of the pre-April rules of full recoverability then the agreement must have been entered into on or before 31 March 2013.[18] In relation to collective CFAs (CCFAs) there must have been an agreement specifically for the purposes of the provision to a person of advocacy or litigation services under the CCFA in connection with those proceedings on or before 31 March 2013.[19] This particular section was to prevent a CCFA being set up that would allow recovery of the success fee (and notional premium) in all future cases even if a cause of action arose after 31 March.

2.3.3 Appeals

The cap of 25% that exists in actions at first instance is removed for appeals.[20] Consequently in an appeal whether by the claimant or the defendant, a solicitor may charge their success fee in the usual way and up to 100% but it is not capped to 25% of the damages. This runs the potential risk of a claimant successfully appealing a decision and then finding that they are worse off by reason of the lawyers applying their full success fee to the sums recovered.

2.3.4 Counsel

The overall cap of 25% seriously restricts the sums available for distribution by way of success fee to both the lawyer and counsel. There

---

[17] Section 1.
[18] Article 6(1)(a).
[19] SI 2013/689, art 6(1)(b).
[20] Article 5(1)(b).

is a growing market in counsels' chambers offering to cap their success fees or, in some cases, not to seek success fees in cases of a certain value. An alternative is to obtain after the event insurance that treats counsel's fees as a disbursement and in that way, if counsel is at no risk when accepting instructions in the case, then there is no requirement for them to have a success fee.

2.3.5 Form

In this latest version of the CFA (unlike previous versions) the only statutory requirement is that it must be in writing. However, as with all contracts, it makes sense to have it signed by both the client and the lawyer to evidence agreement by both. Beyond this the CFA can take any form but of course the risk now is that the CFA must deal with all eventualities; specifically in what circumstances the client may be liable and, for example, but not limited to, a deceitful or uncooperative client.

The Law Society has drafted a model agreement and it still seems most sensible to use this document (reproduced in Appendix 2). However, if one significantly amends it then it is respectfully suggested the words 'Law Society' are removed from it. The Society of Clinical Injury Lawyers (SCIL) has also produced its own model for clinical negligence claims, based upon the Law Society model.

The model agreement is a model; it is not a precedent nor is it a prescribed form. The Law Society disclaimer reads:

> 'This model agreement is not a precedent for use with all clients and it will need to be adapted/modified depending on the individual clients' circumstances and solicitors' business models. In all cases solicitors must therefore ensure that any agreement with a client is made in compliance with their professional duties, the requirements of the SRA and any statutory requirements. The Law Society does not accept any responsibility for any breaches of such requirements in respect of this model agreement which is intended for guidance only.'

David Marshall (one of this book's editors), was part of the working party who drafted the model and he usefully suggests this checklist when considering using the model either generically or on a specific case:

(1) Are you charging a success fee?
(2) How do you set/explain success fees?
(3) Do you want to vary (downwards) the statutory cap?
(4) What are your basic hourly rates?
    (a) Guideline Hourly Rates?

(b) What is the process for increase of rates?
(5) Will you charge a solicitor and client fixed cost?
   (a) Will it be the same as fixed recoverable costs?
   (b) Risk of creating a DBA (damages based agreement)?[21]
(6) Will you charge solicitor and client costs on an hourly rate basis?
(7) Will you offer a separate voluntary cap on all unrecovered costs?
   (a) How much and on what?
(8) Do you want to charge some fees even if you lose?
   (a) 'No win, lower fee' or 'no win, fixed fee'?
   (b) Does the client understand?
(9) Will you ask the client to pay disbursements on account?
(10) Is the client relying on QOCS (qualified one way costs shifting)[22] protection alone?
   (a) Are you advising ATE is obtained? If so, is there a choice?
   (b) What is the cover?
   (c) Is the premium on top of any cap?
   (d) Are you offering a solicitor indemnity?
   (e) Are you charging for it?
   (f) Is your advertising and advice clear about this?
(11) What about counsel's fees and success fees?
(12) What happens to your fees on a Part 36 offer you advise rejecting but is not beaten?
   (a) Does the client pay no costs after the offer, or still pay base costs?
   (b) How does this relate to risk and your success fee?

Through the various CFA regimes and solicitors codes of conduct that existed, the only common threat has been ensuring that the client is given full and proper advice as to the appropriate means of funding their claim. This is very much the case now that the client may well bear a cost if their claim succeeds.

2.3.6 Legal expenses insurance

The Court of Appeal decision in *Sarwa v Alam*[23] remains good law in providing guidance as to the issue of legal expense insurance (LEI) and the solicitor's duty to establish whether satisfactory insurance cover existed. That was a decision within the context of recoverable additional

---
[21] See **3.2.1.2**.
[22] See **4.1**.
[23] [2001] EWCA Civ 1401.

liabilities but it is no less good now that the claimant themselves are likely to forfeit some of their compensation in meeting the additional liabilities. The Court of Appeal determined that a solicitor should ask the client by a standard letter before the first interview to bring copies of motor, household, stand alone, before the event (BTE) insurance policies belonging to the client and/or spouse/partner to the first meeting. If those policies disclosed satisfactory BTE cover, the solicitor should refer the client to the BTE insurer (para 46).

Client passengers should be asked to obtain a copy of their driver's policy where reasonably practical. If the driver's consent is required the client should be asked to obtain it (para 47). Enquiries into the existence of BTE cover should be proportionate. Solicitors 'are not obliged to embark on a treasure hunt' (para 46). A court held it would be disproportionate to investigate BTE cover provided by credit cards, for the present time (para 49). The court did not then and still has not sought to interpret the application of the Insurance Companies (Legal Expense Insurance) Regulation 1990[24] or the definition of proceedings in s 29 of the AJA 1999.

2.3.7 Satisfactory BTE insurance

Satisfactory BTE insurance is perhaps less important than it used to be now that QOCS applies, and therefore it can be viewed as longstop protection for the client both in terms of their liability for disbursements and Part 36 risks. It is unlikely that insurance would be available for the dishonest exceptions of QOCS. Nevertheless, it remains the case that a few simple items should be considered when advising a client:

- Does it cover this type of case?
- Is the indemnity level adequate to protect the client?
- Who has the control of the decision making?
- What ability does the insurer have to rescind cover?

As a business if you can persuade the insurer to allow freedom of choice then you should consider whether you want to work on the case with the client under this policy in view of its terms, including:

- Will you have to bear the disbursements to the conclusion of the case?
- Will you be able to render interim bills for your costs in long-lasting claims?

---

[24] SI 1990/1159.

- Will you be required to bear an unreasonably low hourly rate under the terms of the policy (such that you may need a conditional fee agreement in any event)?
- Will you be required to meet service standards that you may struggle to meet?

If the solicitor objects to the terms of the insurer's policy, it is not necessarily a sufficient reason for advising the client to ignore or reject the policy. The solicitor must either set up an alternative arrangement in which the client is no worse off or, at the very least, the client is offered a clear explanation of their choices in rejecting the BTE cover with another lawyer.

Informed consent remains key. The client may agree with the lawyer any method of retainer as an alternative to using the BTE with another lawyer. However, they must fully understand the extent to which, if at all, they may be potentially worse off, on paper at least, by instructing this law firm.

One leading organisation that provides BTE has already provided a policy where there is an excess equivalent to 25% of the damages to be met by their member. This suggests that in some cases the client will be no worse off instructing lawyers privately than going under the scheme.

The SRA Code of Conduct does not require the client to pursue a claim under their insurance policy or that they must be put in the same position with their solicitors they would be with the policy. What is required is clear and proper advice to the client so that they have informed freedom of choice. They may decide to proceed with a firm, despite being placed in a potentially adverse costs position because, for example, they are a regular user of the firm and want to continue to instruct the firm with whom they are comfortable.

Is all this funding research chargeable? It is not.[25]

2.3.8 Freedom of choice

The Head of Insurance Division of the FSO, Tony Boorman, has said: 'There are good reasons why the customer should want to choose their lawyer. Perhaps the insurer's choice is a solicitor located at a distance, or simply someone not sufficiently skilled in the specialism.'[26]

---

[25] *Motto v Trafigura Limited* [2011] EWCA Civ 1150.
[26] *Litigation Funding*, February 2002.

This was followed by anonymised decision described as that of the case of Mrs A and B Company of 10 January 2003. Here it was ruled that if the language of the policy has the restriction of choice as unclear then the case must be looked at to see if it is a special circumstances case. However, even if the language is unclear then unless there is prejudice to the policy holder in claims such as road accident ones, 'minor personal injury' and routine consumer claims should stay with the panel firm.

> 'I would expect insurers to agree the appointment of the policy holder's preferred solicitors in cases of large personal injury and claims that are necessarily complex such as medical negligence ... significant boundary or employment disputes.'

2.3.9 Appointment by the BTE firm concerned

In the event of instruction by a BTE insurer, careful attention should be paid both to the terms of the policy and the terms of any agreement for instruction provided by the BTE provider. Increasingly BTE providers require solicitors to meet very vigorous service standards that may include matters as specific as the number of telephone rings permitted before the phone is answered; the time for returning and answering correspondence, as well as more general reporting requirements to the insurance provider. Breach of service standards can potentially enable the provider to withdraw instruction or to consider the indemnity of the policy to your client void, which will be potentially a matter of negligence on the solicitor's part.

2.3.10 What retainer?

Having established the service standard requirements (which should be clearly set out on the file) there remains the issue of the retainer. The code of conduct requires there to be a proper enforceable retainer between the solicitor and the client because the insurer is providing an indemnity for the client, which does not form a definitive professional relationship or re-charging relationship. The enforceable retainer may be in the form of standard terms and conditions, providing they are not a sham, ie in other words to contract with the client they will pay your charges win or lose, when in reality you are offering a no win no fee relationship.

However if the LEI provider will indemnify a reduced hourly rate only if the claim was made on the policy, where one seeks to obtain a full hourly rate recovery from the opponent (but seeking to limit the charges for the losing claim indemnity amount) a discounted CFA may be the better option.

2.3.11 Terms and conditions of business

It is possible to have a standard terms and conditions of business between the solicitor and the client. This would provide for the hourly rate to be charged, win or lose. By reason of the indemnity principle it is not possible to have a different rate if the claim should lose than if it should win unless a CFA is used. Any such attempt will otherwise lead to an unenforceable retainer.

2.3.12 Discounted CFA

A discounted CFA remains the most acceptable retainer with a client who has a BTE policy where there is any element of restriction of indemnity towards the claimant's own solicitor's costs. The CFA provides for the full hourly rate to be charged if the case is successful, and if the case is lost or abandoned, the lower discounted rates.

This method of charging received the Court of Appeal's endorsement in the case of *Gloucester CC v Evans*.[27] It is simply not possible to have two rates outside of a CFA; it breaches the indemnity principle.

2.3.13 Satisfactory BTE but where the insurers will not appoint the firm

The first and most important point is that if it is your intention to seek to continue to represent the client, they must have proper informed consent in allowing you to proceed specifically if you are going to levy the success fee or insurance premium upon their damages when the BTE would not have done so. This can be done either by explaining to the client to what extent, if at all, they may be potentially worse off by instructing you with a CFA or, alternatively, attempting to ensure the client is no worse off by instructing the solicitor in that way than going with the BTE and the panel firm. The simplest way to proceed is with be a CFA lite which offers the client a no win no fee relationship if the claim fails, together with no liability to meet costs or disbursements in the event of a claim succeeding. The CFA lite provides that the client's liability is limited to only that which is recovered from the opponent. Under the usual CFA lite there are limited circumstances in which a client would find themselves liable. These arise in situations in which they default their obligations under the agreement. These may be omitted but it does not seem worth it. In reality, the client's default in these situations would almost inevitably avoid the cover under a BTE policy anyway so in that respect the liability remains the same.

---

[27] [2008] EWCA Civ 21.

Even using a CFA lite the client remains liable for the defendant's costs in the limited situation provided by QOCS. This liability does not arise unless and until the court proceedings are commenced. At that point the solicitor may then put an ATE policy in place (for which they would have to bear the costs) or, alternatively, seek to invoke the freedom of choice element to the BTE cover if and when proceedings need to be issued. In that way, the client has the assurance of knowing that they have no potential liabilities, win or lose, prior to the issue of proceedings and therefore mirroring the positions if they had BTE. In the event that proceedings have to be issued then the solicitor will seek to invoke BTE cover which could take effect from that point only and enable the case to continue with the client in the same position they would be if they had been with the BTE panel firm.

2.3.14 Self insurance

Many learned observers used to argue that it was illegal for the solicitor to act as insurer to the client. They contended that by law an insurer must be a suitable body within the meaning of the Financial Services and Markets Act 2000. However, the case of *Sibthorpe v Southwark*[28] is to have allayed all of those fears.

The claimant's solicitors represented their claimant in a housing disrepair case with a CFA but without the backing of an ATE policy. The CFA specified a 10% success fee and represented that the solicitor would indemnify their client against payment of their opponent's costs in the event that they were unable to obtain an insurance policy.

The council argued the indemnity clause fell foul of the law of champerty. They said it is unlawful for solicitors to agree to conduct litigation on terms which gives them a financial interest in the outcome unless specifically permitted by legislation. It was common ground that there was no legislation allowing a solicitor to underwrite a client's liability for adverse costs.

The court held that the CFA was enforceable and binding. Lord Neuberger MR said:

> 'We should accede to the argument that it would be inappropriate in the 21st century to extend the law of champerty ... judicial observations strongly suggest that champerty should be curtailed not expanded, and, given that champerty is based on public policy, it is hard to see how

---
[28] [2011] EWCA Civ 25.

arrangements such as the indemnity, at the very least in connection with litigation such as that in these cases, are against the public interest or undermine justice.'

So on the face of it indemnifying the client against adverse costs is both legal and enforceable albeit of little relevance in the new world of QOCS. Of course with the recent experience of solicitors' firms going out of business, that may be a risky position for a litigant to be in. They would remain liable for their opponent' costs.

2.3.15 Advising on insurance

The lawyer must advise the client whether an ATE policy is required and if so, which one is recommended. Helpful sources include *Litigation Funding* published monthly by the Law Society which produces a chart listing most of the main products available and brokers such as www.thejudge.co.uk and Marsh UK Limited.

The solicitor's Code of Conduct require appropriate advice to be given but this does not mean that the solicitor is expected to be an insurance broker. In other words, the lawyer is not expected to know and advise on every product in the market, but to be able to satisfy a court or more likely the SRA that the product recommended was a reasonable one in all the circumstances.

2.3.16 Disbursements

The client and lawyer should agree who is responsible for the disbursements both as the case progresses and in the event of a loss.

Flatman v Germany[29] and *Tinseltime Ltd v Roberts & Ors*[30] should remove the concerns that solicitors may have in funding or partially funding the case. In the former approval was given by the Court of Appeal to a solicitor in effect funding disbursements:

> 'In my judgment, therefore, the legislation does visualise the possibility that a solicitor might fund disbursements and, in that event, it would not be right to conclude that such a solicitor was "the real party" or even "a real party" to the litigation. As for the policy imperative argued by Mr Brown, after the event insurance is not a pre-requisite of bringing a claim on a CFA (see *King v Telegraph Group* [2005] 1 WLR 2282 at paragraph 100 and *Floods of Queensferry Ltd v Shand Construction Ltd* (supra) at paragraph 37). The fact that a litigant can (or cannot) afford an

---

[29] [2013] EWCA Civ 278.
[30] [2012] EWHC 2628 (TTC).

expert report or the court fee says nothing about his or her ability to fund the costs incurred by opponents in an unsuccessful claim and, indeed, Eady J (at paragraph 25 of his judgment) recognised that the solicitor could advance disbursements with a technical (albeit improbable) obligation for repayment.'

In the latter the Court gave helpful guidance that showed clear thought as to the reality of a solicitor running a case under a CFA:

'In my judgment the authorities establish the following principles:
(1) The starting point in any case must be the first principle stated by Lord Brown in Dymocks, namely that the ultimate question is whether in all the circumstances it is just to make a non-party costs order, that this is a fact-specific enquiry, and that it must be recognised that in a particular case the court may have to balance a number of different considerations, some of them conflicting.
(2) The starting point when considering the position of a solicitor is that it must be shown that he has in some way acted beyond or outside his role as a solicitor conducting litigation for his client to make him liable for a non-party costs order.
(3) The starting point when considering the position of a solicitor acting under a CFA is that the fact that he stands to benefit financially from the success of the litigation, in that otherwise he will not be able to recover his profit costs or his success fee, does not of itself mean that he has acted in some way beyond or outside his role as a solicitor conducting litigation for his client.
(4) The starting point when considering the position of a solicitor acting under a CFA who has agreed to fund disbursements under the CFA should be no different from the case of a solicitor who has not, since both arrangements are permitted and are regarded as meeting a recognised legitimate public policy aim. The position is no different where the solicitor knows that the client is impecunious and that there is no ATE policy in place; that is because acting for clients who are impecunious does not take the solicitor outside his role as such and, indeed, it is consistent with the recognised public policy aim of promoting access to justice, and because there is no obligation on a solicitor acting under a CFA to ensure that ATE insurance cover is in place when his client is impecunious.'

2.3.17 Completing the agreement

Only when the lawyer is satisfied that the client understands what he is signing should he be encouraged to sign the CFA. The lawyer should ensure that the CFA is properly completed before the client and lawyer sign the agreement. Care needs to be taken if the CFA is signed away from the solicitor's own place of business, or following discussions that take place away from their own place of business. The Cancellation of

Contracts made in a Consumer's Home or Place of Work etc Regulations 2008[31] came into force on the 1 October 2008 and applies to all CFAs entered into on this basis since that date. Where the Regulations apply then the client has a right to cancel the contract within a 7-day period. The solicitor must give the client written notice of this right, setting out various prescribed information. Failure to do so is a criminal offence and the CFA will be unenforceable. Regulation 5 provides that the regulations apply to a contract between a consumer and a trader:

(1) which is for the supply of goods or services to the consumer by a trader; and
(2) which is made:
- during a visit by the trader to the consumer's home or place of work, or to the home of another individual;
- during an excursion organised by the trader away from his business premises; or
- after an offer made by the consumer during such a visit or excursion.

Under reg 5, the Regulations apply to contracts for the supply of goods or services to the consumer by a trader. Contracts for the provision of legal advice or other legal services would therefore come within the Regulations. The only remedy if one falls foul of these regulations is to terminate the CFA and to re-issue a new one compliant with them.

The SRA Code of Conduct says:

> 'If you have not met the client, you must consider whether the Consumer Protection (Distance Selling) Regulations 2000 apply. These regulations provide for a period during which the client can cancel their instructions without cost. You should include information about this right in the terms of business.'

Where they do, reg 16 applies:

> '16 The right to cancel:
> - starts the day the contract is concluded
> - ends seven days after the day following delivery, provided the supplier provides the written/durable information no later than the time of delivery'.

It means that the CFA needs to be delivered to the client already signed to trigger the 7-day notice period.

---

[31] SI 2013/1816.

This is dealt with in detail at **1.7**.

2.3.18 Calculating the success fee

Once a firm has conducted its risk assessment and decided to accept the case it should determine the appropriate success fee (the uplift to be applied to the base costs). The Conditional Fee Agreements Order 2013 states that the maximum success fee is 100%.[32]

The prescribed success fees that previously existed under the CPR have been removed for all cases with CFAs entered into after 1 April 2013. Nevertheless a firm may decide to continue to use those prescribed success fees as they were based on national statistics and therefore should insulate the lawyer from any complaint from the client as to the amount of the success fee that is being taken from their damages. For the same reason, a solicitor might choose to consider using a two stage success fee as recommended in the case of *Ku*.[33] A first success fee at the commencement of the claim and a second, rebated or reduced success fee once liability has been admitted or trial itself is fixed. Conversely there are some lawyers who subscribe to the idea that all success fees should be 100% and will be mitigated by the 25% cap on deduction of damages.

2.4 EXCEPTIONAL CASES

2.4.1 Assignments of CFAs

The issue of the assignment of CFAs has become an important topic following the implementation of the Jackson Reforms which has led to the demise of many law firms and the loss of the recovery of additional liabilities. The most common situations in which this arises are:

- solicitor changes firms;
- firm transfers the case to another firm;
- transfer of business from a general partnership to an LLP or limited company;
- merger/take over;
- insolvency;
- client dissatisfaction;
- minors; and

---

[32] Conditional Fee Order 2013, SI 2013/698, art 3.
[33] *KU v Liverpool City Council* [2005] 1 WLR 2657.

- patients.

Assignment is a continuation of the original contract but with the benefit and burden subsequently transferred from one (or sometimes both) of the original contracting parties to a new party. It is as if the original contract were made between the subsequent parties at the date of the original contract.

This is to be contrasted with novation which is where a new party takes over the benefits and burdens of an original contracting party, but the contract is in effect a new contract between one of the previous contracting parties and a new contracting party.

Prior to 1 April 2013 it would rarely make much of a difference whether the transfer of rights and obligations was an assignment or a novation. However, a new CFA signed after 1 April 2013 will be governed under the new regime even if an earlier CFA relating to the same case was a pre-commencement funding arrangement. It seems likely that a novation would constitute a 'new CFA'. Whereas it seems likely that an assignment of an existing CFA (ie one which was signed before 1 April 2013) after 1 April 2013 may be valid so that all the costs are still assessed under the old CFA regime.

Generally contracts are assignable in law and equity. But there are two general exceptions to this rule.

2.4.1.1 Personal Contracts

The benefit of personal obligations cannot be assigned. A contract is only assignable in cases where it can make no difference to the person on whom the obligation lies to which of two persons he is to discharge it. Thus the fact that one or other party relies on the personal attributes, skill, taste, judgment, knowledge or expertise of the other may indicate that the contract is a personal one so far as he is concerned the benefit of which is not assignable. It is arguable that contract with a solicitor is a personal contract.

2.4.1.2 The burden (as opposed to the benefit) of a contract cannot be assigned.

Tolhurst v Portland Cement[34]

> 'It is, I think, quite clear that neither at law nor in equity could the burden of a contract be shifted off the shoulders of a contractor on to those of another without the consent of the contractee.'

Southway v Wolff[35]

> 'If A wishes to assign the burden of the contract to C he must obtain the consent of B, upon which the contract is novated by the substitution of C for A as a contracting party.'

A novation does not assist in preserving the pre-1 April 2013 position because it is effectively a new contract made after that date.

The conditional benefits principle provides an exception to the general rule that the burden of contracts cannot be assigned.

Tito v Wadell[36]

> 'An instrument may be framed so that it confers only a conditional or qualified right, the condition or qualification being that certain restrictions shall be observed or certain burdens assumed, such as an obligation to make certain payments. Such restrictions or qualifications are an intrinsic part of the right: you take the right as it stands, and you cannot pick out the good and reject the bad. In such cases it is not only the original grantee who is bound by the burden: his successors in title are unable to take the right without also assuming the burden. The benefit and the burden have been annexed to each other ab initio, and so the benefit is only a conditional benefit.'

In subsequent cases, the courts have stressed that this exception to the general rule must be applied restrictively and will rarely apply.

However, it was applied in the one reported case relating to assignment of CFAs: *Jenkins v Young Bros*.[37] A solicitor had, in the name of her then firm, entered into a CFA with a client. While the litigation proceeded she moved firms twice. On each occasion the benefit of the CFA was assigned by the former firm to the subsequent firm.

---

[34] [1902] 2 KB 660 and [1903] AC 414.
[35] [1991] 57 BLR 33.
[36] [1977] Ch 106.
[37] [2006] 1 WLR 3189, 14.

Rafferty J applied the principle of conditional benefits:

> '[The original solicitors were] under the general burdens of a solicitor acting for a client under a CFA, imposed in part in its section 6, "Our responsibilities", and by rules of professional conduct. [They were] obliged to act in Mr Jenkins's best interests and to secure for him in his claim for damages the best possible outcome. By virtue of the CFA [they were] entitled to the benefit of payment for work done only if his claim were successful. The CFA section "Paying us" reads: "If you win your claim you pay our basic charges, our disbursements and a success fee" and there are provisions for the calculation of costs and for any failure to beat a CPR Pt 36 offer.
>
> It follows that the benefit of being paid was conditional upon and inextricably linked to the meeting by [the solicitors] of its burden of ensuring to the best of its ability that Mr Jenkins succeeded …the condition was relevant to the exercise of the right. In our judgment, upon the facts in this case the benefit and burden of the CFA could be assigned as within an exception to the general rule.'

There was obviously a strong public policy motivation behind the judgment. However, the judge failed to deal with the issue personal contracts. The decision has been criticised.[38]

However, in *Davies v Jones*[39] the decision was cited by the Court of Appeal at least without disapproval:

> 'Plainly an inextricable link between benefit and burden would satisfy the tests formulated in all the earlier cases. That is sufficient for present purposes, though I have some doubt whether the relevant benefit and burden were correctly described.'

2.4.1.3 Specific issues

Minors

Some problems arise as a result of the transitional effect of the new regulations, where a CFA that was in existence prior to 1 April needs to be replaced or is terminated after 1 April. One such example is with a minor. The correct way to advise a minor under a CFA is actually to enter into the CFA with the minor albeit that it is signed on their behalf by the litigation friend. The problem comes if the CFA is entered into with the litigation friend and it isn't clear that it is actually for the client.

---

[38] *Cordery on Solicitors*, section F, para 2198.
[39] [2009] EWCA Civ 1164.

There is no question that a minor who has entered into a CFA prior to 1 April 2013 will recover the success fee for work done during his or her minority. If the minor reaches the age of 18 after 31 March 2013 then the new CFA which he or she must enter into will not have a recoverable success fee. In general contract principles a child's contract is voidable on the child's part unless it is a contract for necessaries. Necessaries include food, drink, clothing, lodging and articles purchased for his own use and also some services (eg for education or apprenticeship). Services (eg for education or apprenticeship) are necessaries. Most of the authorities are nineteenth century, although in *Proform Sports Management Ltd v (1) Proactive Sports Management Ltd (2) Paul Stretford*,[40] Hodge J held that whilst Wayne Rooney could enter into a valid and enforceable apprentice contract with Everton FC at the age of 15, his contract with a football agent was not a 'necessary'. Apparently a contract for legal services can be a necessary, although *Chitty* cites only first instance decisions in 1864, 1883 and 1887 as authority.

It is generally argued that a CFA is a contract for necessaries. Nevertheless, it is good practice for a minor on coming of age to ratify ongoing contracts in which they are a party. The Law Society guidance states that:

> 'Contracts enter into with a minor are not binding unless it is for necessaries. A contract for legal services could be argued to be for necessaries. Thus any CFA entered into with a minor would bind the minor on the attainment of majority at 18. Thus any CFA would continue after the minor reached 18. Further, even if the CFA entered into with a minor was not a contract for necessaries (and could thus be avoided by the minor its reaching 18), the minor could ratify the contact after he reached 19.'

The problem where the CFA is entered into directly with the litigation friend personally, as opposed to as an agent for the child, is that the CFA must be terminated automatically once the child reaches majority.

Consequently in relation to CFAs entered into before 1 April 2013 with a minor, either by themselves or through the litigation friend as agent, then a new CFA is not required and the current agreement will continue to bind the former minor. This, of course, presumes, as the Law Society suggests, that a CFA is a contract for necessaries. However, a cautious approach would have the minor ratifying the terms of the CFA as they attain majority.

---

[40] [2006] EWHC 2903 (Ch), [2007] 1 All ER 542.

For those cases where the CFA is entered into in the name of the litigation friend personally and not as an agent for the child then the Law Society guidance is:

> 'if the contract has been entered into with a "next friend" personally as opposed to as agent for the child, then it is automatically terminated once the child reaches majority. However, there is probably nothing to stop the next friend assigning the contract to the child once the child reaches majority. This would mean the original CFA would continue.'

So either the minor on attaining majority would enter into a new post-1 April CFA or they would seek an assignment of the existing CFA from the litigation friend. However, as will be seen below, there is a question mark over assignment and that an alternative more cautious approach is to require the minor to enter into a new CFA post 1 April 2013 and accept that one is going to lose the success fee for the work post 1 April. The question of course as to whether a CFA has been entered into by the litigation friend personally or as an agent is going to have to be factually interpreted in each individual case.

Patients

A similar analysis will apply as for minors, but there are potentially additional difficulties.

Under the Mental Capacity Act 2005 (MCA 2005), capacity is issue specific, so the point is whether the proposed claimant has capacity to understand a conditional fee agreement. This begs a number of questions as to the extent to which the contract has to be understood. The law presumes that everyone has capacity to contract unless a lack of capacity is established. The burden is on the person claiming lack of capacity.

As with minors, it is arguable that a CFA is a contract for necessaries. For protected parties these are defined by s 7 of the MCA 2005 as goods or services 'suitable to a person's condition in life and to his actual requirements' and s 7 provides that the protected party 'must pay a reasonable price for them'.

If a CFA is not a 'necessary', the capacity of a protected party to enter into contract is a more complicated issue than for a child. It cannot safely be entered into with an agent on behalf of the protected party as the proposed claimant would also not have the capacity to appoint an agent. In these circumstances, the contract is voidable at the protected party's option, but the voidable contract can be ratified expressly or by conduct if the protected party regains capacity. *Baldwyn v Smith*[41] provides that the court (now the Court of Protection) may order that a voidable contract made by a protected party before his affairs became subject to its jurisdiction be adopted and thus validated. A deputy appointed by the Court of Protection might be able to take this action himself, but care must be taken to ensure that such action is within the terms of the Order appointing him and also, if he is a solicitor with the same firm, that there is no potential conflict of interest.

The difficulties that solicitors may face when dealing with instructions from potential protected parties were recognised long before any controversy regarding CFAs. The Master of the Court of Protection issued a practice note on 9 August 1995 which recites the contractual issues, but goes on to stress that 'nevertheless incapacitated people may need solicitors to act for them and them alone' and confirms that 'the solicitor's authority to act for him can be expressly confirmed by the Court of Protection'.

It is unlikely that the Court of Protection will welcome applications for the appointment of deputies in cases where there are no assets (except a possible right of action) simply to ratify a retainer. However, where a deputy is to be appointed in any event, it is sensible to ask for an Order that expressly authorises him to ratify the existing retainer and enter into such further arrangements relating to the conduct of the litigation as may be necessary.

It may be prudent if there is any doubt as to capacity to have the CFA executed by the client and a potential litigation friend as well. Following medical examination, a decision can then be taken as to whether to apply to the Court of Protection for ratification.

If the client becomes a protected party after having entered into the CFA, slightly different considerations apply. Supervening lack of capacity renders non-agency aspects of the retainer voidable (so they continue and can be ratified), but revokes forthwith the agency aspects of the retainer (although this too is subject to subsequent ratification).

In *Drew v Nunn*,[42] the court suggested that revocation is only if it is 'lunacy so great so that the person who suffers from it has no contracting mind'. The agent's apparent authority continues and he may become liable for breach of warranty of authority to third parties.[43] The

---

[41] [1900] 1 Ch 588.
[42] (1879) 4 QBD 661.
[43] *Yonge v Toynbee* [1910] 1 KB 215.

termination does not affect accrued rights up to that date. The patient can ratify the acts of the solicitor as his agent in the proceedings subsequently if he regains capacity.

In *Findley v Jones (1) and MIB (2)*,[44] the claimant had been referred to his solicitor via TAG. A CFA was signed. Less than a year later, because of fears as to whether TAG CFAs complied with the CFA Regulations 2000 the client signed a second CFA with his solicitors. The first CFA was not terminated expressly. The claimant had suffered a serious head injury in the accident. During the course of the litigation it was drawn to the solicitors' attention that whilst he could function to an extent he was probably a protected party of the Court of Protection. It was accepted that until that became known the retainer was valid. The claimant's sister agreed to become litigation friend but did not formally sign a CFA or ratify either of the existing CFAs.

Treitel[45] states:

> '4–018 Where the contract is one which would be discharged by the death of a party, it may likewise be discharged by that party's supervening incapacity ... the relationship of principal and agent is terminated by the insanity of either party ... [*Drew v Nunn* [1879] 4 QBD 661; *Yonge v Toynbee* [1910] 1 KB 215].'

Treitel goes on to say that effect of the doctrine is to discharge the contract 'forthwith without more and automatically'.[46] And section 24.04 of the Guide to Professional Conduct of Solicitors 1999, which was current at the time of the claimant's incapacity in answer to the question 'what do I do if my client loses capacity in the course of the retainer?' states:

> 'The retainer will be determined by operation of law. However, you should contact, eg, relatives, the Public Trust Office or the Official Solicitor so that the relatives or the relevant agency can take reasonable steps to protect the client's interests.'

Master Hurst found that the first CFA was unenforceable as the solicitor's interest had not been notified in accordance with *Garrett*. The second CFA was potentially enforceable. Master Hurst held:

> 'For the reasons given above I find that the CFA with the Claimant came to an end as a result of his lack of capacity on 4 February 2004. Mr Mallalieu argues that where a party has no capacity to contract at the

---
[44] Unreported, SCCO Master Hurst, 13 January 2009.
[45] *Frustration and Force Majeure* (2nd edn, 2004).
[46] Treitel, 15–002.

outset, capacity may be attained at a later stage, and a party may ratify the earlier contract. He accepts that a contract for necessaries may be enforceable in such circumstances, despite the lack of capacity. In this case, however, he submits, and I accept, the matter turns on what happens when a party with capacity has entered into a contract which provides for continuing mutual obligations, but then that party loses capacity to manage his own affairs. This is a situation covered by both *Yonge v Toynbee* and *Drew v Nunn*, and which is spelt out by the Law Society in its guidance. I find, therefore, that as from 4 February 2004 the Claimant was no longer able to give instructions, and the contract was at that point frustrated. The question whether the legal services amount to "necessaries" cannot in my judgment save the contract.'

The litigation friend can adopt the retainer and, as Master Hurst points out, the simplest course would be to formally adopt the CFA. Although the litigation friend may have thought she was bound by the same terms, there was no letter and she did not sign a CFA. Whilst a private paying retainer could be simply adopted by a litigation friend by conduct, the CFA Regulations 2000 required a CFA to be signed to be enforceable. Relying somewhat imaginatively on the dissenting judgment of Maurice Kay LJ in *Crane v Cannons Leisure*[47] that the costs regime under the AJA 1999 must not operate 'unjustly', Master Hurst concluded:

'In my judgment it would certainly be unjust if these Solicitors were deprived of their reasonable costs because of the lack of signature of the second CFA by Mrs Findley-Clarke. That breach of the Regulations does not have a materially adverse effect on the protection afforded to her as a client, nor upon the administration of justice. I should regard it as adversely affecting the administration of justice if the Defendant in these proceedings was able to walk away without having to pay any costs to the Claimant's Solicitors.'

The MIB decided not to pursue an appeal.

Dissatisfied clients

If the solicitor and client relationship has broken down, the original solicitor may be reluctant to agree to instruct the new solicitor as an agent and thus retain the existing CFA with its recoverable additional liabilities. In which case, the client must be warned that in changing solicitor, success fees may cease to become recoverable.

---

[47] [2007] EWCA Civ 1352, [2008] 2 All ER 931.

If an after the event policy is linked to the earlier CFA there may be an additional problem as the client may lose the benefit of this policy on transfer of solicitor, but the transitional provisions appear to deprive the client of the benefit of QOCs.

However, it cannot be right to effectively force a client to stick with a solicitor in which he has lost confidence. One option might be to threaten the first solicitor with a complaint to the legal services ombudsman. If there are genuine service complaints against the first solicitor, it might be possible to seek an award for inadequate service from the ombudsman to compensate for the irrecoverable success fee. The threat of an application to the ombudsman might be sufficient to persuade the first firm to agree to assign the existing CFA.

If you decide to assign, care must be taken in drafting the assignment to potentially take advantage of Jenkins. Because there is a risk the court will not follow Jenkins, it might be wise to have a 'belt and braces' of a compliant post-1 April 2013 CFA in case.[48]

Death

If the person dies then, by law, their contract automatically terminates with them. So if the case is to be continued through the instruction of personal representatives then a new CFA will need to be entered into, which will fall under the new provisions.

2.5 DEFECTIVE CFAS

There is concern that the new CFA regime may be troubled by the sort of technical challenges that hampered pre-November 2005 CFA's. If that is to be the case then lawyers may have to revisit the law from that time to try to cure potential problems. Time alone will tell as to whether the potential remedy of 'materiality' as set out in *Hollins*[49] and as amended in *Myatt*[50] will prevail. Lord Dyson said:[51]

> 'the only mitigation of this strict approach is that, as was made clear in *Hollins v Russell*, the breach must be material in the sense described at para 107 of the judgement. Thus, literal that trivial and immaterial departures from the statutory requirements did not amount to a failure to

---

[48] *Forde v Birmingham City Council* is authority, albeit High Court only, for the proposition that you can have more than one retainer at the same time as a fall back if one fails.
[49] Ibid.
[50] Ibid.
[51] Paragraph 31.

satisfy the statutory conditions. It is unnecessary to decide whether the test stated at para 107 was no more than an application for principle that the law is not concerned with very small things.'

Thus, the remedy in *Hollins* appears to be confined to failures to comply with the strict requirements of the statutory provisions that are trivial when judged against the statutory conditions, regardless of whether or not the client is affected. This leaves open the suggestion that if the defect is minor, perhaps in relation to omitting the date or a signature or perhaps a simply misprint, then the court may consider the document remains affective as the defect is too minor to render the whole document defective.

2.5.1 Rectification

The courts have looked at deeds of rectification and variation as well as equitable rectification all with varying results.

In *Brennon v Associated Asphalt*[52] the court examined whether a deed of rectification could be used to remedy a defect, but where the deed of rectification was executed after the costs order had been made at the end of the trial. Perhaps unsurprisingly the court considered that the deed was ineffective to rectify the apparent defect in the document as the case had concluded and all rights for which the deed was sought to be varied had been exercised. The question whether such a deed may be effective before a costs order is made is left open, but even if it is possible it must also raise the question as to whether it is appropriate for the client to have independent advice in so doing whether external evidence of the true agreement is necessary to reflect the rectified CFA? The two may, of course, go hand in hand. Given that the client is being asked to help their solicitor cure a defect in the agreement so that he can charge the client where no such ability existed before (by reason of the defect) one can see why the answer is almost certainly yes.

2.5.2 Deed of variation

The courts were asked to look at this in *Oyston v RBS*[53] where a deed was made after the judgment and making of a costs order. (The CFA was held to be unenforceable because it provided for a success fee which could exceed 100%.) After the date of judgment on costs the client and his solicitors entered into a deed of variation which removed reference to any success fee above 100%. It was argued, among other things, that

---

[52] [2006] EWHC 90052 (Costs) 18 May 2006.
[53] [2006] EWHC 90053 (Costs) 16 May 2006.

variation after the date of judgement can be of no effect against the paying party and the variation should not be allowed as it imposes an additional burden on the paying party. Senior Costs Judge Hurst accepted these arguments, but declined to express a view about the effectiveness of deeds made before judgment because that issue was not argued before him.

2.5.3 Equitable rectification by the court

The judgment of District Judge Flanagan in *Morrish & Co v No-one*[54] is apparently the only report known of a court being asked to intervene to rectify a CFA because it received defects prior to it being disclosed to the paying party. In this case the CFA omitted the date of the accident and the defendant's name which in relation to the pre-2006 CFA's would have rendered the document defective. The court granted the equitable remedy of correcting these omissions on the basis that it was clear that both the client and the solicitor knew all along what the CFA intended. The remedy backdated the correction to the original date of the CFA and was supported with the client's consent and witness statements. Ironically the necessity for this correction would seem to run contrary to the comments above that these were such minor omissions as not to require rectification as they were not material defects. However, clearly it helps to err on the side of caution. However, the paying party may seek to set aside such an order on the grounds it is not suitable to circumvent effective regulations where the defect was material and not capable of resolution.

2.5.4 Terminate the existing CFA and start again

This is likely to be the most effective and perhaps most widely used remedy. Permission of the client is not required for the termination of the CFA and it is argued that independent advice for the client is not required here. Termination is possible because it would seem to be the case that it is not reasonable to expect a solicitor to continue to act under a retainer that they know to be defective. What is the client's remedy if they are unhappy with this? If they are unhappy that the solicitor is seeking to 'renege' from a defective retainer but then seeking to set up an effective retainer the client could of course seek representation elsewhere in which case they will find themselves required to enter into an effective retainer with costs obligations in any event.

---

[54] APIL Focus vol 13, issue 1, February 2003 (DJ Flanagan, Leeds County Court).

Before the new CFA is executed it is wise to seek the agreement of any relevant ATE provider that they will continue to provide indemnity under the new arrangements. If the CFA is one that does not involve recovery of additional liabilities (which seems almost inevitable as it is unlikely that post 2005 would need such remedy) then notice of funding is not going to be required.

2.5.5 Retrospectivity

In *Kellar v Williams*[55] there was a fee paying agreement with solicitors which was varied after a costs order was made. It was not a CFA. The Privy Council held it was open to the client and to his solicitors to vary the agreement by changing the method of calculating the fees payable as long as there was consideration for the change. However, the paying party could not be ordered to accept the variation if it produced a higher figure for costs because the amendment came into existence subsequent to the costs order and so could be disregarded by the paying party if he wished. *Kellar* was considered in the context of a CFA by *Crook v Birmingham City Council*[56] where the solicitor's CFA was challenged and subsequently entered into a contentious business agreement with the client which confirmed the client remained liable under the CFA. The consideration for this was the solicitor giving up their right to retain the compensation pending the outcome of the costs assessment. Master Campbell suggested that the decision in *Kellar* prevents a successful solicitor from being 'wise after the event' and increasing his charges to the client when he knows a costs order has been made against the other side. However, in using a CFA they were not attempting to impose a greater burden on their client (and consequently the defendants) than existed before the outcome of the claim was known. Accordingly he upheld the new arrangement. In *Musa King v Telegraph*,[57] Master Hurst stated:

> 'There is no doubt that, as between the claimant's solicitors and their client, the CFA may be backdated. This would, in my judgement, be sufficient to satisfy the court that there was a proper retainer between the client and his solicitors before the signing of the CFA ...'

It should be noted, however, that Senior Costs Judge Hurst was looking at a situation with a CFA that was to have retrospective effect only, related to a period 18 days earlier and at the commencement of the case. It remains open to question whether he might have been quite so dogmatic in a situation where the solicitor asked the client to assist him

---

[55] [2004] UKPC 30.
[56] Unreported, 21 August 2006 (SCCO).
[57] [2005] EWHC 90015 (Costs).

in reclaiming the right to effect a charge for work that he had otherwise lost the right to charge by reason of an earlier defective CFA. Master Hurst's apparent remedy for the retrospective CFA was to suggest that no success fee could be charged for the retrospective period although his reasoning, it is respectively submitted, seems questionable. It may be that there was confusion between the right to charge the client the success fee in the absence of an effective notice as was previously required by the CPR[58] to give the paying party sufficient notice that they must pay the success fee, because contractually there seemed little wrong with the agreement. In remedying a defective CFA from the paying party this point may well be academic. In *Holmes v Alfred McAlpine*,[59] the claimant's solicitors had told the client in June 2000 that they would represent him under a CFA with no success fee. However, in August 2000 the client was required to sign a CFA dated July 2000 that this time included a 25% success fee and no reference to retrospectivity in the narrative. Burton J decided this was a non-material breach but went onto say:

> 'I would emphasize, however, the backdating of documents as was done in this case is generally wrong. It is wrong to seek to give an agreement retrospective effect by backdating it ... if it is agreed that a written agreement should apply to work done before it is entered into, it should be correctly dated with the date on which it is signed and expressed to have retrospective effect, ie to apply to work done before its date ... backdating is liable to mislead third parties, and is liable to lead to suspicion that it was done in order to mislead third parties, including a court before which the agreement is to be placed.'

It is noteworthy that there remains no appellant authority on this subject and Senior Costs Judge Hurst was only asked to consider retrospectivity in very limited circumstances and certainly not in the circumstances designed to assist a solicitor being able to recover the right to charge that they had previously lost. John Foy QC[60] has advised APIL of the possibility of using a contentious business agreement to work retrospectively and a new CFA for the future work. He concluded, however, that a retrospective CFA for both the past and future work is the better option:

> 'A solicitor may enter into a retrospective contentious business agreement pursuant to section 59 of the Solicitors Act 1974 and a further new CFA to cover future costs. The difficulty with the CBA route is that it places the claimant in a potentially worse position that he was under the old CFA (where enforceable or not) because he now has a liability for costs in a

---

[58] CPR, r 44.15.
[59] [2006] EWHC 110 (QB).
[60] APIL PI Focus vol 70, issue 1.

losing case which he did not previously have. As well as the normal solicitor's client care requirements, it may be a case where the client should be told to take independent advice, which in practice wouldn't make it unworkable.

There is no doubt that a retrospective CFA can be entered into. The wording of section 59 makes this clear. However, if the retrospective CBA is permissible why not a retrospective CFA? Section 59, of course will not apply but what is the objection to such an agreement? One answer might be that there is no consideration given by the solicitor for such an agreement. If it is perfectly plain that the existing CFA was unenforceable then there may not be consideration (see later for a possible argument) and the best advice is probably to accept the position, enter a new CFA and at least get paid for future work. But if there is uncertainty about whether the existing CFA is enforceable or not, the advice is to enter into a retrospective CFA which is a CFA lite permissible but virtue of (CPR) 43.2(3) with a nil uplift and a new CFA with an uplift to cover future work. Then there is consideration. In consideration for terminating the existing CFA, under which the claimant may have a liability for costs and success fee, and enter into a new one, the solicitors will not have any right to a success fee incurred prior to the date of the retrospective CFA. The claimant is not prejudiced because the light provision means he will not in any circumstances have to pay any costs, whereas before he may have been liable.

A further objection might be that no notice of funding has been given to the defendant pursuant to (CPR) 44.15 at the time the costs were incurred. However, this is not uncommon. Notices are often given when proceedings are commenced and will relate to costs already incurred. In the case of a nil uplift CFA the additional liabilities reduced. The ATE premium is the same as when notice was originally given and the success fee has gone, so there is no possible prejudice to the paying party (except a possible windfall if the previous CFA had been found to be unenforceable).

There is no public policy reason why this remedy should not be adopted. The solicitors cannot be expected to go on working when there is a chance they may not be paid at all. The claimant is not worse off and may well be better off. The administration of justice is not affected. Indeed it must be in the interest of the administration of justice that solicitors can be confident of being paid a proper amount for their work.'

It is suggested therefore that the best way forward if a solicitor has doubt about whether the CFA is enforceable is to enter into a new retrospective CFA lite with a nil uplift and a new CFA for future costs with a success fee. The original CFA can be terminated by the client. If it is allowed to run without termination with a view to arguing it is enforceable, the danger that it will nonetheless be held to be unenforceable in those circumstances it may be harder to establish consideration for the new agreement.

In *Forde v Birmingham City Council*,[61] the High Court held the second of two conditional fee agreements to be valid and enforceable, even though it was retrospective and the retrospective period covered a period prior to 1 November 2005, when there was a different regime in place.

2.5.5.1 Recoverability of ATE

It is important to note that even if one continues to represent a client under a pre-April CFA where recoverability of additional liabilities would have been permitted, if the contract for after the event insurance is not taken out until after 1 April then it will fall foul of the LASPO provisions and the ATE premium will not be recoverable and will have instead to be funded either by the client or their lawyer.

Extensions of insurance entered into before April is less clear at the moment. It is argued that if one simply seeks to vary an existing ATE contract; in other words one that was entered into before 1 April then that would remain a recoverable premium. It is inevitable that there will be some challenge to that view but it is presently permitted there is a difference between entering into a new contact or varying an earlier one.

2.5.6 Price increase clause

The Law Society model CFA has historically provided the lawyer with the ability to review their hourly rate and to notify the client of any change in the rate in writing: 'We will review the hourly rate in X each year and we will notify you of any change in the rate in writing.'

There is current thinking that a consumer clause of this kind may breach the Unfair Contract Terms Regulations 1999 (UCTR). Under Sch 2 of UCTR the clause falling within the following description would be 'indicative' of being unfair:

> '(I) providing for the price of goods to be determined at the time of delivery or allowing the seller of goods or supplier of services to increase their price without in both cases giving the consumer the corresponding right to cancel the contract if the final price is too high in relation to price agreed when the contract was concluded.'

---

[61] [2009] EWHC 12 (QB1).

There is an argument therefore that says that this clause as currently used by the Law Society in its model agreement would fall foul of UCTR because it does not give the client the right to cancel if they do not wish to agree the increase. If the clause were determined to be unfair it does not render the CFA unenforceable simply the price increase clause.[62]

Therefore it may be preferable to set the hourly rates annual in the CFA; another is to continue to reserve the right to review the hourly rate but indicate that any proposed increase will be discussed and implemented with the agreement of the client; although it is difficult to see why a client would agree to it. Nor does it provide what will happen if the client declines to agree to the increase. Does the solicitor use this to withdraw from the contract completely or are they bound to accept an hourly rate that may be out of date?

2.5.7 Notice

As there are no longer any recoverable liabilities, notice to the opponent of the CFA is no longer required.

---

[62] Regulation 8.

CHAPTER 3

DAMAGES-BASED AGREEMENTS

3.1 INTRODUCTION

3.1.1 Contingency fees in the United Kingdom

For many years public policy, expressed through the offences of champerty and maintenance and enforced through court decisions and practice rules, prevented lawyers from having a financial interest in the outcome of a case. Although the crime was abolished in the 1960s, any such agreement remained unenforceable at law. Fears about an ever-reducing access to justice led to a fundamental change of view. But the means by which this policy change was implemented, conditional fee agreements, was a very 'English' compromise. Parliament did not want to introduce a US-style system of contingency fees for fear of creating a 'compensation culture'. The 'loser pays' costs rule was to be maintained. And 'success fees' for risk were to be linked to the costs by way of an uplift on base costs and not to the damages recovered.

A conditional fee agreement is itself on a wide definition a 'contingency fee agreement' as the fee (and the amount of the fee payable) is contingent upon the outcome. However, as Lord Justice Jackson said in his Final Report, contingency fees in the narrower sense are:

> 'fees which (a) are payable if the client wins and (b) are calculated as a percentage of the sum recovered.'

Even after the introduction of conditional fee agreements, solicitors remained prohibited from acting on the basis of a contingency fee for contentious business, save insofar as this was lawful under statute (ie a conditional fee agreement complying with s 58 of the Courts and Legal Services Act 1990) or at common law. For example, the Solicitor's Code of Conduct 2007 read:

'2.04 Contingency Fees

(1) You must not enter into an arrangement to receive a contingency fee for work done in prosecuting or defending any contentious proceedings before a court of England and Wales, a British court martial or an arbitrator where the seat of the arbitration is in England and Wales, except as permitted by statute or the common law.'

And the House of Lords *in Awwad v Geraghty & Co (a firm)*,[1] decided that contingency fee agreements for contentious business which did not comply with statute (ie at that time only conditional fee agreements) were unenforceable at common law so that no costs could be recovered under them at all. If an unenforceable conditional fee agreement cannot be enforced against the client then, because of the indemnity principle, costs cannot be recovered against the third party who would otherwise be liable under the order for costs.

However, employment tribunal claims (where there is generally no cost shifting) were generally accepted as 'non-contentious business' for the purposes of the Solicitors Act 1974. Contingency fees were therefore permitted for such work by the Law Society. The growing involvement of claims management companies in such claims led to the regulation of such arrangements in 2010 by way of an amendment to the Courts and Legal Services Act 1990. Regulations were introduced to allow contingency fee agreements in the narrower sense (ie calculated as a proportion of the sum recovered) and called 'damages-based agreements'.[2]

3.1.2 Overseas experience

Contingency fees are of course widely used in the US. As Lord Justice Jackson recorded in Chapter 60 of his Interim Report:

'3.1 Contingency fee arrangements have been called a "hallmark" of the US legal system and their use dates back to at least 1786. Today, contingency fee arrangements are most commonly utilised by individual litigants in tort claims or breach of contract claims. A well-regarded (although now somewhat dated) empirical study found that individual litigants use contingency fee arrangements in approximately 87% of all tort claims and 53% of all contractual claims. In contrast, approximately 88% of organisational litigants use hourly or flat fees.'

This arrangement is not unregulated. As Lord Justice Jackson goes on to describe:

---

[1] [2001] QB 570, [2000] 1 All ER 608, [2000] 3 WLR 1041, CA.
[2] Damages-based Agreements Regulations 2010, SI 2010/1206.

'2.3 About half the states in the United States limit contingency fees in some way – from imposing sliding scales, to capping percentages, to requiring court review for reasonableness. Most states that limit contingency fees do so in the context of medical malpractice, personal injury, wrongful death or tortious conduct cases.'

Of course, the main difference between the legal systems in the US and the UK is that under the so-called 'English Rule' costs usually 'follow the event' so that the 'loser pays', whereas under the so-called 'American Rule' each side usually (although not invariably) bears their own cost of the litigation, win or lose. This difference gave rise to the need for 'after the event insurance' to accompany conditional fee agreements in the UK and, after 1 April 2013, the introduction of a limited form of the 'American Rule' for personal injury litigation, namely 'qualified one-way cost shifting' (see Chapter 4). However, the application of the English Rule also leads to complications over how the recovered between the parties costs are dealt with in conjunction with a contingency fee based on the damages. There are two possibilities:

- the 'success fee model' whereby the contingency fee is paid on top of the recovered between the parties costs; or
- the 'Ontario model' where the recovered between the parties costs are set against the amount of the contingent fee.

The Ontario model was of interest to Lord Justice Jackson because it provided a real life example of a system which applied contingency fees in an environment where the English Rule of cost recovery applies. He describes this in Chapter 61 of the Interim Report:

'Contingency fee agreements are a common feature of civil litigation in Canada, including in Ontario. Where the reward for success is a multiple of the regular fee, contingency fee agreements are conceptually similar to CFAs in England and Wales. However, the permissible multiples are higher and there is no principle of recoverability beyond the ordinary fee for the solicitors' work. As mentioned above, this form of contingency fee agreement is generally confined to class actions. The alternative form of contingency fee agreement (which is generally used outside the realm of class actions) provides for the plaintiffs' lawyers to receive a percentage of any sums recovered. Such contingency fee agreements are principally used in personal injury actions. The contingency fee charged is often in the region of 20% (although in some cases it may go up to 30%). I understand from practitioners that in such cases the costs awarded by the court often turn out to be very close to 15% of the damages. Thus in a typical personal injuries case (where the defendant agrees or is ordered to pay damages and costs) the claimant may end up losing about 5% of his damages as a contribution to costs. This does not appear to be a source of general concern or complaint. Contingency fee agreements (with the reward for the lawyers being a percentage of the sum recovered) are sometimes used outside personal injury litigation, for example in contract claims. I am told that contingency fee agreements are now beginning to be used in commercial litigation.'

3.1.3 The Civil Justice Council

There had been a growing interest in allowing contingency fees in England and Wales in the new millennium. It was perhaps thought that having crossed the Rubicon of allowing fees to be paid to lawyers contingent upon the outcome (with conditional fee agreements), there was no real conceptual difference in allowing the lawyer to charge a fee based on the damages recovered.

In 2005 the Civil Justice Council's first report 'Improved Access to Justice – Funding Options and Proportionate Costs', recommendation 10 was as follows:

> 'In contentious business cases where contingency fees are currently disallowed, American style contingency fees requiring the abolition of the fee shifting rule should not be introduced. However, consideration should be given to the introduction of contingency fees on a regulated basis along similar lines to those permitted in Ontario by the Solicitors Act 2002 particularly to assist access to justice in group actions and other complex cases where no other method of funding is available.'

And in 2007 in a second report, also somewhat confusingly titled 'Improved Access to Justice – Funding Options and Proportionate Costs', recommendation 4 was as follows:

> 'In multi party cases where no other form of funding is available, regulated contingency fees should be permitted to provide access to justice. The Ministry of Justice should conduct thorough research to ascertain whether contingency fees can improve access to justice in the resolution of civil disputes generally.'

3.1.4 The Jackson review

Lord Justice Jackson in his Interim Report set out the pros and cons of contingency fee agreements. He summarised the arguments raised in favour as follows:

- '• the principle of no win–no fee has been established by CFAs, so there can be no principled objection to contingency fee agreements.
- • Contingency fee agreements are simpler than CFAs. They are easier to understand and would avoid some of the problems of CFAs.

- Contingency fee agreements offer less scope for conflicts of interest than CFAs.
- Many clients would prefer contingency fee agreements to CFAs.
- If CFAs are permitted as well as the existing funding mechanisms, this can only increase access to justice.
- Under a contingency fee agreement, the fees payable to the lawyer are always, and by definition, proportionate.
- Contingency fees give the lawyer a direct incentive to maximise recovery for his client.
- There is no danger of contingency fees creating a US type situation here. In England and Wales (a) juries do not assess damages and (b) judges are not elected.
- Contingency fees would "remove from a reluctant judiciary the difficult task of seeking to regulate costs on a case by case basis".
- Contingency fees work well in employment tribunals. They also work well in appeals to the VAT and Duties Tribunal.
- There can be no possible objection to sophisticated clients (e.g. large plcs with inhouse counsel) entering into contingency fee agreements, if that is what both they and their solicitors want to do.'

And he summarised the arguments raised against contingency fees as follows:

'- Contingency fee agreements are liable to give rise to greater conflicts of interest between lawyer and client than in the case of CFAs.
- It is wrong in principle for the lawyer to have an interest in the level of damages.
- If CFAs and contingent fees co-exist, lawyers would conduct lower value claims on CFAs and higher value claims on contingent fees. This dual system would maximise recovery for lawyers and give rise to a conflict of interest between lawyer and client.
- If part of the contingent fee is not recoverable from the other side (as is the case in all jurisdictions where contingent fees are currently permitted), then clients will lose part of their damages. This is unacceptable in personal injury cases especially in so far as damages represent the cost of future care.
- Contingent fees create an incentive to settle a case early.
- Contingent fees will only be viable if the level of general damages for personal injuries increases. That is not going to happen, as is apparent from the nonimplementation of the Law Commission's 1998 report.
- Contingent fees are only acceptable in the US because damages are extremely high and include non-compensatory elements. This is not the case here.
- The introduction of contingency fees would be damaging to the solicitors profession.

- The introduction of contingent fees would be contrary to the existing professional culture, which makes the Commercial Court attractive to overseas litigants.'

Lord Justice Jackson pointed out that if introduced, regulation would be required:

'It appears to be generally accepted that if contingency fees become permitted, they should be regulated. Views differ as to the appropriate form of regulation. On one view, it is sufficient if the client takes independent advice before entering into a contingency fee agreement. On the alternative view, there ought to be fairly detailed rules about what a contingency fee agreement must and must not include (re percentage recovery, resolution of disputes etc.).'

In the Final Report, Lord Justice Jackson concluded:[3]

'Having weighed up the conflicting arguments, I conclude that both solicitors and counsel should be permitted to enter into contingency fee agreements with their clients on the Ontario model. In other words, costs shifting is effected on a conventional basis and in so far as the contingency fee exceeds what would be chargeable under a normal fee agreement, that is borne by the successful litigant.'

His reasoning for the recommendation was:

'it is desirable that as many funding methods as possible should be available to litigants. This will be particularly important if my earlier recommendations are accepted, that CFA success fees and ATE insurance premiums should become irrecoverable.'

3.1.5 Civil Justice Council Working Party

The Ministry of Justice accepted Lord Justice Jackson's recommendations. In the case of contingency fees, however, it commissioned the Civil Justice Council to set up a Working Group to examine the practical issues and to report before it finalised legislation and regulations.

The Working Party reported on 25 July 2012.[4] A key point was that they felt that Lord Justice Jackson's suggestion of an independent lawyer to advise clients on the funding arrangement was not pursued. They also felt that, subject to review, existing professional regulation should provide adequate consumer protection:

---

[3] 'Review of Civil Litigation Costs: Final Report', December 2009, Chapter 12, para 4.2.
[4] 'Report of the Working Party on Damages Based Agreements (Contingency Fees)'.

'Members of the WP who are representatives of the Solicitors Regulation Authority (SRA) and the Bar Standards Board (BSB) have advised that their respective regulations already deal with professional and ethical issues of conflict generally and in respect of the now well established "no-win, no-fee" method of funding civil cases. However, the WP recommends (6) that the SRA and BSB review their current guidance to ensure that the use of new DBAs is adequately covered alongside the existing guidance in relation to CFAs.'

The Working Group's report is considered further below at **3.6**.

3.2 DAMAGES-BASED AGREEMENTS: STATUTORY REQUIREMENTS

3.2.1 Legal Aid, Sentencing and Punishment of Offenders Act 2012 (LASPO)

The Ministry of Justice implemented the Jackson recommendations on contingency fees by way of damages-based agreements (DBAs), contingency fees on the narrow basis which are lawful under s 45 of LASPO.

Section 45 of LASPO operates to amend the provisions of the original statute, the Courts and Legal Services Act 1990. Section 58AA of that Act (as amended) deals with DBAs and was originally introduced to deal with DBAs for employment tribunal cases.

The revised s 58AA, with explanatory commentary, is set out at **3.2.1.1**.

3.2.1.1 A compliant DBA is 'not unenforceable'

'58AA (1) A damages-based agreement which satisfies the conditions in subsection (4) is not unenforceable by reason only of its being a damages-based agreement.

(2) But (subject to subsection (9)) a damages-based agreement which does not satisfy those conditions is unenforceable.'

Subsection (1) follows the wording used for conditional fee agreements in s 58 of the Courts and Legal Services Act 1990, providing that this kind of contingency fee is lawful and thus 'not unenforceable' (as it would be at common law), provided that it complies with the statutory requirements. This wording is likely to be construed in the same way as s 58 was construed in the case-law relating to conditional fee agreements. In particular, the decision of the Court of Appeal in *Garrett v Halton BC; Myatt and others v NCB*[5] will probably be followed:

> 'To adopt language appropriate to a breach of contract, the statutory language refers only to breach, and not to causation or loss. Subject to the principle that the law is not concerned with very small things, a breach of contract is a breach even if it causes no loss.
>
> The primary statutory purpose of the requirements was to provide protection to claimants. In these circumstances, it seems to us that it would be extraordinary if the court were required to hold that, however egregious the breach, it was not material if it had not in fact caused the client to suffer any loss.'

The Court felt that the test previously set out in *Hollins v Russell* (ie materially adverse effect on the protection afforded to the client or the administration of justice)[6] was no more than an application of the principle that the law is not concerned with very small things.

It is therefore essential that solicitors strictly comply with the requirements of the statute or regulations. If they do not, the DBA is likely to fall outside the statutory protection and be an unlawful and unenforceable contingency fee agreement at common law.

3.2.1.2 What is a DBA?

> '58AA(3) For the purposes of this section a damages-based agreement is an agreement between a person providing advocacy services, litigation services or claims management services and the recipient of those services which provides that—
> (i) the recipient is to make a payment to the person providing the services if the recipient obtains a specified financial benefit in connection with the matter in relation to which the services are provided, and
> (ii) the amount of that payment is to be determined by reference to the amount of the financial benefit obtained;
> ...
>
> 58AA(7) In this section—
>
> "payment" includes a transfer of assets and any other transfer of money's worth (and the reference in subsection (4)(b) to a payment above a prescribed amount, or above an amount calculated in a prescribed manner, is to be construed accordingly);

---

[5] [2006] EWCA Civ 1017, [2007] 1 WLR 554, [2007] 1 All ER 147.
[6] [2003] EWCA Civ 718, [2003] 4 All ER 950, [2003] 1 WLR 2487, [2003] 3 Costs LR 423.

"claims management services" has the same meaning as in Part 2 of the Compensation Act 2006 (see section 4(2) of that Act).

(7A) In this section (and in the definitions of "advocacy services" and "litigation services" as they apply for the purposes of this section) "proceedings" includes any sort of proceedings for resolving disputes (and not just proceedings in a court), whether commenced or contemplated.'

The concept of 'payment' (as a defined statutory term rather than an ordinary English word) is introduced here. It is widely defined so that any transfer of value (money or money's worth) is included.

The solicitor must be careful not to turn an intended conditional fee agreement into a damages-based agreement by mistake. A damages-based agreement is defined by the statute as an agreement where the solicitor's fee is determined by reference to the sums recovered. This might, for example, be arguable even in the case of an agreement expressed to be a conditional fee agreement if the solicitor agrees to charge as solicitor and client costs the fixed recoverable costs in fast track personal injury cases (which are calculated by reference to the damages) plus a success fee (a percentage uplift on such costs). It is far from certain that this would in practice turn a conditional fee agreement into a damages-based agreement, but there will almost inevitably be such a challenge by paying parties. The problem is that the Damages-based Agreements Regulations 2013 have different statutory requirements which will be difficult to meet if the solicitor thinks that he is entering into a conditional fee agreement. The agreement would, however, probably be a conditional fee agreement if the solicitor reserves the right to charge solicitor and client costs (either a fixed fee, not linked to the damages, or at hourly rate) on top of the fixed recoverable costs.

Solicitors should also be wary of complicated 'hybrid' agreements seeking to maximise their fees in various circumstances. Not only may this not be in the best interests of the client, it may also have the effect of rendering the entire retainer unenforceable.

The statute applies to the provision of litigation services defined elsewhere (s 119 of the Courts and Legal Services Act 1990) as:

'any services which it would be reasonable to expect a person who is exercising, or contemplating exercising, a right to conduct litigation in relation to any proceedings, or contemplated proceedings, to provide.'

The effect of s 58AA(7A) appears to mean that work done prior to the issue of court proceedings is caught by the statutory provisions. In other words, it does not appear to be possible to enter into a contingency fee which does not comply with the statute and regulations for pre-proceedings work only. This is notwithstanding the provisions of subsection 9:

> '58AA(9) Where section 57 of the Solicitors Act 1974 (non-contentious business agreements between solicitor and client) applies to a damages-based agreement other than one relating to an employment matter, subsections (1) and (2) of this section do not make it unenforceable.'

The definitions of contentious and non-contentious business in the Solicitors Act 1974 are unfortunately rather circular. But as contentious business is defined as 'business done ... in or for the purposes of proceedings begun before a court or before an arbitrator', it seems that the purpose of subsection 9 is to exclude what is clearly non-contentious solicitor's work (eg property or share transactional work) from this additional statutory regulation, rather than to allow pre-proceedings work to escape regulation. The wording is far from clear, however, and leading commentator Professor Rachel Mulheron reaches a contrary view in 'The Damages-Based Agreements Regulations: Some conundrums in the "Brave New World' of funding".[7]

The statute also applies to damages-based agreements (a contingency fee payable by reference to the damages, ie 'the financial benefit received') in respect of 'claims management services'. These are defined in s 4(2) of the Compensation Act 2006 as:

> 'advice or other services in relation to the making of a claim'

where:

> '"claim" means a claim for compensation, restitution, repayment or any other remedy or relief in respect of loss or damage or in respect of an obligation, whether the claim is made or could be made—
> (i) by way of legal proceedings,
> (ii) in accordance with a scheme of regulation (whether voluntary or compulsory), or
> (iii) in pursuance of a voluntary undertaking'

provided that such 'claims' are 'regulated', which are presently those under the Compensation (Regulated Claims Management Services) Order 2006:

> '(3) The kinds of claim are the following—

---

[7] (2013) 32 CJQ, Issue 2, 252.

(a) claims for personal injuries, within the meaning in the Civil Procedure Rules 1998;
(b) claims under the Criminal Injuries Compensation Scheme established under the Criminal Injuries Compensation Act 1995;
(c) claims for a benefit specified or referred to in article 3 of the Compensation (Specification of Benefits) Order 2006;
(d) claims in relation to employment (including claims in relation to wages and salaries and other employment-related payments, and claims in relation to wrongful or unfair dismissal, redundancy, discrimination and harassment);
(e) claims for housing disrepair (that is, claims under section 11 of the Landlord and Tenant Act 1985 or section 4 of the Defective Premises Act 1972, claims in relation to the disrepair of premises under a term of a tenancy agreement or lease or under the common law relating to nuisance or negligence, but not claims for statutory nuisance under section 82 of the Environmental Protection Act 1990);
(f) claims in relation to financial products or services'

unless (under reg (4)) it relates to a referral 'not undertaken for or in expectation of a fee, gain or reward'.

The statutory provisions relating to damages-based agreements for personal injury claims therefore apply to solicitors providing 'litigation services', barristers providing 'advocacy services' and/or to claims management companies providing 'advice or other services in relation to the making of a claim'.

The Ministry of Justice appear to consider that the claims management services provisions only apply to employment tribunal claims and not to court proceedings (eg for personal injury claims). See, for example, Lord McNally, who stated:[8]

'On why DBA regulations do not contain requirements on termination for civil litigation, as in employment cases, the DBA regulations 2010 made provisions for employment cases which can be taken forward by non-lawyers. Detailed safeguards need to be built in as a result. Civil litigation can be conducted only by lawyers, who are subject to their own professional regulations.'

And Helen Grant MP stated:[9]

'Regulations 5, 6, 7 and 8 replicate the provisions from the 2010 regulations for employment matters. Those detailed provisions on information and other matters are necessary because employment matters

---

[8] *Hansard*, 26 February 2013, col GC133.
[9] *Hansard*, Fifth Delegated Legislation Committee Monday 11 March 2013, col 5.

may be undertaken by non-lawyers, such as claims managers. On the other hand, civil litigation can be undertaken only by qualified legal representatives, who are subject to regulation by their professional bodies and whose conduct may be subject to challenge through those bodies. It is therefore considered that, at this stage, further regulation is not required.'

This may well be right but it is, however, not clear from the actual wording of the various statutes why claims management companies should not enter into DBAs in respect of personal injury claims. If they can, that might in theory mean a claimant could enter into a DBA with the claims management company for up to 25 per cent of general damages and past loss and a further DBA with a solicitor for another 25 per cent of the damages (or indeed a CFA with a success fee capped at another 25 per cent). This is obviously not what the government intended.

3.2.1.3 Requirements prescribed by statute

'58AA(4) The agreement—
(a) must be in writing;
(aa) must not relate to proceedings which by virtue of section 58A(1) and (2) cannot be the subject of an enforceable conditional fee agreement or to proceedings of a description prescribed by the Lord Chancellor;'

This means that any non-family civil litigation can be conducted either under a damages-based agreement or a conditional fee agreement.

The damages-based agreement must be a written agreement. It does not have to be signed by the client, but that is obviously best evidence of compliance.

3.2.1.4 Further requirements prescribed by regulations

'58AA(4)(b) if regulations so provide, must not provide for a payment above a prescribed amount or for a payment above an amount calculated in a prescribed manner;
(c) must comply with such other requirements as to its terms and conditions as are prescribed; and
(d) must be made only after the person providing services under the agreement has complied with such requirements (if any) as may be prescribed as to the provision of information.

(5) Regulations under subsection (4) are to be made by the Lord Chancellor and may make different provision in relation to different descriptions of agreements.

(6) Before making regulations under subsection (4) the Lord Chancellor must consult—
(a) the designated judges,
(b) the General Council of the Bar,
(c) the Law Society, and
(d) such other bodies as the Lord Chancellor considers appropriate.

The damages-based agreement must therefore also comply with regulations made, following consultation, by the Lord Chancellor (ie the Damages-Based Agreements Regulations 2013).

It should be noted that the definition of 'payment' under the Damages-based Agreements Regulations 2013 is different to that under the statute (reg 1(2)):

> '"payment" means that part of the sum recovered in respect of the claim or damages awarded that the client agrees to pay the representative, and excludes expenses but includes … any disbursements incurred by the representative in respect of counsel's fees;'

The fee must be a part of the 'sum recovered', so damages-based agreements cannot be used by defendants (except presumably by reference to damages awarded under a counterclaim, which is unlikely to apply in personal injury litigation).

Counsel's fees must be included within the 'payment' (the fee charged by reference to the damages). So Counsel must agree to act under a damages-based agreement too. It appears that it is not therefore permissible in personal injury litigation for the solicitor to act under a damages-based agreement, but for Counsel to charge on a private paying basis. But 'expenses' (which are defined as disbursements, including expert's fees), can be charged in addition. The Regulations are silent as to whether after the event insurance premiums are 'expenses' and so chargeable to the client in addition. However, the Ministry of Justice's view is that after the event insurance premiums are expenses and so outside the cap. Lord McNally said:[10]

> 'The noble Lord asked whether the cost of ATE insurance is within or outside the 25% cap. This is an expense and is therefore outside the cap.'

Regulation 3 sets out the requirements for the contents of all damages-based agreements, as specified under s 58AA(4)(c) of the Courts and Legal Services Act 1990:

---

[10] *Hansard*, 26 February 2013, col GC133.

'3 Requirements of an agreement in respect of all damages-based agreements

The requirements prescribed for the purposes of section 58AA(4)(c) of the Act are that the terms and conditions of a damages-based agreement must specify—
(a) the claim or proceedings or parts of them to which the agreement relates;
(b) the circumstances in which the representative's payment, expenses and costs, or part of them, are payable; and
(c) the reason for setting the amount of the payment at the level agreed …'

It seems likely that the extensive case-law relating to conditional fee agreements and compliance with relevant parts of the Conditional Fee Agreements Regulations 2000[11] will apply by analogy to the interpretation of these requirements for damages-based agreements.

Regulation 4 sets out the key provisions relating to payment. For all damages-based agreements (other than relating to employment matters):

'4 Payment in respect of claims or proceedings other than an employment matter

(1) In respect of any claim or proceedings, other than an employment matter, to which these Regulations apply, a damages-based agreement must not require an amount to be paid by the client other than—
(a) the payment, net of—
   (i) any costs (including fixed costs under Part 45 of the Civil Procedure Rules 1998); and
   (ii) where relevant, any sum in respect of disbursements incurred by the representative in respect of counsel's fees,

that have been paid or are payable by another party to the proceedings by agreement or order; and
(b) any expenses incurred by the representative, net of any amount which has been paid or is payable by another party to the proceedings by agreement or order.'

So far as para (a)(ii) is concerned, this will not apply to personal injury litigation as counsel's fees are only allowed as disbursements on top of the 'payment'. Presumably, the intention behind 'costs' being set against the contingent 'payment' is to introduce the so-called Ontario model. However, the definition of costs is not, as one would expect, 'recovered between the parties costs' but rather:[12]

---

[11] SI 2000/692.
[12] Regulation 1(2).

'the total of the representative's time reasonably spent, in respect of the claim or proceedings, multiplied by the reasonable hourly rate of remuneration of the representative.'

It may be that this will be interpreted as the amount recovered as reasonable costs between the parties, but the introduction of a completely novel definition of 'costs' does nothing to assist understanding.

3.2.1.5 Additional requirements for personal injury claims

Additional requirements apply to claims for personal injuries. The Regulation adopts the definition from CPR 2.3:

'proceedings in which there is a claim for damages in respect of personal injuries to the claimant or any other person or in respect of a person's death, and "personal injuries" includes any disease and any impairment of a person's physical or mental condition;'

so this includes clinical negligence cases, but would exclude a claim for professional negligence relating to conduct of a personal injury claim.

The additional requirements are:

'(2) In a claim for personal injuries—
(a) the only sums recovered by the client from which the payment shall be met are—
   (i) general damages for pain, suffering and loss of amenity; and
   (ii) damages for pecuniary loss other than future pecuniary loss,

net of any sums recoverable by the Compensation Recovery Unit of the Department for Work and Pensions; and
(b) [in respect of claims or proceedings at first instance], a damages-based agreement must not provide for a payment above an amount which, including VAT, is equal to 25% of the combined sums in paragraph (2)(a)(i) and (ii) which are ultimately recovered by the client.'

So, as is the case for a success fee under a conditional fee agreement, the damages-based agreement fee cannot be applied to sums paid as compensation for future pecuniary loss. The damages-based agreement itself should specify this using wording lifted directly from the Regulation itself so as to ensure compliance.

As is the case with conditional fee agreements, there remains the issue of how this is to be calculated in the case of a global settlement where general damages and past pecuniary loss are not separately specified in any award. It is suggested that the damages-based agreements could contain a voluntary arbitration provision, adapting wording from the Law Society's model conditional fee agreement. In the case of dispute, however, the client would also be entitled to seek assessment of the damages-based agreement fee by way of a solicitor and client assessment of costs.

It should also be noted that there is no facility for 'solicitor and client costs' to be charged on top of the damages-based agreement fee. Nor does it appear to be possible for the client to be charged a (reduced) fee if the case does not succeed. Nor does it appear to be possible for there to be an initial assessment, for example, on a private retainer, followed by a damages-based agreement, unless, perhaps, the private fee is expressly set against the damages-based agreement fee payable within the damages-based agreement itself.

There are a number of additional requirements for 'employment matters' only:

- reg 5 – information to be given before the agreement is made;
- reg 6 – adding causes of action;
- reg 7 – termination; and
- additional requirements under reg 3(c) that the payment shall have 'regard to, where appropriate, whether the claim or proceedings is one of several similar claims or proceedings'.

As an 'employment matter' means 'a matter that is, or could become, the subject of proceedings before an employment tribunal', these provisions will not apply to personal injury litigation.

The explanatory memorandum from the Ministry of Justice explains:[13]

> 'There are different requirements in the regulations as between civil litigation and employment tribunal cases, as civil litigation can only be conducted by authorised lawyers, who act under professional rules of conduct. Employment tribunal matters can be conducted by others, including claims managers, who do not have professional rules of conduct, and additional safeguards are therefore provided in the regulations.'

---

[13] See www.justice.gov.uk/civil-justice-reforms/main-changes.

3.2.1.6 *The indemnity principle applies*

'58AA(6A) Rules of court may make provision with respect to the assessment of costs in proceedings where a party in whose favour a costs order is made has entered into a damages-based agreement in connection with the proceedings.'

The explanatory memorandum from the Ministry of Justice explains:[14]

'Lawyers acting under a DBA will be required to comply with the indemnity principle, which means that their fee would be restricted to what is due under the DBA fee: if the DBA fee is less than the solicitors' costs would be in the absence of a DBA, a losing defendant would only be liable to pay the DBA fee.'

So if recoverable between the parties costs exceed the contingent 'payment' under the damages-based agreement, the solicitor cannot recover the excess from the losing defendant. The costs are capped at the amount of contingent 'payment' under the damages-based agreement. And the higher the recoverable between the parties costs are, the lower the liability of the client to pay anything out of damages to top this up to the maximum contingent 'payment' under the damages-based agreement.

CPR 44.18 provides:

'(1) The fact that a party has entered into a damages-based agreement will not affect the making of any order for costs which otherwise would be made in favour of that party.

(2) Where costs are to be assessed in favour of a party who has entered into a damages-based agreement –
(a) the party's recoverable costs will be assessed in accordance with rule 44.3; and
(b) the party may not recover by way of costs more than the total amount payable by that party under the damages-based agreement for legal services provided under that agreement.'

3.3 LIABILITY FOR ADVERSE COSTS

Although a client will not be liable to pay their own solicitor in the event that the claim fails, there is still the question of their liability for their

---

[14] See www.justice.gov.uk/civil-justice-reforms/main-changes.

opponent's costs. However, the advent of one-way cost shifting after 1 April 2013 means that in personal injury litigation this risk is less than it once was.

After the event insurance may still be available for the client. If it is not taken out and the client has a liability to pay the opponents costs but is unable to meet liability, is the solicitor in some way liable as a funder?

With regard to conditional fee agreements, a number of cases established the so-called Hodgson immunity.[15] It seems likely that by analogy this principle should also apply to solicitors acting under damages-based agreements. However, as the CJC Working Party commented, this is not certain:

> 'The WP therefore recommends (16) that some appropriate mechanism (possibly the CPR) is adopted to extend "Hodgson immunity", or such protection as the Court of Appeal has held exists, from adverse costs to lawyers acting on a DBA.'

There is also the question as to whether a third party funder in the case where there is a damages-based agreement would be bound by the so-called Arkin Principle:[16]

> 'The WP therefore recommends (17) that some appropriate mechanism (possibly the CPR) is adopted to make it clear that the Arkin principle also applies to a TPLF who provides commercial finance in a DBA case. There has been some speculation about the effect of Alternative Business Structures (ABSs) on the liability of TPLFs for adverse costs where the TPLF has an ownership share in the ABS. However, the WP does not feel that this is a matter that could at this stage be the subject of rules or regulation and is best left to the Courts to resolve if and when a question arises in a particular case.'

A solicitor might also provide a personal indemnity in conditional fee cases to the client against the risk of adverse costs if the case is lost.[17] It seems likely that this principle be extended to damages-based agreements, but again this cannot be certain.

---

[15] See, for example, *Hodgson v Imperial Tobacco Ltd* [1998] 2 All ER 673, [1998] 1 WLR 1056, CA; *Myatt v National Coal Board (No 2)* [2007] EWCA Civ 307, [2007] 4 All ER 1094, [2007] All ER (D) 301 (Mar) and *Flatman v Germany; Wedell v Barchester Healthcare Limited* [2013] EWCA Civ 278.
[16] *Arkin v Borchard Lines Ltd* [2005] EWCA Civ 655, [2005] 3 All ER 613.
[17] *Sibthorpe & Morris v LB Southwark* [2011] EWCA Civ 25.

3.4 DBAS IN PRACTICE

Damages-based agreements are not a US-style contingency fee. The so-called 'Ontario' model is intended and operates on the basis that:

- costs shifting applies;
- base costs recovered from a losing opponent belong to the client; and
- the base costs are set off against the agreed contingency fee.

The Damages-Based Agreements Regulations 2013 are poorly drafted and difficult to interpret.

The following chart sets out how the DBA operates and how it does not operate:

25% DBA	Base costs	Damages	Fee	Client retains
SO =	2,000	10,000	2,500 (2,000 + 500)	9,500
NOT	2,000	10,000	4,500 (2,000 + 2,500)	7,500
NOT	2,000	10,000	3,000 (12,000 x 25%)	9,000

Under CPR 44.18 as the indemnity principle also applies, so the recovered costs cannot exceed the damages-based agreement fee. In these circumstances, the client pays nothing extra and keeps all of the damages. If the recovered between the parties costs would have exceeded the contingent fee, the solicitor cannot claim these from the opponent. His costs are capped at the amount of the contingent fee. The following chart sets out how the damages-based agreement operates and how it does not operate:

25% DBA	Value of time	Damages	Fee	Client retains
SO=	5,000	10,000	2,500	10,000
NOT	5,000	10,000	5,000 (2,500 + 2,500)	7,500
NOT	5,000	10,000	5,000 (inter partes)	10,000

3.5 CFA V DBA

The question of whether solicitor or client will be better or worse off in a particular case with a conditional fee agreement or a damages-based agreement is a complex one, dependent upon the likely amount of compensation and the costs to be incurred in achieving this. The following chart sets out some examples:

Example 1: big, quick win

	CFA (with 100% SF)	DBA (25% cap)
Damages	£5,000,000	£5,000,000
GDs + past loss	£1,000,000	£1,000,000
Time value	£10,000	£10,000
Base costs	£10,000	£10,000
'SF'	£10,000	£240,000
Total costs	£20,000	£250,000
Retained Damages	£4,990,000 (- SF of £10,000)	£4,760,000 (- 25% + £10,000 recovered)

Example 2: big, slow win

	CFA (with 100% SF)	DBA (25% cap)
Damages	£5,000,000	£5,000,000
GDs + past loss	£1,000,000	£1,000,000
Time value	£200,000	£200,000
Base costs	£200,000	£200,000
'SF'	£200,000	£50,000
Total costs	£400,000	£250,000
Retained Damages	£4,800,000 (- SF of £200,000)	£4,950,000 (- 25% + £200,000 recovered)

Example 3: small, costly win

	CFA (with 25% SF)	DBA (25% cap)
Damages	£3,000	£3,000
GDs + past loss	£3,000	£3,000
Time value	£2,000	£2,000
Base costs	£2,000	£750
'SF'	£500	£0
Total costs	£2,500	£750
Retained Damages	£2,500 (- SF of £500)	£3,000 (- 25% + £750 recovered)

Example 4: small, cheap win

	CFA (with 25% SF)	DBA (25% cap)
Damages	£3,000	£3,000
GDs + past loss	£3,000	£3,000
Time value	N/A	N/A
Base cost	£700	£700
'SF'	£175	£50
Total costs	£875	£750
Retained Damages	£2,825 (- SF of £175)	£2,950 (- 25% + £700 recovered)

There is no obligation on any individual solicitor or firm to offer a choice of conditional fee agreement or damages-based agreement. However, the possibility of others offering a damages-based agreement probably should be mentioned when advising the client about funding options. Lord Justice Jackson said:

> 'A number of opponents of contingency fees fear that solicitors would exploit the new regime by selecting the arrangement most favourable to themselves. There is always a danger that solicitors will negotiate retainer terms which are favourable to themselves, but I do not accept that the danger is greater in this situation. If the solicitor is willing to proceed on either a CFA or a contingency fee basis, then he has a duty to advise the client of the implications of each. If the solicitor is only willing to proceed on one or other basis, then no question of selection arises.'

However, he had envisaged a further safeguard for the client, namely an independent solicitor to advise on the funding agreement. Following the report of the CJC Working Party, this was ruled out by the Ministry of Justice and may well have been practically impossible. How would the independent solicitor advise as the benefit or disbenefit would largely depend upon how quickly the case settled. If the advice was so caveated, would it be worth having? Would solicitors think the risk to their professional indemnity policy worthwhile, particularly in the early days?

At present, it seems likely that a damages-based agreement will be disadvantageous to the solicitor compared to a conditional fee agreement in most low value claims (unless the small claims limit is raised), and disadvantageous to the client compared to a conditional fee agreement in most large claims. It seems at present unlikely that damages-based agreements will become a major part of the personal injury funding landscape, but until the practical reality of life after 1 April 2013 becomes clear, it is impossible to be certain how the market will develop.

3.6 CONTENT OF A DBA

The CJC Working Party decided not to recommend or draft a proposed prescribed form of damages-based agreement:

> 'In the same way that the WP has not drafted the wording of a statutory instrument or the detail of rules and regulations it has not drafted a model DBA. Any attempt to do so would have been an impossible task given the wide variety of cases that may be funded by a DBA. However annex 6 proposes the essential provisions that should be included in a lawful DBA. Once again the WP is alert to the danger of encouraging satellite litigation and avoiding further Costs Wars. It is therefore not attracted to the detailed list of 'dos and don'ts' in a DBA under the Ontario Solicitors Act Regulations 195/2004. In the 15 years since CFAs have been lawful the legal profession's various specialist litigation associations have produced their own varieties of model CFA. The WP therefore recommends (15) that the same steps should be taken by the specialist associations and professional bodies in relation to model DBAs.'

The Law Society has not to date drafted a model damages-based agreement. The uncertainties around the drafting of the regulations and ensuring compliance with them make drafting a precedent problematic. This is compounded by the draconian effect of even minor non-compliance – assuming that the line taken for conditional fee agreements in *Garrett v Halton BC; Myatt and others v NCB*[18] is followed for damages-based agreements – the agreement will be unenforceable against the client. As with the costs wars relating to conditional fee agreements when the Conditional Fee Agreement Regulations 2000 were in force, it is not likely to be clients challenging the drafting but defendants (or more likely their insurers) using the

---
[18] [2006] EWCA Civ 1017, [2007] 1 WLR 554, [2007] 1 All ER 147.

indemnity principle to knock out the client's agreement and relieve themselves of having to pay any between the parties costs at all.

For these reasons, no precedent damages-based agreement is offered by the publishers of this work. But those who are drafting a damages-based agreement may find helpful the summary prepared by Sir Rupert Jackson of the minimum matters to be contained in a damages-based agreement:[19]

- the definition of success;
- how the representative's award was to be calculated;
- by whom disbursements are to be paid;
- as between representative and client, who was to be responsible for adverse costs;
- how settlement disputes between representative and client should be resolved;
- in what circumstances either representative or client could terminate the DBA.

The CJC Working Party also provided signposts to other issues to be covered (CJC WP Annex 6A):

> 'The contents obviously also need to be considered against the background of the DBA Regulations and whether there will be prescribed contents. Even if they are not prescribed, one would expect to see within a DBA the requirements set out in Regulation 2 of the DBA Regulations 2010.
>
> Subject to that, the normal provisions of a CFA are:-
> 1. Definitions. This is an important element, particularly in defining the claim and success under the agreement.
> 2. What is covered by the agreement. This was a regulatory requirement and is included within the standard CFA, although the Regulations have been repealed.
> 3. What is not covered by the agreement.
> 4. The payment of fees to the firm. This covers both the limitation of the firm's fees, which in a DBA will be a limitation on the percentage. It also sets out what is defined as a success. If there is to be a limit on the percentage then that limit will be on cash recovered, as set out in the DBA Regulations, so that success for those purposes will be cash-based rather than simply obtaining judgment. A CFA is often based on obtaining judgment rather than success in recovering

---

[19] Terms of Reference to CJC Working Party, Annexure 1 to the Report of the CJC Working Party on Damages-Based Agreements 25 July 2012 at www.judiciary.gov.uk/Resources/JCO/Documents/CJC/Publications/Pre-action%20protocols/contingency-fees-working-party-report1.pdf.

money. That will change because of the provisions of Section 44(2) of LASPO for CFAs. The other important element of the calculation of the success fee for a CFA is the reasons why it has been set at the amount it has. Those reasons are then set out in the schedule. This would need to be included for DBAs with particular emphasis on those DBAs which are not subject to a maximum percentage. If the percentage is uncapped then clearly the solicitor will have to explain why they have proposed a predetermined percentage of the damages recovered.

5. Termination. The complicated part of the CFA is often the termination provisions. This covers both termination by the client and the firm and what may happen as a result of that termination.

6. Recovery of costs. The standard agreement provides what happens when an order for costs is made in favour of the client. One important element of that is what happens in the event of summary assessment. Under the standard CFA the costs can be recovered when they are summarily assessed during the course of the proceedings. There is no reason why this should not be similarly applied to the DBA.

7. Payment of interim or provisional damages and liabilities for the other side's costs. Rather like summary assessment, the standard CFA includes what may happen on the recovery of interim or provisional damages. This clause also deals with the payment of costs by the client to the other side. Again this is a fairly vital element in a CFA because the solicitor will want to ensure that the other side's costs are paid on a summary assessment, failing which there may be a strikeout or a stay. The position may be different if a Sibthorpe agreement has been entered into. This would provide for the solicitor effectively to indemnify the client and clearly that element would have to be set out in any standard agreement.

8. The firm's responsibilities.
9. The client's responsibilities.
10. Removal from record of an action.

These are just some initial thoughts.'

One matter which needs to be considered is whether in the event of termination (or in any other circumstances), an alternative quantum meruit remuneration based on hours worked and hourly rates is ever appropriate (it is not clear to the writer that it is even lawful under the Regulations).

3.7 THE FUTURE

Damages-based agreements have not been met with immediate enthusiasm. As we have seen, this is because of a combination of poor drafting, novelty and statutory restriction on their practical availability.

So far as personal injury litigation is concerned, it seems at the time of writing unlikely that solicitors will embrace them as a practical alternative when conditional fee agreements are available.

It seems that damages-based agreements are most likely to be effective in an environment where there is no cost shifting. The absence of cost shifting means the fee is certain and there is little or no risk of challenge by a paying party. In civil litigation these circumstances are most likely to arise in the small claims track. If at any point in the future the Ministry of Justice proceeds to increase the small claims limit the personal injury litigation (currently cases with general damages in excess of £1,000 are generally exempted) to say £5,000, £10,000 (the current small claims track limit for non-personal injury cases) or even £25,000 (the current fast track limit), then damages-based agreements may become the principal method of funding.

One factor that may lead to increasing encouragement of the use of damages-based agreements in the future is the obvious one that the fee must be proportionate by definition to the amount of damages. As Professor Michael Zander put it[20] and was quoted by Lord Justice Jackson in his Final Report:[21]

> 'A contingency fee as a percentage of the damages, by definition, gives a proportionate relationship – though whether the proportion is reasonable would obviously depend on its level, which may or may not be regulated. Sometimes, no doubt, contingency fees can produce a disproportionate reward for the lawyers, but it seems this is not as common as is sometimes suggested.'

It may therefore be the ultimate policy objective for lawyers to be able to charge a proportionate fee (whether to the client or as recovered costs) along the lines of the damages-based agreement.

---

[20] 'Will the Revolution in the Funding of Civil Litigation in England Eventually Lead to Contingency Fees?' (2002) 52 Depaul Law Review 259 at 294–295.
[21] At p 189.

CHAPTER 4

QUALIFIED ONE-WAY COSTS SHIFTING

Victoria Walne

4.1 INTRODUCTION

Qualified one-way costs shifting (QOCS) is the regime whereby a losing claimant will not usually (except in defined circumstances) be liable for the winning defendant's costs, but a winning claimant can usually expect to recover his costs from a losing defendant.

Prior to QOCS, the general rule in English litigation was a system of the loser paying the winner's costs: two-way costs shifting. This presumption could be displaced by the operation of CPR Part 36 in respect of settlement offers, by CPR Part 38, in relation to discontinuance of a claim post-service of proceedings or in accordance with the court's overarching discretion as to costs.

The QOCS regime was introduced (by changes to the Civil Procedure Rules effective from 1 April 2013) in respect of personal injury cases, following Lord Justice Jackson's wide-ranging review of civil litigation costs and funding published in December 2009. It was implemented at the same time as the abolition of recoverability of additional liabilities (principally the success fee element of a conditional fee agreement and the premium of an after the event (ATE) insurance policy) from a losing party. Whilst the QOCS regime is presently limited to the personal injury arena, the wider funding changes implemented by the Legal Aid, Sentencing and Punishment of Offenders Act 2012 (LASPO) apply across civil litigation generally.

Prior to QOCS, defendants bemoaned the high cost of paying ATE insurance premiums and success fees in cases in which they were unsuccessful. In personal injury litigation, despite the majority of claims which were pursued being either won by the claimant or settled out of court, defendants were liable to pay a successful claimant's ATE insurance premium (taken out to protect him against the risk of an adverse costs order if the case was lost).

In the personal injury litigation arena, defendant insurance companies saw QOCS as a trade-off for the abolition of recoverability of additional liabilities. Paying out ATE insurance premiums in most cases was more expensive than the financial benefit gained from the right to recover their own legal costs in cases won by defendants (or discontinued post-service of proceedings by claimants). The advantages to insurance companies of not paying ATE insurance premiums therefore outweighed the prospect of not being able to recover their own costs in cases in which they were successful.[1]

4.2 JACKSON REPORT

In his review of costs and funding, which commenced in 2008 and was published in 2009, Lord Justice Jackson recommended, amongst 107 other matters, that Access to Justice Act 1999, s 29 and related rules (allowing recoverability of ATE insurance premiums by way of costs) should be repealed and that 'those categories of litigants who merit protection against adverse costs liability on policy grounds should be given the benefit of qualified one way costs shifting'.

He specifically recommended the implementation of QOCS for personal injury litigation, listing within his report the factors[2] he considered supported the recommendation, as follows:

> '(1) Claimants are successful in the majority of personal injury claims. Defendants seldom recover costs, so they derive little benefit from two way costs shifting.
>
> (2) Personal injuries litigation is the paradigm instance of litigation in which the parties are in an asymmetric relationship.
>
> (3) The principal objective of recoverable ATE insurance premiums is to protect claimants against adverse costs orders. One way costs shifting would be a less expensive method of achieving the same objective.
>
> (4) One way costs shifting is not a novel concept in personal injuries litigation. Between 1949 and 2000, the vast majority of personal injury claims proceeded under a one way costs shifting regime, namely the legal aid shield.'

---

[1] See the examples cited by LJ Jackson at pp 185–187 of his 2009 report. There was no overall consensus in the defendant camp, however, local authorities, for example, preferred recoverability of ATE to QOCS.
[2] Chapter 19, para 1.3, pp 184–185.

He went on to say that whilst in clinical negligence cases the success rate of claimants is lower, the other factors are present and, as the level of ATE insurance premiums is 'significantly higher' in clinical negligence cases than in ordinary personal injury cases, factor (3) above 'gains greater force'.

Jackson LJ considered that there was no place for QOCS in commercial, construction and other similar litigation, on the basis that the 'parties are generally in a contractual relationship and there is symmetry in their legal positions'. He considered that any commercial party was able to insure, if they wanted to, at their own expense, against adverse costs liability. Lord Jackson felt that QOCS was appropriate where 'the parties are in an asymmetric relationship'. In respect of personal injuries litigation, Lord Jackson positively recommended QOCS, stating, 'it must be accepted that [personal injury] claimants require protection against adverse costs orders. Otherwise injured persons may be deterred from bringing claims for compensation'.

Jackson LJ also considered other types of litigation and gave examples of other areas of law which may be appropriate for QOCS, such as 'claimants in housing disrepair cases, claimants in actions against the police, claimants seeking judicial review and individuals making claims for defamation or breach of privacy against the media'. In his review, he considered that further consultation was required as to whether professional negligence litigation was appropriate for a QOCS regime, although he voiced his opinion that 'this may be difficult to justify outside clinical negligence'. He went on to say that 'most persons who employ solicitors, accountants, architects etc could afford to take out before-the-event insurance, if they chose to do so'.

4.3 QOCS IN PRACTICE

Jackson LJ concluded:

> 'it seems to me inevitable that, provided the costs rules are drafted so as (a) to deter frivolous or fraudulent claims and (b) to encourage acceptance of reasonable offers, the introduction of one way costs shifting will materially reduce the costs of personal injuries litigation.'

Following publication of his report, in the consultation, drafting and implementation process, the proposed definition of QOCS and, in particular the circumstances in which one-way costs shifting would be 'qualified', underwent many changes. A definition of 'qualified' in the government's November 2010 impact assessment was as follows: where the claimant 'is judged to have acted unreasonably in relation to the claim, is sufficiently wealthy, and/or the defendant is an uninsured individual or otherwise of limited means'.

However, the final rules provided for no financial test to determine a claimant's eligibility to benefit from QOCS. Similarly, QOCS applies regardless of whether the defendant is insured or has other means to pay the opposing party's costs. Whilst the government considered requiring all losing claimants to make a minimum payment to defendants (with the stated intention of deterring unmeritorious claims), the final rules make no provision for a minimum contribution payable to successful defendants. This is a policy decision which appears to have been grounded in the risk that any minimum payment requirement would risk discriminating against the poorer members of society thereby inhibiting access to justice.

The starting point for QOCS is CPR, r 44.13 which provides that the regime applies to claims for damages for personal injury. A claim for damages for personal injury is not defined in the QOCS section of the CPR (rr 44.13 to 44.17) but is likely to be defined in accordance with CPR, r 2.3 where a claim for personal injuries means proceedings in which there is a claim for damages in respect of personal injuries to the claimant or any other person or in respect of a person's death and 'personal injuries' include any disease or any impairment of a person's physical or mental condition. This includes claims for personal injury arising out of clinical negligence.

The definition does not include a claim for professional negligence against a solicitor in relation to representation in an underlying personal injury claim. However, reference is made to the Civil Justice Council's June 2012 report to the Ministry of Justice in which it was stated:

> 'while this is clearly not a "claim for personal injuries" ... there would nevertheless appear to be the asymmetry in the relationship between claimant and defendant (here, the adviser) which Sir Rupert considered as a necessary (and perhaps sufficient) justification for the imposition of QOCS. Furthermore, in loose terms the new action could be said in some way to involve a personal injury dispute, albeit at an underlying level. For these reasons in the main we would recommend that the MoJ takes soundings from relevant stakeholders in order to decide whether these claims are or are not to benefit from QOCS protection ... We believe that a positive decision on the status of these cases for QOCS purposes is necessary both as a matter of clarity and in order to prevent litigation – whether satellite or otherwise – on the point.'

At the time of publication, the position remains to be clarified.

The QOCS regime applies to proceedings which include a claim for damages under the Fatal Accidents Act 1976 or a claim for damages which arises out of death or personal injury and survives for the benefit of an estate by virtue of the Law Reform (Miscellaneous Provisions) Act 1934, s 1(1).

QOCS, specifically, does not apply in relation to applications for pre-action disclosure (CPR, r 44.13) or where the claimant has entered into a pre-commencement funding arrangement (CPR, r 44.17). A pre-commencement funding arrangement is a conditional fee agreement or collective conditional fee agreement entered into before 1 April 2013 which provides for a success fee and/or an insurance policy taken out before 1 April 2013 where the party is seeking to recover an insurance premium (CPR, r 48.2). Mesothelioma claims in personal injury litigation and insolvency-related proceedings, publication and privacy proceeding are excluded from this definition.

The, perhaps unintended, consequence of this provision, is that QOCS is likely to apply retrospectively to cases where no relevant funding arrangement exists even where the claim has been ongoing for some time; so, for example, it will apply to a personal injury claim which was commenced prior to 1 April 2013 but which was privately funded by the client or a third party and/or funded through before-the-event insurance. Therefore, a claimant privately funding his own personal injury claim commenced, say, in 2009 and with extensive legal costs incurred on both sides, would, if his claim is concluded post 1 April 2013, escape liability to pay the defendant's legal costs if unsuccessful, despite both sides having the expectation of two-way costs shifting through the majority of the claim (assuming none of the QOCS qualifications applies).

QOCS applies to parties making a counterclaim or additional Part 20 claim for damages for personal injury (CPR, r 44.13(2)).

In summary, claimants will lose the protection of QOCS if:
(1) the claim is found to be fundamentally dishonest on the balance of probabilities;
(2) the claimant has not bettered a Part 36 offer made by the defendant during the claim (but the claimant will only be ordered to pay the defendant's costs up to the amount of damages actually awarded);
(3) the case has been struck out on the grounds that:
 (a) the claimant has disclosed no reasonable grounds for bringing the proceedings;
 (b) the proceedings are an abuse of the court's process; or

(c) the conduct of the claimant (or a person acting on the claimant's behalf and with the claimant's knowledge of such conduct) is likely to obstruct the just disposal of the proceedings.

Subject to (1) to (3) above, the claimant will not lose QOCS protection on discontinuance of the claim post-issue of proceedings. If this were not the case, claimants whose prospects of success decline during the progress of a claim might otherwise find themselves in a position where they would be financially better off to continue with an unmeritorious claim to trial solely to retain the benefit from QOCS protection. Claimants will continue to benefit from QOCS protection during the appeal process. This is on the basis that the high threshold to overcome in securing the court's permission to appeal would act as a control on unmeritorious appeals.

4.4 QOCS AND PART 36 OFFERS

The introduction of the QOCS regime in April 2013 did not change a claimant's potential liability towards a defendant in respect of costs where the claimant fails to beat at trial a defendant's Part 36 offer. CPR, r 36.14(2) provides that, where a claimant fails to obtain a judgment more advantageous to them than a defendant's Part 36 offer, the court will (unless it considers it unjust to do so) order that the defendant is entitled to his costs (plus interest) from the expiry of the 'relevant period' to trial. CPR, r 36.2(2)(c) defines the 'relevant period' as the period specified in the defendant's offer letter of not less than 21 days within which the defendant will be liable for the claimant's costs if the offer is accepted. The court's discretion to disapply the operation of Part 36 in 'unjust' circumstances is narrowly applied.[3]

CPR, r 36.14A clarifies that 'in relation to any money claim or money element of a claim, "more advantageous" means better in money terms by any amount, however small, and "at least as advantageous" shall be construed accordingly'.

Therefore, a claimant will usually lose QOCS protection if he is awarded less than the amount of the defendant's money offer of settlement by whatever amount, however small. The implementation of CPR, r 36.14A (effectively overturning the Court of Appeal's decision in *Carver v BAA plc*[4]) largely removed (subject to the court's wide-ranging discretion as to costs) the element of subjectivity in the application of

---

[3] See, for example, *SG v Hewitt* [2012] EWCA Civ 1053.
[4] [2008] EWCA Civ 412.

Part 36 offers. CPR, r 44.14 confirms that any such costs order against the claimant can be enforced without the court's permission, ie by automatic effect following judgment. Therefore there is little room for the court's discretion in the operation of Part 36 in displacing QOCS, save where the effect of Part 36 is unjust (CPR, r 36.14(2)).

However, a claimant's costs liability to a defendant in relation to Part 36 offers is limited to the amount of damages actually awarded: CPR, r 44.14(1) states that subject to rr 44.15 and 44.16 (claims which are found to be 'fundamentally dishonest' or struck out by the court) orders for costs made against a claimant may be enforced without the permission of the court but only to the extent that the aggregate amount in money terms of such orders does not exceed the aggregate amount in money terms of any orders for damages and interest made in favour of the claimant.

CPR, r 36.10(4)(b) provides that where a Part 36 offer is accepted after the expiry of the relevant period, if the parties do not agree liability for costs, the court will make an order as to costs. CPR, r 36.10(5) states that in those circumstances, unless the court orders otherwise, the claimant will be entitled to the costs of the proceedings up to the date on which the relevant period expired and the offeree (the claimant) will be liable for the offeror's (the defendant's) costs for the period from the date of expiry of the relevant period to the date of acceptance.

CPR, r 44.14(2) states that orders for costs made against a claimant may only be enforced after the proceedings have been concluded and the costs have been assessed or agreed.

The effect of CPR, rr 36.10 and 44.14(2) is that a claimant's late acceptance of a defendant's Part 36 offer does not automatically give rise to an adverse costs order against the claimant; that is initially a matter for the parties, but, absent agreement, the court is likely to order the claimant to pay the defendant's costs from the expiry of the relevant period to the date of actual acceptance of the offer (but limited to the amount of damages and interest actually agreed).

CPR, r 44.14(3) states that an order for costs against a claimant 'shall not be treated as an unsatisfied or outstanding judgment for the purposes of any court record'. This means that any such judgments will not be entered on the register of outstanding judgments.

4.5 STRIKE OUT APPLICATIONS

Aside from the operation of Part 36, there are two types of exceptions to QOCS, namely exceptions which are automatic and exceptions which require the permission of the court to be enforced.

Where a claim has been struck out (on specified grounds relating to the substance of the claim) a claimant will automatically lose the protection of QOCS. CPR, r 44.15 provides that orders for costs against the claimant may be enforced to the full extent of such orders without the permission of the court where proceedings have been struck out on the grounds that:

(1) the claimant has disclosed no reasonable grounds for bringing the proceedings;
(2) the proceedings are an abuse of the court's process; or
(3) the conduct of:
    (a) the claimant; or
    (b) a person acting on the claimant's behalf and with the claimant's knowledge of such conduct,
    is likely to obstruct the just disposal of the proceedings.

With regard to strike out CPR, r 3.4(2) provides that:

'(2) The court may strike out a statement of case if it appears to the court –
(a) that the statement of case discloses no reasonable grounds for bringing or defending the claim;
(b) that the statement of case is an abuse of the court's process or is otherwise likely to obstruct the just disposal of the proceedings; or
(c) that there has been a failure to comply with a rule, practice direction or court order.'

There is a difference between a substantive strike out (CPR, r 3.4(2)(a) and (b)) and a technical strike out (CPR, r 3.4(2)(c)). The fact that CPR, r 3.4(2)(c) – in relation to technical strike-outs – is not mirrored in CPR, r 44.15, unlike CPR, r 3.4(2)(a) and (b), indicates the underlying intention that QOCS protection should be lost only for a substantive strike out and not a technical strike out. However there is an additional provision in CPR, r 44.15 which provides for QOCS to be displaced following a strike out where conduct by or on behalf of the claimant 'is likely to obstruct the just disposal of the proceedings'.

An exaggerated claim is unlikely to be sufficient for a finding of 'fundamental dishonesty' under CPR, r 44.16(1) to disengage QOCS (see below). However, it is possible that in the circumstances of a 'merely' exaggerated claim, a defendant could succeed in an application to strike out for abuse of process under CPR, r 3.4(2)(b) which would in turn, automatically, displace QOCS under CPR, r 45.15(b). The Court of Appeal acknowledged its power to do so in *Summers v Fairclough Homes Limited*[5] but refused to exercise its discretion in the specific circumstances of that case, and emphasised that such power should only be exercised in very exceptional circumstances.

4.6 'FUNDAMENTAL DISHONESTY'

Where a defendant alleges fraud, then the court's permission is required before QOCS will be displaced. CPR, r 44.16(1) provides that orders for costs made against the claimant may be enforced up to the full extent of such orders with the permission of the court where the claim is found on the balance of probabilities to be fundamentally dishonest.

The concept of 'fundamental dishonesty' is new to English litigation. The requirement for a finding of 'dishonesty' to be 'fundamental' implies that there are degrees of dishonesty in relation to claims, the implication being that only the most dishonest claims will lose QOCS protection. This in turn however implies a subjective assessment of the extent of any finding of dishonesty, which, it is submitted, will inevitably require satellite litigation to clarify. Semantically, however, the adjective 'fundamental' would indicate that, in order for a claimant to lose the benefit of QOCS in these circumstances, the alleged dishonesty must go to the foundation or root of the claim. Whilst the parameters of 'fundamental dishonesty' await clarification, it is submitted therefore that 'mere' exaggeration of the extent of an injury and/or an element of the damages claim should not be enough to displace QOCS but rather the threshold is intended to catch sham accidents.

However as para 12.6 of CPR PD 44 specifically states that costs orders against claimants in such circumstances can exceed the amount of any order for damages, interest and costs made in favour of the claimant, it is clear that the rules envisage that a finding of 'fundamental dishonesty' can be made against the claimant in circumstances where damages have in fact been awarded.

In its June 2012 report[6] to the Ministry of Justice, the Civil Justice Council recommended the following test for a finding of fundamental

---

[5] [2012] UKSC 26.
[6] Response to Ministry of Justice Commissioning Note entitled 'Implementation of Part 2 of the Legal Aid, Sentencing and Punishment of Offenders Act 2012: Civil

dishonesty, namely that it is the defendant's burden to prove on the balance of probabilities the following four matters:

(a) that the statements and representations relied on were made;
(b) that they were false;
(c) that they were likely to interfere with the course of justice in some material respects; and
(d) that at the time they were made, the maker had no honest belief in their truth and knew of the likelihood that they would interfere with the course of justice.

It is likely that there will be a requirement for any such allegation of fraud to be specifically pleaded by the defendant. Pursuant to para 12.4(a) of CPR PD 44, the court will usually order the issue to be determined at the trial of the substantive claim. The burden is on the defendant to prove fraud to the civil standard, namely on the balance of probabilities.

A finding of 'fundamental dishonesty' will invalidate any legal expenses insurance (either before the event or after the event insurance) that the claimant may have. This means that, where a claimant lacks the financial means to meet a costs order, a finding of fraud is unlikely in practice to put the defendant in a better position with regard to recovering costs from the claimant.

As a well-pitched Part 36 offer (which is not accepted and not bettered by a claimant at trial) displaces QOCS, it is submitted that this is the appropriate tool for a defendant who suspects an exaggerated claim, rather than reliance on CPR, r 44.16(1) which would more appropriately cover claims which are dishonest to the core.

Paragraph 12.4(b) of CPR PD 44 states that where the proceedings have been settled, the court will not, save in exceptional circumstances, order that issues arising out of an allegation that the claim was fundamentally dishonest be determined in those proceedings.

Pursuant to para 12.4(c) of CPR PD 44, where the claimant has served a notice of discontinuance, the court may direct that issues arising out of an allegation that the claim was fundamentally dishonest be determined notwithstanding that the notice has not been set aside pursuant to CPR, r 38.4.

Litigation Funding and Costs – Issues for Further Consideration by the Civil Justice Council' (June 2012). http://www.judiciary.gov.uk/JCO%2FDocuments%2F CJC%2FPublications%2Fconsultation+responses%2FCJC-response-to-MOJ-pt2-legal-aid-sentencing.pdf.

Paragraph 12.4(d) of CPR PD 44 provides that the court may, as it thinks fair and just, determine the costs attributable to the claim having been found to be fundamentally dishonest.

4.7 MIXED CLAIMS

CPR, r 44.16(3) provides that the court may make an order for costs against a person other than the claimant for whose financial benefit the whole or part of the claim was made.

Paragraph 12.2 of CPR PD 44 gives examples of claims made for the financial benefit of a person other than the claimant or a dependant within the meaning of the Fatal Accidents Act 1976, s 1(3), including subrogated claims or claims for credit hire.

The court's permission is required to enforce a costs order in a 'mixed claim', namely proceedings which include a claim for the benefit of someone other than the injured claimant or, alternatively or additionally, the claim is made for the benefit of the claimant other than for damages for personal injury.

There are in practice two types of mixed claims. The first type is a claim in which damages for personal injury is sought in addition to a non-monetary or non-personal injury element, such as housing disrepair or public nuisance. This is covered by CPR, r 44.16(2)(b) which refers to a claim made for the benefit of the claimant other than a claim for personal injury.

The second type of mixed claim is a claim for damages for personal injury only but where an element of the damages award is sought by a party other than the claimant, for example, subrogating insurers (in respect of the costs of repairing damage to the claimant's vehicle, for example, or in relation to credit hire claims). This is covered by CPR, r 44.16(2)(a) which refers to proceedings which include a claim made for the financial benefit of a person other than the claimant. CPR, r 44.16(3) allows the court to make a costs order against the 'third party' (eg the subrogating insurers or credit hire company) in such circumstances, ie the rules prevent them from benefitting from QOCS.

There are, however, specific exclusions to a type 2 mixed claim namely:
(a) claims for gratuitous care and assistance advanced by a claimant on behalf or friends and family;[7]

---

[7] Paragraph 12.3 of CPR PD 44 clarifies that gratuitous provision of care within the meaning of r 44.16(2)(a) includes the provision of personal services rendered

(b) claims in which an employer has a financial interest arising from its contractual right to recover payments they have made to the injured claimant in respect of earnings whilst the claimant was unable to work; and

(c) claims in which a medical insurer has a financial interest arising from its contractual right to recover payments they have made to the injured claimant in relation to treatment or other medical expenses.

In relation to these three exceptions, such claims will be treated as non-mixed personal injury claims and QOCS will apply in the usual way.

In mixed claims (ie claims covering both personal injury and a non-personal injury element), the claimant will only benefit from QOCS if they have an interest in the non-personal injury aspect of the claim. Therefore, QOCS protection applies to all aspects of a type 1 mixed claim. Regarding a type 2 mixed claim, it will depend on the specific circumstances.

Where in a type 2 mixed claim the claimant does not have an interest in an element of the claim, QOCS protection is split so that the element of the claim in which the claimant does not have a direct interest does not benefit from the QOCS regime. Paragraph 12.5 to CPR PD 44 specifically states that in a type 2 mixed claim, the court will usually order any person other than the claimant for whose financial benefit such a claim was made to pay all the costs of the proceedings or the costs attributable to the issues. This is intended to ensure that credit hire companies in particular cannot benefit from QOCS protection. Such costs orders can exceed the amount of any orders for damages, interest and costs made in favour of the claimant (para 12.6 of CPR PD 44).

Where a claim is made for the financial benefit of a person other than the claimant, an order for costs against the claimant may be enforced up to the full extent of the order with the permission of the court and to the extent that the court considers it just (CPR, r 44.16(2)). Paragraph 12.5 of CPR PD 44 states that in a type 2 mixed claim, costs orders in relation to the element of the claim pursued for a third party's interest will be enforced against the claimant 'exceptionally'.

---

gratuitously by persons such as relatives and friends for things such as personal care, domestic assistance, childminding, home maintenance and decorating, gardening and chauffeuring.

In such proceedings, where a person other than the claimant has a financial interest in the claim, the court may make an order for costs that person. CPR, r 46.2 applies in such circumstances, namely that the person against whom the costs order is contemplated must be added as a party to the proceedings (for the purposes of costs only) and must be given a reasonable opportunity to attend the hearing at which the court will consider the matter further.

CPR, r 44.16(2)(c) allows the full extent of a costs order to be enforced against a claimant in a type 1 or type 2 mixed claim with the court's permission and to the extent the court considers it just. Therefore, this provision allows the court to disapply QOCS in these circumstances but the court has discretion here, and the extent to which the court considers it 'just' to do so. The question which is likely to be at the forefront of the court's consideration is the extent to which it appears that the personal injury element of the claim is being pursued in its own right as opposed to being tagged onto, for example, a credit hire claim or a housing disrepair claim, with a view to benefiting from the QOCS regime. The court will similarly have discretion with regard to the application of QOCS in a claim which begins life as a mixed claim, but where at a later stage the personal injury element is abandoned. It is submitted that the application of the court's discretion in such circumstances is likely to be dependent on the interplay between the two elements of the claim, their relative proportions to the case as a whole and the stage at which the claim for personal injury is discontinued.

4.8 QOCS AND ATE INSURANCE

Following the implementation of LASPO 2012, ss 46 and 47 a party can no longer recover an after the event insurance premium from the losing party (except, in part, in clinical negligence claims). The QOCS regime was intended to operate as a balance to the removal of recoverability of additional liabilities, including the ATE insurance premium.

Subject to the availability of ATE insurance post 1 April 2013, this does not prevent a party from taking out an ATE insurance premium, but paying for the premium him/herself.

A claimant may choose to take out ATE insurance to effectively ring-fence their damages in the event of a failure to beat a defendant's Part 36 offer. There is no cap on the amount of a claimant's damages which may be eroded by an order to pay costs to a defendant who has made an unbeaten Part 36 offer: depending on the stage in the claim when the offer was made, a claimant, whilst successful, may lose all damages awarded at trial if less than a defendant's Part 36 offer of settlement.

Such ATE insurance policies may also provide costs cover in the event of a defendant's successful strike out application and/or in respect of own disbursements if the case is lost. However, ATE insurance is unlikely to be available to protect a party from the displacement of QOCS resulting from a finding of 'fundamental dishonesty'.

4.9 DISCONTINUED CLAIMS

Under the pre-QOCS regime a claimant who served notice of discontinuance usually became liable for the defendant's costs of the proceedings up to that date. CPR, r 38.6 states that unless the court orders otherwise, a claimant who discontinues is liable for the costs which a defendant against whom the claimant discontinues incurred on or before the date on which notice of discontinue was served on the defendant.

However, this is reversed under the QOCS regime so that a claimant discontinuing a claim will usually continue to benefit from QOCS subject the defined qualifications outlined above.

It is noted however that the Civil Justice Council's June 2012 report to the Ministry of Justice on QOCS recommended changes to CPR, r 38.6 which at the date of publication have not been implemented.[8]

Given that QOCS is not lost if a claimant discontinues a claim but a claimant does however lose QOCS where the defendant successfully applies to strike out the claim, defendants are likely to look to take the initiative to apply more often to strike out unmeritorious or fraudulent claims rather than reactively waiting for a claimant to abandon proceedings.

4.10 APPEALS

QOCS applies to appeals against a relevant judgment. The reasoning behind this is that the requirement to obtain permission to appeal

---

[8] Response to Ministry of Justice Commissioning Note entitled 'Implementation of Part 2 of the Legal Aid, Sentencing and Punishment of Offenders Act 2012: Civil Litigation Funding and Costs – Issues for Further Consideration by the Civil Justice Council' June 2012 (Section 6).

(namely establishing reasonable prospects of the appeal succeeding) acts as a control against appeals by claimants which lack merit.

CPR, r 52.9A provides that in any proceedings in which costs recovery is normally limited or excluded, an appeal court may make an order that the recoverable costs of an appeal will be limited to the extent which the court specifies.

The position remains to be clarified in a type 1 mixed claim, ie a claim with both a personal injury and non-personal injury element, where only the non-personal injury aspect of the claim is subject to an appeal. It is submitted that QOCS will in practice apply only to appeals where the ongoing dispute is classified as a claim for personal injuries under CPR, r 2.3, so not to appeals only of the non-personal injury element of a claim even if though the claim began life as a mixed claim. In relation to an appeal in a type 2 claim, where only the element of the claim which does not directly benefit the claimant is appealed (eg a credit hire claim), it is very likely that QOCS will not apply to the appeal.

CHAPTER 5

FIXED RECOVERABLE COSTS

5.1 INTRODUCTION

5.1.1 Solicitor and client costs, fixed costs and fixed recoverable costs

Solicitors, like any other trade or profession facing a project of uncertain size, length and complexity, have always been wary of agreeing fixed or capped fees with their clients. These have become commonplace in simple non-contentious transactions such as residential conveyancing. However, in litigation, resistance to fixed fees has continued.

Fixed fees are easier to implement and to police for 'between the parties' costs and for costs paid by a public body such as the Legal Services Commission. Most proposals for fixed fees relate to this. The solicitor retains the right as a matter of contract in a free market to agree whatever rate he chooses with his client. The fact that clients may decide to negotiate a fixed solicitor and client fee based on any fixed 'between the parties' fee does not derogate from this point of principle. Many commentators and legislators seem, however, to have misunderstood this distinction.

The SRA Code of Conduct does requires as an Outcome:

> 'O(1.13) clients receive the best possible information, both at the time of engagement and when appropriate as their matter progresses, about the likely overall cost of their matter;'

And as an indicative behaviour:

> 'IB(1.14) clearly explaining your fees and if and when they are likely to change;'

It does not require the solicitor to offer fixed costs to the client even where the costs recoverable from the opponent are fixed.

Recoverable costs belong to the client and not to the lawyer in the absence of any agreement to the contrary. These are fixed recoverable costs, not fixed solicitor and client costs.

The solicitor can agree with the client if he wishes that he will accept the fixed recoverable costs in full settlement of the client's liability for costs (if the relevant fixed costs scheme applies and there is no exceptionality escape). The indemnity principle is unlikely to be a problem here. Section 51 of the Supreme Court Act 1981 gives the power to impose fixed costs. Fixed costs are payable by the opponent come what may if the scheme applies. In *Nizami v Butt*,[1] Simon J upheld Master O'Hare's decision that as the costs are fixed by the Civil Procedure Rules (CPR), they are payable irrespective of the liability of the claimant to pay costs to his solicitor. In other words, the indemnity principle should be abrogated and the fixed costs payable by the defendant even if there is a breach of the indemnity principle.

Alternatively, the solicitor can agree with the client that he will charge on his normal hourly rate basis. He must warn the client that the client will only recover the fixed recoverable costs if the scheme applies and there is no exceptionality. But if the solicitor's time comes to less than the fixed costs he should then account to the client for the balance.

After 1 April 2013, success fees are not recoverable as costs from the opponent. If charged, they are payable by the client. A success fee is defined by statute as an uplift on the solicitors normal fees. This could be an uplift on an hourly rate, or on a fixed solicitor and client fee. If the fixed solicitor and client fee is calculated by reference to the damages, there is a risk that the solicitor has inadvertently created a damages-based agreement (see Chapter 3).

5.1.2 Lord Woolf and beyond

Fixed fees for the fast track were strongly advocated by Lord Woolf in his reports on Access to Justice (1996–1998). Indeed he considered them integral to his vision of the fast track. After implementation thorough the introduction of the Civil Procedure Rules in 1999, the Lord Chancellor's Department commissioned research (by Tamara Goriely) but was persuaded that it was too early (in 1999) to introduce the fixed costs before the new CPR procedures bedded in. However, the Department never said that it was abandoning them. (The only fixed costs following Woolf were fixed recoverable costs for the trial itself on

---

[1] [2006] 2 All ER 140.

the fast track. This awarded a variable amount of costs to the advocate depending on the 'value of the claim'.)

Some form of fixed or capped costs or scale existed for lower value claims (eg county court lower scale and Scale 1) before the CPR, so the principle was not revolutionary.

In 2003 the 'predictive' costs regime for low value road traffic accident (RTA) claims was introduced, but this dealt only with costs in cases settled pre-issue. In 2010 this was supplemented by the 'new claims process' which fixed (lower) costs for road traffic accident claims where liability was admitted. However, no progress was made towards fixing costs for other kinds of accident claim or towards fixing costs in the fast track once court proceedings were issued.

The Civil Justice Council reported in August 2005 with a recommendation to introduce fixed costs in the fast track.[2]

In his final report on the Review of Civil Litigation Costs published in January 2010, Lord Justice Jackson made wide-ranging proposals for the fixing of fast track costs and set out detailed tables for road traffic, employers' liability (EL) accident and public liability (PL) claims. The government implemented these with effect from 31 July 2013.

5.1.3 Swings and roundabouts?

The principle behind fixed cost regimes is usually avowed to be one of 'swings and roundabouts'. By charging a fixed fee either of a single amount, or an amount variable by reason of the damages, for cases of a similar kind, the solicitor is anticipated to break even on a 'book' of such cases. Some cases would earn higher costs on an hourly rate basis; some would earn lower costs. This principle easily governs some contractual arrangements between solicitors and clients with bulk instructions (eg solicitors acting for defendant insurance companies). It is less easy to see how this can apply to solicitors acting for numerous individual claimants. Why should a claimant whose case is concluded quickly and cheaply not benefit from this? Why should a claimant whose case takes a long time not pay the price for this?

The real reasons for implementation of fixed costs in the fast track are instead ones of practicality and politics. The practical issue is that it is time-consuming for a court to determine the 'correct' fee for work

---

[2] Napier, Hurst, Musgrove and Peysner *Improved Access to Justice – Funding Options & Proportionate Costs* (Civil Justice Council, August 2005).

which is relatively low value and routine. The political issue is that fixed costs allowed proportionality to be imposed upon low value cases so that 'horror stories' of excessive costs for low value claims will become a thing of the past.

5.1.4 CPR format

The Civil Procedure Rules Committee has adopted a reasonably consistent format for the rules governing fixed recoverable costs from the outset. All such provisions appear in CPR Part 45.

The first part of each rule sets out the circumstances in which the fixed costs are payable, the second part sets out a table with a calculation of the fixed sums and the third part sets out any escape or exception.

5.1.5 Budgets

It should be noted that the cost budget provisions in CPR Part 3 do not apply to the fast track. This is because the Rules Committee assumed that fixed fees will apply to the fast track making budget completely unnecessary.

Of course, fixed recoverable costs have only been introduced so far for personal injury litigation.

5.2 FIXED RECOVERABLE COST REGIMES IMPLEMENTED PRIOR TO 2013

5.2.1 Small claims track

The following rule applies to the allocation of personal injury cases to the small claims track (CPR, r 26.1):

'(1) The small claims track is the normal track for–
(a) any claim for personal injuries where –
  (i) the value of the claim is not more than £10,000; and
  (ii) the value of any claim for damages for personal injuries is not more than £1,000.'

Although the government has regularly indicated that it would review the £1,000 limit for general damages, this figure has remained since 1999. The government has recently announced that following consultation the current limit will remain at least for the foreseeable future although it will be kept 'under review'.

CPR, r 27.14 relates to costs on the small claims track:

> '(2) The court may not order a party to pay a sum to another party in respect of that other party's costs, fees and expenses, including those relating to an appeal, except –
> (a) the fixed costs attributable to issuing the claim which –
> (i) are payable under Part 45; or
> (ii) would be payable under Part 45 if that Part applied to the claim;
> (b) in proceedings which included a claim for an injunction or an order for specific performance a sum not exceeding the amount specified in Practice Direction 27 for legal advice and assistance relating to that claim;
> (c) any court fees paid by that other party;
> (d) expenses which a party or witness has reasonably incurred in travelling to and from a hearing or in staying away from home for the purposes of attending a hearing;
> (e) a sum not exceeding the amount specified in Practice Direction 27 for any loss of earnings or loss of leave by a party or witness due to attending a hearing or to staying away from home for the purposes of attending a hearing;
> (f) a sum not exceeding the amount specified in Practice Direction 27 for an expert's fees;
> (g) such further costs as the court may assess by the summary procedure and order to be paid by a party who has behaved unreasonably ...
> (i) in an appeal, the cost of any approved transcript reasonably incurred.'

If proceedings are not issued, a similar principle applies to the question of whether costs are payable following the issue of Part 8 proceedings for recovery of legal costs. In other words, if less than £1,000 is recovered in respect of the general damages, the costs rules relating to the small claims track will apply. However, CPR, r 27.14(h) expressly provides for:

> '(h) the Stage 1 and, where relevant, the Stage 2 fixed costs in rule 45.18 where –
> (i) the claim was within the scope of the Pre-Action Protocol for Low Value Personal Injury Claims in Road Traffic Accidents ('the RTA Protocol') or the Pre-action Protocol for Low Value Personal Injury (Employers' Liability and Public Liability) Claims ('the EL/PL Protocol');
> (ii) the claimant reasonably believed that the claim was valued at more than the small claims track limit in accordance with paragraph 4.1(4) of the relevant Protocol; and
> (iii) the defendant admitted liability under the process set out in the relevant Protocol; but

(iv) the defendant did not pay those Stage 1 and, where relevant, Stage 2 fixed costs.'

So, if the claim is for less than the small claims limit, or was not reasonably expected to exceed it, the claimant will not generally recover any solicitor's costs.

5.2.2 Fixed trial costs in the fast track

The actual cost of the trial itself on the fast track has not since 1999 been subject to detailed or summary assessment. Instead, fixed costs were applied. This awarded a variable amount of costs to the advocate depending on the 'value of the claim'. If the claimant won the case, this meant the total amount of the judgment excluding interest and costs and any reduction for contributory fault. If the costs are to be awarded to the defendant, the value of the claim is the amount specified in the claim form (excluding interest and costs); or, if none was specified, then the maximum amount the claimant reasonably expected to recover according to the statement of value in the claim form.

Solicitors had to decide whether to undertake the advocacy in fast track trials or to brief counsel. If counsel was briefed, the solicitor sought where possible to limit the liability of the client to pay no more by way of brief fee than the amount recoverable as fixed costs on the other side. However, in a CFA case which goes to trial, the solicitor may have significant fees dependent upon a successful outcome. In such circumstances, the solicitor sometimes briefs a more experienced counsel at greater expense as insistence on the fixed trial fee might be a false economy if the trial is lost through the inexperience of counsel.

5.2.3 'Predictive costs' regime: accidents 6 October 2003–31 July 2013

This fixed recoverable costs regime applied to low value road traffic accidents which occurred after 6 October 2003. The dispute must have arisen from a road traffic accident (defined below) where the agreed damages did not exceed £10,000, and if the claim had been issued it would not have been suitable for the small claims track.

A road traffic accident was defined as one 'resulting in bodily injury to any person or damage to property caused by or arising out of, the use of a motor vehicle on a road or other public place in England and Wales' where 'motor vehicle' meant 'a mechanically propelled vehicle intended for use on roads' and 'road' meant 'any highway and any other road to which the public has access and includes bridges over which a road passes'.

The scheme continued to apply after 30 April 2010 to all low value road traffic claims that fell outside the portal process described in **5.2.2** (eg all cases where liability was denied) or which fell out of the portal process (eg where the insurer failed to make payments in the timescale required).

Subject to exceptional circumstances, the only costs which are allowed were:

(a) fixed recoverable costs calculated in accordance with r 45.9;

(b) disbursements allowed in accordance with r 45.10; and

(c) (if incurred prior to 1 April 2013) a success fee allowed in accordance with r 45.11.

The fixed recoverable costs under CPR, r 45.9 were calculated as follows:

- £800 plus
- a sum equal to 20% of the damages agreed up to £5,000 plus
- a sum equal to 15% of the damages agreed between £5,000 and £10,000 plus
- VAT.

Fixed recoverable costs under the scheme were to be calculated by reference to the agreed damages. In calculating those, account had to be taken of:

(1) general and special damages and interest;

(2) interim payments made must be included;

(3) where the parties have agreed an element of contributory negligence, the amount of damages attributed to that negligence must be deducted;

(4) but not Compensation Recovery Unit (CRU) payments and NHS expenses.

In *Swatton v Smithurst*,[3] following a road traffic accident the claimant hired a replacement car. His insurers, the car hire company and the defendant insurers negotiated between themselves, with no solicitors

---

[3] (Unreported) 3 February 2005, Oxford County Court, His Honour Judge Charles Harris QC.

involved. The claimant's solicitors and the defendant's insurers negotiated only about general damages and a tiny claim for special damages. There was no mention of car hire charges or vehicle damage repair charges. The court held that a solicitor should only be entitled to be paid for doing what he has been retained to do. The scheme clearly envisaged the use and remuneration of solicitors, not other negotiating agents. But in *Cook v Graham*[4] the judge rejected the defendant's argument that fixed costs should be calculated only by reference to the value of matters in dispute, rather than by reference to all of the damages recovered due to work by the claimant's solicitors.

It is however possible to recover the following items:

(1) the cost of obtaining:
   - medical records;
   - a medical report;
   - a police report;
   - an engineer's report; or
   - a search of the records of the Driver Vehicle Licensing Authority;
(2) the amount of an (ATE) insurance premium; and
(3) any other disbursement that has arisen due to a particular feature of the dispute.

The predictive costs regime continues to apply to road traffic accidents up to £10,000 which occurred before 31 July 2013 and which fall out of the portal. However, the rules relating to it no longer appear in the CPR, so it is necessary to refer to previous versions.

5.2.4 The first portal (road accident cases only, claim notifications 30 April 2010–29 April 2013)

The RTA claims process introduced by the Ministry of Justice (MoJ) came into effect on 30 April 2010 (the portal). This applied initially to all RTA cases valued up to £10,000. The fees were fixed for three stages.

The 'portal' claims process was divided into three stages. At each stage claimant solicitors received fixed costs. Stage 1 required the claimant's solicitor to complete in full a claims notification form (CNF) which was sent to the defendant's insurer electronically via a web-based portal system. At the end of stage 1, fixed recoverable costs of £400 was to be paid immediately (and not at the end of the claim) where liability is

---

[4] (Unreported) 2005, Liverpool County Court.

admitted. This was regardless of whether or not contributory negligence is alleged (save for failing to wear a seatbelt).

Once submitted, the defendant's insurers had 15 business days in which to respond electronically with their substantive position on liability. The exception to the '15-day rule' is the Motor Insurers' Bureau (MIB) which has 30 days to respond in relation to liability.

Stage 2 covered the issues of medical evidence, offers to settle and negotiations. The fixed recoverable costs applicable to the end of stage 2 were £800.

Stage 3 was determination of the quantum by the court. For a paper hearing only the fixed recoverable cost was £250 and for oral hearings it was £500. If settlement was reached between the issue of the claim and before the trial commences then fixed recoverable costs of £250 applied.

Statistically, these 'low-value' motor cases have formed the vast majority of claims in the past and these rules were intended to have a significant impact on the handling of claims, particularly the speed and the cost at which they are dealt with.

A report by Professor Paul Fenn into the effect of the portal published in July 2012 suggested that although costs had fallen slightly, damages had fallen more.

The claims process was engineered to be more streamlined. However, the effect on claimant solicitors in relation to recoverable costs was also evident. The most that could be received for costs under the portal regime is £1,700, whereas the earlier 'predictive costs' scheme would provide a maximum of £2,550 for a £10,000 claim.

The stage model has been retained for the new portal.

5.2.5 MIB schemes

5.2.5.1 *Uninsured drivers*

The applicable usual fixed recoverable cost schemes apply to cases which fall within the scope of the Uninsured Drivers Agreement, but not cases that fall within the scope of the Untraced Drivers Agreement which have their own scale.

For example, CPR PD 45 states:

'The Section applies to cases which fall within the scope of the Uninsured Drivers Agreement dated 13 August 1999.'

5.2.5.2 Untraced drivers

If a driver who is responsible for an accident is untraced under the meaning of the Motor Insurers' Bureau (Compensation of Victims of Untraced Drivers) Agreement 1 June 2004, there are no potential court proceedings (as there is no known defendant) and any claim has to proceed by way of an application to the MIB.

The following fixed cost regime applies to untraced driver claims:

> '10. (1) MIB shall, in a case where it has decided to make a compensation payment under clause 8, also include in the award a sum by way of contribution towards the cost of obtaining legal advice from a Solicitor or Barrister in respect of–
> (a) the making of an application under this Agreement;
> (b) the correctness of a decision made by MIB under this Agreement; or
> (c) the adequacy of an award (or a part thereof) offered by MIB under this Agreement
>
> that sum to be determined in accordance with the Schedule to this Agreement.
>
> (2) MIB shall not be under a duty to make a payment under paragraph (1) unless it is satisfied that the applicant did obtain legal advice in respect of any one or more of the matters specified in that paragraph.'

The 'contribution' towards legal costs is set out in the Schedule and is expressed as a percentage of the eventual award.

'SCHEDULE: MIB's CONTRIBUTION TOWARDS APPLICANT'S LEGAL COSTS

1. Subject to paragraph 4, MIB shall pay a contribution towards the applicant's costs of obtaining legal advice determined in accordance with paragraph 2.

2. That amount shall be the aggregate of–
(a) the fee specified in column (2) of the table below in relation to the amount of the award specified in column (1) of that table,
(b) the amount of value added tax charged on that fee,
(c) where the applicant has opted for an oral hearing the amount awarded under clause 24(4) and
(d) reasonable disbursements.

TABLE

Amount of the award (1)	Specified fee (2)
Not exceeding £150,000	15% of the amount of the award, subject to a minimum of £500 and a maximum of £3000
Exceeding £150,000	2% of the amount of the award

3. For the purposes of paragraph 2–

"amount of the award" means the aggregate of the sum awarded by way of compensation and interest under clauses 8 and 9, before deduction of any reimbursement due to be paid to the Department for Social Development through the Compensation Recovery Unit (CRU) of that Department (or to any successor of that unit), but excluding the amount of any payment due in respect of benefits and hospital charges.

"reasonable disbursements" means reasonable expenditure incurred on the applicant's behalf and agreed between the applicant and MIB before it is incurred (MIB's agreement not having been unreasonably withheld) but includes Counsel's fees only where the applicant is a minor or under a legal disability.

4. The foregoing provisions of this Schedule are without prejudice to MIB's liability under the provisions of this Agreement to pay the costs of arbitration proceedings or an arbitrator's fee.'

5.3 THE SECOND PORTAL (THE 2013 AMENDMENTS)

In December 2102, following consultation, the Ministry of Justice announced that it proposed to extend the portals horizontally, to incorporate employers liability and public liability claims, and also vertically so that cases up to £25,000 would be included. The Ministry of Justice set out a table of the proposed fees, but the implementation process was the subject of unsuccessful judicial review proceedings brought by APIL.

Immediately after the hearing of the unsuccessful judicial review, the Ministry of Justice announced that it was proceeding with the new costs for the portal scheme for road traffic accidents up to £10,000 with effect from 30 April 2013 and with the other changes to the portal and fixed costs in the fast track with effect from 31 July 2013.

5.3.1 Road traffic cases

For road traffic accident cases up to £10,000, where the claims notification form was submitted after 30 April 2013 (whatever the date of the accident) the new portal fees set out in **5.3.2** apply to the claim.

5.3.2 The portal for accidents after 31 July 2013

The horizontal extension of the portal was effected by amendments to the pre-action protocol for personal injury claims. These required all road traffic, employer's liability and public liability personal injury cases up to £25,000 to be commenced in the portal using a claims notification form.

If the case remains within the portal then the fees payable are as follows (CPR, r 45.18):

Type & Damages	Stage 1	Stage 2	Stage 3 Type A	Stage 3 Type B	Stage 3 Type C
RTA<10,000	£200	£300	£250	£250	£150
RTA 10,001–25,000	£200	£600	£250	£250	£150
EL/PL<10,000	£300	£600	£250	£250	£150
EL/PL 10,001–25,000	£300	£1,300	£250	£250	£150

Type A: Legal Representative's costs

Type B: Advocate's costs if an oral hearing is required

Type C: the costs for the advice on the amount of damages where the claimant is a child

Where the claim is valued at more than £10,000, CPR, r 45.23B provides in addition for a payment equal to a stage 3 type C fixed fee where 'an additional advice has been obtained from a specialist solicitor or from counsel' and 'that advice is reasonably required to value the claim'.

Disbursements are also payable under CPR, r 45.19 as follows:

> '45.19 (1) The court –
> (a) may allow a claim for a disbursement of a type mentioned in paragraphs (2) or (3); but
> (b) will not allow a claim for any other type of disbursement.

5.3.5 Failure to follow the protocol

CPR, r 45.24 sets out draconian penalties for failing to follow the protocol where it was applicable. If the claim was:

- not commenced in the portal when it should have been (eg by the claimant wrongly valuing the claim in excess of £25,000);
- or the court finds that it fell out of the protocol because of unreasonable behaviour or inadequate information supplied by the claimant:

> 'then the court may order the defendant to pay no more than the fixed costs in rule 45.18 together with the disbursements allowed in accordance with rule 45.19.'

In *Patel v Fortis Insurance Ltd*,[5] the claimant's solicitors exited the portal on the basis that the defendant had failed to send an acknowledgement in time. The court decided otherwise and felt their conduct was unreasonable and contrary to the spirit of the protocol so that they were limited to the fixed portal costs. These amounted to £1,927.50 where they had been claiming £16,483.16.

It follows that where there is any reasonable doubt as to whether the claim is worth £25,000 or less, the safest course is to commence the claim within the portal and then exit rather than declining to follow the protocol, following the normal pre-action protocol and then issuing CPR Part 7 proceedings.

5.3.6 Cases that fall out of the protocol

Where a case falls out of the protocol, CPR, r 45.28 provides that 'the court will, when making any order as to costs ... take into account the Stage 1 and Stage 2 fixed costs that have been paid by the defendant'.

5.4 FIXED RECOVERABLE COSTS IN THE FAST TRACK

For accidents after 31 July 2013, if the claim exits the portal but is allocated to the fast track on issue, or would have been so allocated had proceedings been issued, then a new fixed cost regime applies. This does not apply to disease cases where costs in cases exiting the portal will continue to be assessed on the standard basis.

Unlike portal costs, which are fixed for bands damages up to £10,000 and between £10,000 and £25,000, the fixed costs for the fast track (or

---
[5] [2011] EWCC Leicester 23 December LTL 11 January 2012.

for cases exiting the portal and settling pre-proceedings where the appropriate track would have been the fast track) are calculated as a fixed sum plus a sum equal to a percentage of the damages agreed or awarded.

5.4.1 Fast track fixed recoverable costs

The following tables set out the details:

Pre-issue personal injury fixed recoverable costs outside the portal

Damages Type	£1,000–£5,000	£5,001–£10,000	£10,001–£25,000
RTA	£550 or, if less; £100	£1,100	£1,930
+ a sum =	20% Damages	15% Damages > £5,000	10% Damages > £10,000
EL	£950	£1,855	£2,500
+ a sum =	17.5% Damages	12.5% Damages > £5,000	10% damages > £10,000
PL	£950	£1,855	£2,370
+ a sum =	17.5% Damages	12.5% Damages > £5,000	10% Damages > £10,000

Post-issue personal injury fixed recoverable costs in the fast track

Stage type	Issued – post-issue; pre-allocation	Issued – post-allocation; pre-listing	Issued – post-listing; pre-trial
RTA	£1,160	£1,880	£2,655
+ a sum =	20% damages	20% damages	20% damages
EL	£2,630	£3,350	£4,280
+ a sum =	20% damages	25% damages	30% damages
PL	£2,450	£3,065	£3,790
+ a sum =	17.5% damages	22.5% damages	27.5% damages

If the case goes to trial, the following costs are also payable:

Trial advocacy fees

Damages agreed or awarded	Not more than £3,000	More than £3,000, but not more than £10,000	More than £10,000, but not more than £15,000	More than £15,000
Trial advocacy fee	£500	£710	£1,070	£1,705

5.4.2 The stages

CPR, r 45.29C (RTA) and CPR, r 45.29E (EL and PL) sets out when one stage moves to another:

> '"on or after" means the period beginning on the date on which the court respectively—
> (i) issues the claim;
> (ii) allocates the claim under Part 26; or
> (iii) lists the claim for trial; and
> (b) unless stated otherwise, a reference to "damages" means agreed damages; and
> (c) a reference to "trial" is a reference to the final contested hearing.'

5.4.3 Disbursements

The following provisions allow for recovery of the following categories of disbursements in addition to the fixed costs:

> '45.29I
>
> (1) The court—
> (a) may allow a claim for a disbursement of a type mentioned in paragraphs (2) or (3); but
> (b) will not allow a claim for any other type of disbursement.
>
> (2) In a claim started under either the RTA Protocol or the EL/PL Protocol, the disbursements referred to in paragraph (1) are—
> (a) the cost of obtaining medical records and expert medical reports as provided for in the relevant Protocol;
> (b) the cost of any non-medical expert reports as provided for in the relevant Protocol;
> (c) the cost of any advice from a specialist solicitor or counsel as provided for in the relevant Protocol;
> (d) court fees;
> (e) any expert's fee for attending the trial where the court has given permission for the expert to attend;

(f) expenses which a party or witness has reasonably incurred in travelling to and from a hearing or in staying away from home for the purposes of attending a hearing;
(g) a sum not exceeding the amount specified in Practice Direction 45 for any loss of earnings or loss of leave by a party or witness due to attending a hearing or to staying away from home for the purpose of attending a hearing; and
(h) any other disbursement reasonably incurred due to a particular feature of the dispute.

(3) In a claim started under the RTA Protocol only, the disbursements referred to in paragraph (1) are also the cost of—
(a) an engineer's report; and
(b) a search of the records of the—
   (i) Driver Vehicle Licensing Authority; and
   (ii) Motor Insurance Database.'

5.4.4 Children

Unlike within the portal, there is no provision under fast track fixed costs for any additional sums to be paid in children cases to reflect the need for an advice to the court and attending an approval hearing. The defendant is not required to pay anything over and above the fixed recoverable costs payable under the scheme in general.

5.4.5 Escape

The figures for fixed costs in the fast track were averages calculated by Professors Fenn and Rickman from costs data supplied to them by claimants and defendants. The Ministry of Justice deducted a sum of about £700 from these figures to represent the 'saving' from the ban on referral fees, and then added inflation since the figures were published. However, in the table published in the final Jackson report, it is noted that the average should not apply to cases which come in at more or less than 20% of the average.

Accordingly, the Civil Procedure Rules make provision for an escape from the fast track fixed recoverable costs rules.

Under CPR, r 45.29J the claimant must first persuade the court that 'there are exceptional circumstances making it appropriate to do so'. In such circumstances the court may:

'(a) summarily assess the costs; or
(b) make an order for the costs to be subject to detailed assessment.'

A second stage is applied on the actual assessment under CPR, r 45.29K. The claimant must persuade the court on assessment that the costs are at least 20% greater than the amount of the fixed recoverable costs. If the claimant fails to do so, the court will allow the lesser of the assessed costs and the fixed recoverable costs. So far as the costs of the costs only proceedings are concerned then under CPR, r 45.29L, the court may:

'(i) decide not to award the party making the claim the costs of the costs only proceedings or detailed assessment; and
(ii) make orders in relation to costs that may include an order that the party making the claim pay the costs of the party defending those proceedings or that assessment.'

The claimant must therefore persuade the court that there are exceptional circumstances and that the costs allowed on assessment of 20% or more above the amount of the fixed recoverable costs.

Just as under the predictive costs scheme the best method of escape was to issue court proceedings and not to use the escape provisions within the rules, the best way to escape from fast track fixed costs is to get the case allocated to the multitrack. No doubt defendants and courts will be alert to this. However, to be suitable for the fast track the case should be capable of determination by the court in a single day's hearing (so this may render in practice many multi-defendant cases unsuitable) and there should be no need for oral expert evidence (and this may render in practice unsuitable most cases where there are issues as to causation). Value is not the only determinant for allocation to track.

5.4.6 Defendant's costs

Defendant's costs in the fast track are capped rather than fixed (although of course under qualified one-way cost shifting the claimant will rarely be ordered to pay the defendant's costs even if the cases lost).

CPR, r 45.2F provides that defendant's fast track costs are calculated in accordance with the same tables as for claimants, but the reference to the 'value of the claim' is instead as set out below:

'"the value of the claim" is—
(a) the amount specified in the claim form, excluding—
 (i) any amount not in dispute;
 (ii) in a claim started under the RTA Protocol, any claim for vehicle related damages;
 (iii) interest;
 (iv) costs; and

(v) any contributory negligence;
(b) if no amount is specified in the claim form, the maximum amount which the claimant reasonably expected to recover according to the statement of value included in the claim form under rule 16.3; or
(c) £25,000, if the claim form states that the claimant cannot reasonably say how much is likely to be recovered.'

But this operates as a cap, not a fixed fee:

'(a) the court will have regard to; and
(b) the amount of costs order to be paid shall not exceed,

the amount which would have been payable by the defendant if an order for costs had been made in favour of the claimant at the same stage of the proceedings.'

Under CPR, r 45.29F(8) and (9), if the claimant fails to beat a defendant's Part 36 offer, the fixed cost provisions do not apply and the defendant is entitled to costs on the standard basis.

Under CPR, r 45.29F(10) if the defendant is awarded its costs notwithstanding qualified one-way costs shifting under CPR, r 44.15 (claim struck out) or r 44.16 (fundamental dishonesty) (see Chapter 4), the fixed cost provisions do not apply and the defendant is entitled to costs on the standard basis.

5.4.7 Costs of interim applications

The costs of interim applications are allowed on top of the fixed recoverable costs sum.

However, these costs are not subject to summary or detailed assessment but are instead also fixed by CPR, r 45.29H:

'Where the court makes an order for costs of an interim application to be paid by one party in a case to which this Section applies, the order shall be for a sum equivalent to one half of the applicable Type A and Type B costs in Table 6 or 6A.'

In other words, at the time of writing, the fixed costs allowed for any interim application in the fast track is £125 plus VAT.

5.4.8 Offers

CPR Part 36 has been revised to apply to fast track proceedings notwithstanding the new fixed recoverable costs rules.

5.4.8.1 Defendant's offers

With regard to defendant's offers, qualified one-way costs shifting does not apply to protect the claimant (see Chapter 4):

> **'44.14**
>
> (1) Subject to rules 44.15 and 44.16, orders for costs made against a claimant may be enforced without the permission of the court but only to the extent that the aggregate amount in money terms of such orders does not exceed the aggregate amount in money terms of any orders for damages and interest made in favour of the claimant.'

The claimant is however, entitled to the costs for the stage applicable at the date on which notice of acceptance was served. So if the defendant makes a Part 36 offer at the beginning of a stage and the claimant accepted after 21 days but before the end of the stage, the claimant is still entitled to his costs of that stage as well as any earlier stage.

If the offer is accepted after the end of the applicable period, the claimant will still be entitled to his costs of the proceedings up to the stage the offer was served, but is liable to pay the defendant's costs after the date of expiry. The defendant's costs will be calculated as follows:

> '(10) Where the court makes an order for costs in favour of the defendant—
> (a)   the court will have regard to; and
> (b)   the amount of costs ordered shall not exceed,
>
> the fixed costs in Table 6B, Table 6C or Table 6D in Section IIIA of Part 45 applicable at the date of acceptance, less the fixed costs to which the claimant is entitled under paragraph (4) or (5).'

CPR, r 36.14A makes similar provision in the event of a claimant failing to beat a defendant's Part 36 offer at trial.

5.4.8.2 Claimant's offer

As usual, the provisions of Part 36 so far as claimant offers are concerned, only come into play if the claimant goes to trial and obtains a judgment which is more advantageous that he claimant's own offer.

Rule 36.14 continues to apply so that, unless the court thinks it unjust, it will:

(a)   order interest on the damages awarded to the claimant at a rate not exceeding 10% above base;

(b) award costs to the claimant on the indemnity basis;
(c) award the claimant interest on those costs at a rate not exceeding 10% above base; and
(d) award an additional amount of damages being 10% of the damages (the £75,000 cap is unlikely to apply to a claim in the fast track).

The interest provisions (on both damages and costs) run only from the last date on which the defendant could have accepted the Part 36 offer. It therefore follows that the earlier that an appropriate Part 36 offer can be made, the better the prospects that the claimant can obtain the full benefit of these costs provisions.

The variations to CPR, r 36.14 under CPR, r 36.14A appears only to apply to a claimant's failure to beat a defendant's offer at trial. In these circumstances, if a claimant beats his own offer a court should order indemnity costs instead of fixed costs. 'Proportionality' does not expressly apply.

However, the rules are not entirely crystal clear. In any event, indemnity costs are not a 'blank cheque' ('the court will not ... allow costs which have been unreasonably incurred or are unreasonable in amount') and the court might well take the amount of the applicable fixed costs into account even when assessing costs on the indemnity basis. However, on an assessment on the indemnity basis 'the court will resolve any doubt which it may have as to whether costs were reasonably incurred or were reasonable in amount in favour of the receiving party'.

Solicitors must therefore be alert to making Part 36 offers at appropriate levels, revising them when appropriate and doing so at the earliest possible stage.

These provisions apply to issued cases in the fast track, and also to cases which have exited the portal but settle pre-proceedings.

5.5 LONDON WEIGHTING

In respect of predictive, portal and fast track fixed costs, where the claimant:
(a) lives or works in London (including Bromley, Croydon, Dartford, Gravesend and Uxbridge); and
(b) instructs a firm of solicitors who practise in that area,

add 12.5% to the total fixed costs figures.

5.6 MULTIPLE CLAIMANTS

Where there is more than one potential claimant in relation to a dispute and two or more claimants instruct the same firm of solicitors, the provisions of the section apply in respect of each claimant.

5.7 COUNSEL

It should be noted that, contrary to their submissions to Jackson, counsel have not been treated as 'disbursements' under the various fixed recoverable costs schemes. In other words, if a solicitor decides to instruct counsel then any payment to counsel has to come out of the fixed costs payable. Counsel's fees are not payable in addition to the fixed costs.

5.8 WORKING WITH FIXED RECOVERABLE COSTS

A fixed costs regime across the whole fast track up to £25,000 creates numerous challenges for solicitors' practices to operate economically. Solicitors must first decide whether they wish to:

- agree with clients to work for the fixed recoverable costs only;
- work on hourly rate basis with clients only able to recover the fixed recoverable costs as a contribution towards the total costs; or
- agree to any solicitor and client costs either as an absolute figure or a percentage of the damages recovered under a conditional fee agreement.

Even if solicitors reserve the right to charge on a full hourly rate basis, damages in most personal injury cases are relatively low. It is unlikely that any solicitor undertaking work in the fast track could operate as if there had been no change to the costs regime.

Solicitors must consider varying their working practices. This may include better use of information technology, using lower grade staff and giving only a no-frills service for such cases. Some cases for some clients might be rejected if it appears that the work required is likely to exceed the fixed recoverable costs (examples might include work for protected parties, children, claims with multiple defendants, clients who is the first language is not English, overly 'consumerist' clients). A fixed recoverable costs system certainly benefits clients with simple cases against those with complicated ones and it incentivises solicitors to cherry pick.

5.9 FIXED RECOVERABLE COSTS: THE FUTURE

There is no inbuilt mechanism in the rules for increasing the fixed recoverable costs under any of these provisions. The likelihood is that they will remain without change for long periods and become further devalued. However, one of the terms of reference of the Civil Justice Council's costs committee is:

> 'To monitor the operation of the costs rules, in consultation with the Ministry of Justice, and where appropriate, to make recommendations.'

It is also possible that fixed recoverable costs will be extended further, either by way of increasing the scope of the fast track or by imposing fixed recoverable costs for those at the lower end of the multitrack. There are no concrete proposals to this effect at present.

There is a clear tension between the mechanism of fixed recoverable costs in fast track where the amount of costs is clearly fixed to the amount of the sum awarded or agreed to be paid by way of damages, in contrast to the test of proportionality in the multitrack whether judges to take account of the 'sums in issue'. This may lead to peculiar difficulties in the assessment of costs of cases at the bottom end of the multitrack compared with the top end of the fast track.

5.10 SUMMARY OF APPLICABLE FIXED RECOVERABLE COSTS SCHEMES

	RTA Damages £1,000–£10,000	Damages £10,000–£25,000	PL Damages £1,000–£25,000	EL Accident Damages £1,000–£25,000	EL Disease Damages £1,000–£25,000
Accident 6 October 2003–30 April 2010	PCS	Standard	Standard	Standard	Standard
Accident 1 May 2010–29 April 2013, admitted	Portal 1	Standard	Standard	Standard	Standard
Accident 1 May 2010–29 April 2013, denied	PCS	Standard	Standard	Standard	Standard
Claim 30 April–31 July 2013, admitted	Portal 2	Standard	Standard	Standard	Standard
Accident 30 April–31 July 2013, denied	PCS	Standard	Standard	Standard	Standard
Accident after 31 July, admitted	Portal 2	Portal 2	Portal 2	Portal 2	Portal 2

	RTA		PL	EL Accident	EL Disease
	Damages £1,000–£10,000	Damages £10,000–£25,000	Damages £1,000–£25,000	Damages £1,000–£25,000	Damages £1,000–£25,000
Accident after 31 July, denied	FT Fixed	FT Fixed	FT Fixed	FT Fixed	Standard

Standard: Standard basis costs assessment

PCS: Predictive costs scheme (see **5.2.3**)

Portal 1: First portal (described in **5.2.4**)

Portal 2: Second extended portal (described in **5.3**)

FT Fixed: Fast track fixed recoverable costs scheme (described in **5.4**).

CHAPTER 6

COST ORDERS

6.1 PROPORTIONALITY

Proportionality is arguably now the main theme of the costs and case management regime of the Civil Procedure Rules. In 1996, then Master of the Rolls, Lord Woolf, published his *Access to Justice Report 1996*[1] in which he set out a number of principles that would underpin the civil justice system going forward. The original nine key elements did not include the term 'proportionate', but in his second report, he focused on controlling the costs of litigation, both in terms of time and money including, where necessary, limiting the amount of work that had to be done on a case.[2] The original part one of the Civil Procedure Rules stated:

> '1.1(1) These rules are a new procedure rule code with the overriding objective of enabling the court to deal with cases justly.
>
> 2. Dealing with the case justly includes, so far as is practical –
> (a) ensuring that the parties are on an equal footing;
> (b) saving expense;
> (c) *dealing with the case in ways which are proportionate [emphasis added]* –
>   (i) to the amount of money involved;
>   (ii) to the importance of the case;
>   (iii) to the complexity of the issues; and
>   (iv) to the financial position of each party ...'

Lord Woolf's first opportunity to comment judicially on proportionality came in March 2002 in *Home Office v Lownds*.[3] Here he set out his guidance that if the overall costs were considered to be disproportionate then the costs would be assessed on the basis that each item is necessary,

---

[1] Access to Justice Final Report, Lord Woolf, Master of the Rolls, July 1996 *Final report to the Lord Chancellor on the civil justice system in England and Wales*.
[2] Access to Justice Report 1996, section II: Case Management, chapter 2, fast track: general, para 23.
[3] [2002] EWCA Civ 365.

eg the judge was to apply a test of necessity to each item of work. As will be seen below, Sir Rupert Jackson's proposals swept this element away and effectively reversed *Lownds*.

In *Lownds* the defendant had appealed a decision of a circuit judge who had dismissed an appeal from a costs order at first instance in a case in which the claimant Lownds had sued the Secretary of State for the Home Office for clinical negligence caused while he was a prisoner. The claimant settled for damages of £3,000 and his costs were assessed at £16,784 including VAT. In fact the majority of the costs had been incurred before the CPR had come into force on 26 April 1999 but the points of principle that the Court of Appeal decided to look at included whether the costs to be awarded might or should be reduced if they were disproportionate to the amount claimed in the action and whether those costs should then be reduced if they were disproportionate. The Court of Appeal decided that the proportionality of costs recovered by the claimant should be determined having regard to the sum that it was reasonable for him to believe he might recover at the time he made his claim. It was then held that the proportionality of the costs incurred by the defendant should be determined with the regard to the sum that it was reasonable for him to believe that the claimant might recover should the claim succeed.

The Court of Appeal produced a two-stage approach for judges assessing costs. To begin with they would look at the global assessment and then would go on to consider each item in turn. If on the global assessment, the costs claimed were proportionate then the court would allow each item providing it was reasonably incurred and was a reasonable amount. However, on a global assessment, if those costs were disproportionate then the court had to assess each item and then would only allow those that are necessary as well as reasonable.

Therefore, until 2013, necessity would prevail over proportionality. However, following the implementation of Sir Rupert Jackson's Review of Civil Litigation, all work undertaken after 1 April 2013 will be assessed on an item-by-item basis and will then be followed by a global assessment. In practical terms, if on an item-by-item assessment, the costs are proportionate then the court will still have to go on to consider whether the total costs are proportionate and if not it will have to amend the bill accordingly. The result is that the two-stage hurdle that a receiving party will have to overcome is to satisfy a court that the costs are reasonable and proportionate before they are allowed. In simple terms 'proportionality trumps necessity'.

6.1.1 Post 1 April 2013

The overriding objective, as originally drafted by Woolf LJ (see **6.1**), has been amended to include 'and at proportionate cost'.[4] The newly amended rule now reads:

'1.1(1) These Rules are a new procedure rule code with the overriding objective of enabling the court to deal with cases justly and at a proportionate cost.

(2) Dealing with the case justly *and at proportionate costs* includes, so far as is practical [*emphasis added*] –
(a) in showing that the parties are on an equal footing;
(b) saving expense;
(c) dealing with the case in ways which are proportionate –
 (i) to the amount of money involved;
 (ii) to the importance of the case;
 (iii) to the complexity of the issues; and
 (iv) to the financial position of each party;
(d) ensuring that it is dealt with expeditiously and fairly;
(e) allotting to it an appropriate share of the court's resources, while taking into account the need to allot resources to other cases; and
(f) enforcing compliance with rules, practice directions and orders.'

This is a clear signal that whilst access to justice is acknowledged by the rule makers, it is qualified and reflects the position in other areas of legal practice. The problem that has always existed in personal injury litigation is that the claimant rarely had a vested interest in the costs of litigation as they would be shielded from liability to costs through the availability of legal aid, trade union support or conditional fee agreement (with after-the-event insurance). This contrasts significantly with litigants in other areas of law, where the fact that there was a cost to litigants winning or losing would mean that they took a greater interest in the costs that were incurred on their behalf. It is almost inconceivable in other areas of civil litigation, perhaps with the exception of high level commercial litigation, that any willing litigant would be prepared to incur significantly more in costs than they were hoping to recover. This is why the new rules are such an anathema to the personal injury lawyer when many other non-personal injury civil litigators may well be scratching their heads to understand what all the fuss is about.

---

[4] CPR, r 1.1.

6.1.2 Transitional provisions

Cases issued before 1 April 2013 will continue to be governed by pre–1 April CPR. This means that the costs judge has the unenviable task of undertaking an assessment of costs in a case that straddled 1 April on a two-stage basis. They apply a traditional older *Lownds* approach to assessment for work undertaken before 1 April but are then required to interpret the new rule on work after 1 April. The new rule appears at CPR, r 44.3.

> '(2) Where the amount of costs appears to be assessed on the standard basis, the court will:
> (a) only allow costs which are proportionate to the matters in issue. Costs which are disproportionate in amount may be disallowed or reduced even if they were reasonably or necessarily incurred ...
> ...
>
> (5) Costs incurred are proportionate if they bear a reasonable relationship to:–
> (a) the sums in issue in the proceedings;
> (b) the value of any non-monetary relief in issue in the proceedings;
> (c) the complexity of the litigation;
> (d) any additional work generated by the conduct of the paying party; and
> (e) any wider factors involved in the proceedings, such as reputation or public importance.'

As Sir Rupert commented in his report:

> 'I propose that in an assessment of costs on the standard basis, proportionality should prevail over reasonableness and the proportionality test should be applied on a global basis. The court should first make an assessment of reasonable costs, having regard to the individual items of the bill, the time reasonably spent on those items and the other factors listed in CPR 44.5(3). The court should then stand back and consider whether the total figure is proportionate. If the total figure is not proportionate, the court should make an appropriate reduction.'

What each of these items means is open to debate. Litigators should be prepared to guide the court to these elements either at the time the budget is being awarded (where there is no agreement between the parties) or on detailed assessment. However, it seems very likely that judges will probably have regard to (a) or (b) only, depending on the nature of the case. It will be hard work to divert the judge's attention to (c)–(e). However, good practice would dictate (particularly in the event of provisional assessment which is a paper-based assessment only) that where a case is at risk of being deemed disproportionate, the claimant's solicitor will need to give attention to each of these items in their bill.

The lack of definition or guidance from a practice direction means, for example, that in a common a scenario such as a multi-defendant case, the claimant has no way of knowing what level of costs can be recovered where there are two defendants who blame each other. Is there a 100% or 50% or 25% loading for example? In cases with multiple injuries where it may be necessary to involve medical experts from more than one discipline, but where the injuries themselves are not cumulatively valued, what sort of loading will take place? There are increasing numbers of cases involving foreign law that are brought before the courts of England and Wales following the application of Rome II.[5] This renders even a modest slipping or tripping case more expensive because of the need for foreign law to assist a court either in determining liability or more often quantum. The first indication of what the court considers proportionate will be at the time the budget is set and that may be too late if a judge is not sufficiently generous in the loading that he or she applies to the budget to enable the claimant to win their case. It is also unclear when and to what extent the Court of Appeal will provide detailed guidance for the various types of litigation that will be before the court.

It is unfortunate therefore that there is no practice direction to enable the parties and the court to follow and to provide guidance as to what is proportionate. The Civil Justice Council's working party which comprised representatives of all users of the court (claimants, defendants, insurers, funders, district, circuit and costs judges, counsel and solicitors) produced a practice direction that would have assisted. However, at a meeting in October 2012 where there was optimism that this practice direction would be implemented, the delegates to the gathering were presented with what became known as a 'virtual lecture' which subsequently was entitled 'Sir Rupert Jackson's third implementation lecture'. This followed his review of the recommendations of the working party. He commented:

> 'There is no need for an elaborate practice direction ... subject to any drafting improvements which may be made by the Rule Committee, the rule is sufficiently clear. Apart from making the amendments to the costs practice direction proposed in chapter 3, paragraphs 5.22 to 5.23 (which result in overall shortening) there is no need for any further practice direction.'

---

[5] The Rome II Regulation (EC) No 864/2007.

However, it is understood that others in the Court of Appeal now take a different view and are keen for a case to reach them to be able to offer some guidance. This is reflected in the comments of Lord Neuberger, Master of the Rolls at the time that these rules came into force:[6]

> 'The law on proportionate costs will have to be developed on a case-by-case basis. This may mean a degree of satellite litigation while the courts work out the law ... It should focus the minds of all involved on the need to consider the costs and benefits of each step proposed to be taken in proceedings.'

Embodied in the rules is the sort of case planning anticipated by Lord Woolf as referred to in his judgment in *Lownds*. In *Lownds* he quoted with approval[7] the words of Her Honour Judge Alton in *Stevens v Watts*:[8]

> 'In modern litigation, with the emphasis on proportionality, there is a requirement for parties to make an assessment at the outset of the likely value of the claim and its importance and complexity, and then to plan in advance the necessary work, the appropriate level of person to carry out the work; the overall time which will be necessary and appropriate spend on the various stages in bringing the action to trial and the likely overall cost. Whilst it was not unusual for costs to exceed the amount in issue, it was, in the context of modest litigation such as the present case, one reason for seeking to curb the amount of work done, and the cost by reference to the need for proportionality.'

This is a very useful, succinct guide to the steps to be taken when accepting instructions from a litigant in terms of assessing the value of the claim, taking into account the elements of CPR, r 44.3 and then applying an appropriate case plan (with perhaps the removal of the word 'necessary' and thereafter calculating an appropriate amount of investment in the case).

As Lord Neuberger commented 'not least because parties will need to be made fully aware of the fact that certain steps taken may, or will, be at their own cost, or may be futile'.

---

[6] *Proportionate Costs Fifteenth Lecture in the Implementation Programme*, The Law Society, 29 May 2012.
[7] 'I would respectfully endorse every word of those comments of Judge Alton' per Lord Woolf.
[8] [2000] LTL July 14. This was a case from the Birmingham County Court in June 2000 and was first quoted with approval in *Jefferson v National Freight* [2001] EWCA Civ 2082.

Traditionally, in non-personal injury litigation, litigants were more likely to suffer expenditure whether their case was won or lost. However, following the advent of non–recoverable success fees in personal injury cases, there is now a real likelihood that claimants will incur expense within the litigation, for which the claimant should be made aware. The claimant's solicitor, who proposes to indemnify their client, may have to recognise that the stricter regime will mean that there is a greater likelihood of costs being assessed off their bill. This will be at their own expense and seriously impact upon the profitability of the individual case and eventually the profitability of undertaking the work generally.

In practice, until there is Court of Appeal guidance, claimant lawyers should:

- case plan in every multi-track case. Budgeting as provided for by the CPR will mean this is important in any event;
- assess the sums being claimed;
- bear in mind all the various additional factors set out in CPR, rr 1.1(2), 44.3(5) and 44.4(3);
- warn the client that the costs of steps the lawyer considers necessary to win or increase the compensation may not be allowed between the parties, but that if the client consents the money can still be spent at the client's cost and risk;
- recoverable costs are not the same as solicitor and client costs;
- at an assessment, rely upon the process outlined in the Final Report – a detailed item-by-item assessment followed by a global view; do not allow the judge to form a global view on proportionality before the assessment begins;
- consider escaping proportionality by a well-judged Part 36 Offer in every case which if beaten will lead to indemnity costs (to which proportionality does not apply).

6.2 BUDGETING

Sir Rupert Jackson set out in his report an explanation of how budgeting would work:

(i) The parties will prepare and exchange litigation budgets or (as the case proceeds) amended budgets.
(ii) The court states the extent to which those budgets are approved.
(iii) So far as possible, the court manages the case so that it proceeds within the approved budgets.

(iv) At the end of the litigation, the recoverable costs of the winning party are assessed.

There were several pilots in regional commercial courts as well as in defamation work. Despite that many remain critical of the process and the detail required.

The principles of proportionality are defined thus:[9]

> 'only allow costs which are proportionate to the matters in issue. Costs which are disproportionate in amount may be disallowed or reduced, even if they were reasonably or necessarily incurred.'

Although the focus in budgeting relates to the actual process by which a court approves a budget after the defence has been filed and at the time the directions questionnaire and directions fixed, in practical terms the claimant's solicitor will need to work on a budget from the time they take on the claimant's case. The law firm will need to make an assessment as to the likely cost of prosecuting the case and to determine whether it will be possible to profitably represent the claimant within that likely budget and to make adjustments accordingly. While formerly the only assessment was whether the case would win or lose, now a proper assessment is to be made as to the likely costs of undertaking he claim. This brings personal injury litigation into the same world as other businesses where there are properly budgeted projects. From the claimant's solicitor's perspective the budget is about ensuring that their client can access justice, albeit that it will be at a proportionate cost as dictated by CPR, r 1.1. This will inevitably present a challenge to the profitability of both individual cases and of the firm generally. It is therefore vital that claimant lawyers are able to properly budget their cases and to persuade their opponent, or the court, as to the level of those budgets to ensure that these victims continue to have access to justice.

6.2.1 Planning – the firm

Law firms are businesses, and lawyers need to understand the make-up of the business and the product/s they are selling. They need to understand the cost of each part of the process.

In order to do this effectively, a law firm needs to have data on the average costs recovered per case type. In the first instance, that is to enable it to identify the extent to which, if at all, that work was being

---
[9] CPR, r 44.3(2)(a).

done historically, whether proportionately or not. If the overwhelming majority of the work was recovering costs at levels that would not be perceived as proportionate then clearly adjustments are going have to be made to the work process if those cases are going to be continued to be brought. Within that assessment the law firm needs to make adjustments for the loss of success fees which are no longer recoverable from the opponent. That may mean no success fee at all or, it may mean a reduced success fee being taken from the claimant's damages. This is fundamental to the profitability, as in many areas of low value litigation the lawyer would have relied upon the success fee to achieve profit.

It is also vital to understand how long particular cases take to bring to fruition as that will impact upon the profitability of the work through the cash flow. The continued use of counsel will need careful consideration in the context of the ongoing profitability of running cases. Counsel brings an important element of added value to a case; or at least they should do if they are going to continue to have a role. Whilst it may be possible to replace the independent view that they bring to a case with an in house referral, unless the firm feels capable of producing its own advocates then it would need the assistance of counsel. If one is going to use an advocate then the advocate ought to be involved from early in the case to determine how it is presented to the court. It is important that the law firm has regard to the manner in which it uses counsel historically and whether they can continue to use them at that rate. Some firms historically have been very dependent upon counsel input involving them at three or four stages within a case. Each time counsel is involved in the case that results in a reduction of profits to the law firm and that is without even considering the issue of whether or not the counsel expects to share in a success fee or not.

Finally, the issue of disbursements will need careful consideration and firms should review the manner in which they conduct litigation. Court fees continue to increase and they are not judged separately to the remaining costs of the case but are taken into account. By definition a case that progresses to trial will have a significantly higher element of disbursement in it compared to the one that will settle early on and that must be taken into account when determining the budget that can be incurred. Historically because necessity was taken into account these could be set to one side before considering proportionality. Now that necessity is not a factor that the court will take into account when determining proportionality these expensive additions to the cost of the case can have a significant impact.

With an understanding of the work involved in cases, the extent to which counsel and experts will form a part, and the length of time cases take, then a firm will begin to understand its profitability of particular case types and cases generally. It will help to identify the cases that of course will fall into the fixed cost regime and those that fall outside but are likely to run into the ceiling of proportionality; most likely those cases of low multitrack value, for example from £25,001 to £75,000.

6.2.2 The case

At the time that the firm takes on a case a proper case plan should be prepared. As with any project, there are a number of elements to address:

- an assessment as to what is to be achieved;
- the timescale;
- the cost; and
- the tools that are required to carry out the project.

The same project management and assessment must follow in a claimant personal injury case. Having risk assessed the case to the extent of determining whether it can be won and what it will need to enable the case to win, including identifying the potential pinch points and hurdles that will have to be overcome for a successful case, the law firm will need to identify the approximate value of the case. This will be fundamental to determining whether the case goes into the fast track and the portals with their considerably restricted costs recovery regime or, into the multitrack. Here is the extent to which, if at all, proportionality is likely to impose an uncomfortable ceiling to cost recovery.

In the lower value cases the law firm will need to assess whether it needs to reduce the cost of undertaking work. History will show the work was commonly undertaken at a disproportionate cost. Therefore the firm will need to justify to a court why the particular case plan and budget should be allowed in full.

Law firms will need to consider, at a high level, the seniority of lawyers that it attaches to cases and, in turn, which lawyers are appropriate for individual cases. There is of course a large range of work in a typical claimant law firm. There will be the simplest, the most lower value worth (not always the simplest), the high complexity low value worth, and there may be a minority of complex high value high worth cases. What is certain is that few law firms will be able to continue to litigate in the manner that they did prior to 1 April 2013. Even in the most complex high valued cases it is possible to identify significant parts of the case that do not require specialised experienced lawyer input. These are items that can be commoditised. Such areas may include: the initial client instruction taking and file opening; the drafting of pleadings; the preparation of special damage schedules; and costings. All of these are areas that are common across all litigation and where it may be possible to make a saving in terms of the cost of undertaking the work.

It seems likely that turnover in claimant personal injury work will reduce in virtually every law firm; the real test for the law firm, however, is whether or not the profitability can be preserved or improved. In individually assessing the case and identifying the case plan this will identify the work that will need to be undertaken for the claimant to win. There will inevitably be 'necessary' work as the lawyer perceives it yet it is not 'necessary' as defined by the proportionality rules. Key areas and stages of the litigation should be identified and plotted and values attached.

That case plan will underpin the Precedent H budget that will ultimately be submitted to a court. It will be good practice to begin working alongside that document from the date that the case is incepted and not just something that is perceived to be court rule required. In the same way that risk assessment was required by the court rules to support a success fee, in real terms risk assessment was necessary from inception of the case for good case planning.

In determining the manner in which a case can be litigated and whether or not a firm can continue to litigate in the way it has done historically one example for consideration is the pre-action protocol. The pre-action protocol was introduced by Lord Justice Woolf in his rules in 1999. Most observers have considered it to be a helpful addition to the litigation process but many have complained that it has simply shifted the cost burden from the middle to the end of the case to the beginning. However, no data has ever been properly assessed on this point. The point of the pre-action protocol is to narrow the areas of dispute between the parties, if not to resolve the dispute completely. For the vast majority of personable injury cases, the protocol has resulted in a modest number of admissions from a defendant and a similarly modest number of replies which would cause a claimant to abandon their case there and then. The overwhelming majority of protocols in cases have demonstrated a form of table tennis by which each party sends a series of letters back and forth until such time as a claimant decides that they ought to issue proceedings. This is more often than not because of the forthcoming expiry of a limitation period. In the new world that is simply using up a substantial part of the budget. There is therefore a school of thought that suggests that whilst the claimant should and, indeed, must give a detailed letter of claim with sufficient information to enable the defendant to make a proper assessment of the case, if the defendant is not able to make the admission at the first available opportunity then the case should proceed to litigation as quickly as possible. If the defendant is going to seek to engage on a series of arguments in relation to liability or otherwise then they may as well do so within the framework of issued proceedings within a budget. Otherwise, the risk is that the judge, when taking into the account the work to be undertaken, will not leave sufficient in the budget post issue of proceedings for the claimant to do justice to their case.

Personal injury lawyers may have been somewhat relaxed towards the client's interest in the cost of the litigation. They rarely expected to have to pay anything win or lose. That changes now with recoverable additional liabilities. The Solicitor's Regulatory Authority Code of Conduct outcome[10] specifies: 'clients receive the best possible information, both at the time of engagement and when appropriate as their matter progresses, about the likely overall cost of their matter'.

This is supported as an indicative behaviour[11] by the solicitor 'clearly explaining your fees and if and when they are likely to change'.

Under the pre-April funding regime providing an updated estimate on a regular basis was often perceived by the claimant lawyer to be no more than an irritant that caused more questions than it was worth. However, in the post-April world where claimants are more likely to be paying success fees, then the estimates become that much more important and therefore again, all work undertaken in case planning and the budget will be even less of a waste of time because the claimant will need to understand the likely costs involved in determining how much of their compensation they are going to receive and how much will be taken up in terms of success fee.

6.2.3 Teamwork

In most personal injury work if not all, there is an element of teamwork. Few cases are pursued by the claimant's solicitor alone. The vast majority of cases will involve expert input and larger value cases are more likely to involve counsel. These additional factors need to be taken into account before a budget can be supplied to the court. Historically, claimant personal injury lawyers have probably paid scant regard to the estimate of costs that they were required to provide in the allocation

---

[10] SRA Code of Conduct, O(1.13).
[11] SRA Code of Conduct, IB(1.14).

questionnaire (now directions questionnaire) and the pre-trial checklist. However, it will be a foolish lawyer who had a budget approved by the court involving expenditure on counsel and experts where there had not been a proper engagement of the relevant personnel as to the work involved. CPR, r 35.4(2) requires the solicitor to provide an estimate of the costs involved to specify the issues which the expert evidence will address.

Again, it would be a naive solicitor who did that without actually asking the expert themselves to provide that estimate. Similarly, it would be a foolhardy solicitor who instructed counsel to advise on evidence post pleadings or indeed to brief them for trial and to present that counsel with the budget that the court has permitted and to then be told by counsel that it simply does not provide enough work for the counsel to properly participate in the claim. For this reason, when case planning, counsel and experts should be engaged at least to provide estimates at the earliest opportunity even if they are not going to be substantively engaged on the case at that point.

Underlying the budgeting procedure is the requirement from the courts that it should be agreed between the parties and therefore in theory, at least, the court should be asked to intervene in only a minority of cases. This is thought to be optimistic in personal injury with the effect of qualifying one-way cost shifting (QOCS). Nevertheless, it presents an opportunity for the claimant lawyer to engage with their opponent on the case to discuss items such as liability, arguments on fact and law, and quantum and they enable a significant amount of agreement to be reached which may in fact assist the prospects of settlement. In engaging with the defendant it may be an appropriate time to identify areas that are considered to be likely to lead to the unnecessary expenditure of costs. A common example might be the defendant who insists on arguing a limitation defence, either when it is unclear that the claimant is in fact in breach of s 11 of the Limitation Act or more likely, that they will not be applying the s 33 discretion.

6.2.4 Post issue

The rules provide for the filing and service of a budget:[12]

> 'Unless the court otherwise orders, all parties except litigants in person must file and exchange budgets as required by the rules or as the court otherwise directs. Each party must do so by the date specified in the notice served under rule 26.3(1) or, if no such date is specified, seven days before the first case management conference.'

---

[12] CPR, r 3.13.

The form is prescribed:[13]

> 'Unless the court otherwise orders, a budget must be in the form of precedent H annexed to this practice direction. It must be in landscape format with at least 12 point type face. In substantial cases the court may direct that budgets be limited initially to part only with the proceedings and subsequently extended to cover the whole proceedings.'

The precedent document has emerged from a series of cost budgeting pilots across the mercantile and commercial courts in the regions. Nevertheless most practitioners are critical of the format of the document and the manner in which the litigation has been phased; it is difficult to fit certain pieces of work in. The precedent was revised in October 2013 with the 66th Update to the CPR.

It includes the work done to date including pre-action costs, although the section entitled 'pre-issue' is not in fact as was first conceived, for all work pre-issue to be inserted. The pre-issue work should still be apportioned, where possible, between the various phases. The result is that the pre-issue section is only work that does not fit into the phases elsewhere. The intended work is broken down into phases and should be categorised according to:

- issue;
- pleadings;
- case management conference (CMC);
- disclosure;
- witness statements;
- expert reports;
- pre-trial review; and
- ADR.

It involves likely contingencies, disbursements, counsel's fees and expert fees (see the document).

In cases where costs are not to exceed £25,000, only the front summary page needs to be completed. In fact this is simply time saving for the judge considering the budget for the solicitor will need to have completed the other pages themselves anyway to populate the front page.[14]

---

[13] PD 3E, para 1.
[14] CPR, r 3.3.

When completing this document the party needs to consider the assumptions by which they are intending the case to be run. Essentially, the parameters within which they anticipate the case will need to be managed to bring it to fruition. It is important these assumptions are properly detailed because as we will be seeing later whilst the court has power to allow later amendments to the budget to vary it, it will only do so where there have been significant developments. In other words, when it could not have been reasonably foreseen so for example, discovering that the experts are more expensive than intended would not be a good reason for the court to amend and vary the budget. The service of a witness statement by a defendant that produced a new issue that needed to be considered by an existing or new expert might.

By setting out the assumptions that underpin the budget then one bolsters an application to vary at a later stage and avoids the suggestion that any later variation is a cloak for an overspend. It sends out a clear message to the court of the case plan that underpins the budget.

What is unclear at this stage is the extent of the work that a court will permit. In an early unreported decision involving a significant quantum only clinical negligence case, Master Cook determined that the claimant's budget of £1m involved considering every single possible eventuality that could ever occur within a piece of quantum only litigation. It was the Master's view that this was an overestimate and that one should only take into account of what is 'likely' to happen. Nevertheless, it would be a brave claimant's solicitor who did not consider many possible ways in which the case could go although it may be that that work should be dealt with within the contingency elements. If there is a reasonable chance that a particular cost is to be incurred then it should be included in the budget or warned of within a contingency.

6.2.5 Completing the form

If possible, firms should seek to integrate Precedent H into their IT systems. By its very nature as a spreadsheet it is intended for completion on a computer but if it is possible to link that to historic data and work, so that lawyers do not need to populate the form from scratch on each occasion but can take pre-populated assumptions and work and amend it for the specific case then that is likely to be advantageous to the lawyers in the firm in determining the budget. Similarly, it is important that the time recording system links into the budget as it is pointless having the court order a particular budget made up of significant components and for the lawyer then to work on the case ignoring the parameters. If possible, the cost system should also be set up to enable it to record the time within the phases set out under the budget so that when a lawyer undertakes a piece of work on expert reports that it is time recorded under the expert report phase. Finally, ideally it would also be linked into a billing system so that when it was necessary to produce a summary or detailed assessment bills then the work can be pulled straight through. The time recordings should include a traffic light system so that a lawyer is warned when they are getting within a particular margin of the budget that is being permitted. Even with firms that do not have the level of sophistication that permits that as an IT system it should be appropriate that supervision or marking on files is sufficiently clear to enable the steps to be monitored.

When completing the form on an individual case the work should begin with the lawyer whose case it is. Much help can be gleaned from cost draftsmen, whether in house or external. Indeed external costs draftsmen will be able to provide guidance from their wider ranging experience of the type of cases and the work that is generally required or indeed permitted. The work must be divided amongst the phases. Despite having gone through pilots there remain criticisms of what categories are listed and how difficult it is to fit some work in to the appropriate slot. 'Pre-action' work is not actually what it says. It should be divided up amongst the various related phases. So work done with an expert pre-issue should appear in the experts' phase but labelled as incurred work. The court cannot interfere with the incurred work but it can pass comment which may affect recovery at assessment later.

There remains uncertainty where certain work should be listed. Case management where there is a protected person is one such area; it perhaps should be highlighted so the court sees its unusual nature.

The solicitor should begin with their case plan and in turn to recite the key assumptions that are behind the budget. One does not need to set out all the obvious points, such as the issue of proceedings, the trial and the like. However, one should set out succinctly the case theory, the key evidential aspects, and whether leading counsel is required.

The solicitor should engage with counsel if they propose to instruct one and to engage with them on the case plan generally and the extent of their work. Counsel and their clerks should be encouraged to produce their estimates. Many leading chambers have been assembling information packs setting out the likely work involved on certain case types based on previous cases.

The essential expert evidence and the expert to provide it must be identified. Once done they should be engaged to assist on estimates; this will be easier of course where they have already provided a report or have advised generally. It is important to consider all of the work the expert will do and not just their report but also the work that surrounds the expert. This will include conferences, answering questions from both parties, meetings and joint statements and trial. Added to this should be the letters of instruction at all stages as well of course as the advocate's work.

Some consider taking the phases as listed in the spreadsheet and then deconstructing the work into smaller pieces to ensure the estimate has a better base in calculating the work involved.

However, whatever way this is approached the actual estimate of hours will always be a challenge in the absence of precedent. Some will always argue that they should (over)estimate the time to be involved. Others work on identifying parameters of shortest and longest time and perhaps picking the mid-way course. Experience of court decisions will inform this, as will the various nuances of behaviour. For example a solicitor may be convinced the case will settle without trial and so just wants to get through the budget without a judge interfering to too great a level because the full work to trial may be disproportionate.

Also important are contingencies; two are provided for in Precedent H. Unfortunately one cannot simply include a generalised amount, for example 25% in case of underestimate. Rather, as one finds in a construction estimate, the contingency must be specified and with an amount. Perhaps a claimant has a concern about disclosure they may receive from the defendant. They may wish to reserve their right to take a particular step; the court may be happy to include contingencies to circumvent later applications to vary. A significant allowance for other contingencies should also be included.

PD 3E confirms that interim applications can be treated as additional costs if reasonable and do not have to be included in the original budget.

It is essential that no budget should be filed or served without someone other than the conducting lawyer reviewing it. In this way they can ensure a second pair of eyes ensures nothing is missed. Other than in very limited circumstances it is not possible to increase the budget at a later stage and certainly not because of an oversight or general underestimate.

The client should be consulted and the budget approved by them. This may give some protection or comfort to the solicitor if the judge significantly reduces the budget.

Although, the rules provide that the document must be filed 7 days before the hearing (unless the court otherwise orders),[15] it should be borne in mind that the premise of the budgeting is that it is agreed with the opponent. Sufficient time should therefore be provided to allow for the claimant lawyer to be able to send a draft of the budget to their opponent and to engage by telephone with their opponent to see to what extent some or all of the budget can be agreed. It is an opportunity to explore the defendant's case plan; to identify possible areas for agreement; and if necessary to revise the draft before court.

It is good practice to ensure that the budget is reviewed by someone other than the lawyer with conduct of the case and the cost draftsmen, given its importance to the case (it may make or break whether the claimant can in fact prosecute their case) it is submitted that a supervisor should review the budget in conjunction with the individual lawyer before submitting it.

6.2.6 Failure to file a budget

> 'Unless the court otherwise orders,[16] any party which fails to file a budget despite being required to do so will be treated as having compiled a budget comprising only the applicable court fees.'

The first and high profile decision on this rule was in the case of *Mitchell v News Group*,[17] a libel case surrounding the infamous so-called Plebgate case. The claimant through his solicitors filed the budget late and the result was that instead of being granted a budget that they were seeking in the sum of around £500,000, Master McCloud limited the budget to his court fees of around £2,000.

The claimant's solicitors made it clear that the default was their own responsibility and not the culpability of their client and that there were particular reasons such as the modest size of the firm and the fact that significant partners were away on holiday at the time but this did not wash with the Master.

> 'The explanations put forward by the claimant's solicitors are not unusual ones. Pressure of work, a small firm, unexpected delays with counsel and so on. These things happen, and I have no doubt they happened here. However, even before the advent of the new rules, the failure of solicitors was generally not treated as in itself a good excuse and I am afraid that

---

[15] CPR, r 3.13.
[16] CPR, r 3.14.
[17] [2013] EWCA 1537.

however much I sympathize with the claimant's solicitors, such explanations carry even less weight in the post-Jackson environment.'

To no one's surprise, the Court of Appeal took the case from the appeal system to give an early decision to help guide the profession. Giving the leading judgment, the Master of the Rolls Lord Dyson upheld the decision that having failed to file his costs budget in time, Mr Mitchell was to be treated as having filed a costs budget comprising only the applicable court fees, and to refuse relief from sanctions.[18] In doing so and in a judgment of much wider application to the CPR than just costs budgets he spelt out a stark warning to the profession of the new world:

'although it seems harsh in the individual case of Mr Mitchell's claim, if we were to overturn the decision to refuse relief, it is inevitable that the attempt to achieve a change in culture would receive a major setback.'

As we have said before, if a budget is worked on from inception of the case then there should not really be a problem in terms of filing the document in time. This was a point made by Master McCloud and quoted by Dyson LJ:[19]

'Budgeting is something which all solicitors by now ought to know is intended to be integral to the process from the start, and it ought not to be especially onerous to prepare a final budget for a CMC even at relatively short notice if proper planning has been done. The very fact that the Defendants, using cost lawyers, were well able to deal with this in the time allotted highlights that there is no question of the time being plainly too short or unfairly so.'

6.2.7 Cost management orders

Costs management orders were introduced on 1 April 2013:[20]

'(1) In addition to exercising its other powers, the court may manage the costs to be incurred by any party in any proceedings.

(2) The court may at any time make a "costs management order". By such order the court will –
   (a) record the extent to which the budgets are agreed between the parties;
   (b) in respect of budgets or parts of budgets which are not agreed, record the court's approval after making appropriate revisions.

(3) If a costs management order has been made, the court will thereafter control the parties' budgets in respect of recoverable costs.'

---

[18] [2013] EWCA Civ 1537.
[19] Para 17 (quoting paragraph 61).
[20] CPR, r 3.15.

Budgeting is therefore predicated upon the parties agreeing the budgets and indeed if they do the court does not appear to have power to interfere. However, it seems unlikely that agreement will be rife in personal injury matters, so it will remain an adversarial process. Nevertheless the requirement to agree means an opportunity for the parties' lawyers to speak: a valuable tool in every litigator's armoury. Talking is an opportunity to narrow disputes, whether that be small matters such as admitted points or even quantum subject to liability. It also presents an opportunity to warn the opponent of the weaknesses in their case and areas that if they maintain will lead to additional cost burdens for them.

6.2.8 Cost management conferences

Costs management conferences, also introduced on 1 April 2013, are defined as:[21]

'(1) Any hearing which is convened solely for the purpose of costs management (for example, to approve a revised budget) is referred to as a "costs management conference".

(2) Where practicable, costs management conferences should be conducted by telephone or in writing.'

It is presumed that the decision to limit the costs hearing to telephone or in writing is to try to reduce the possibility of satellite costs being generated in a mechanism designed to reduce costs. Nevertheless it remains vitally important that whether by telephone or in writing that all relevant points are made clearly and simply for the judge to be able to follow and absorb when making any decision.

It is almost inevitable that it will not be possible to appeal the decision of a judge on any costs management order because of the level of discretion that is involved which a court is not going to interfere with.

6.2.9 Preparation for the budgeting hearing

It is an interesting dilemma now as to whether the CMC at which the budget will be considered should be dealt with by the case handler themselves or whether they can use an advocate or agent. It is submitted that if anyone other than the conducting lawyer is to deal with the CMC then they have to ensure that their advocate is fully briefed on every eventuality in relation to the case and indeed to the budget.

---

[21] CPR, r 3.16.

It is important that the Precedent H sits on the lawyers' desktop or laptop depending whether they are on the telephone or in court. If there are to be amendments made to the precedent by the court during the budget then it is important they are reflected in the draft spreadsheet and the totals monitored. The risk otherwise is that the lawyer discovers after the case that a significant element of his case has been reduced which in fact makes it very difficult to win the case. There have been reports of courts ordering the parties to attend with laptops.

The lawyer should also consider the management of the case. The judges have been trained that when assessing the budget it should be done in conjunction with the assessments of the management of the case generally. In other words, every step of the case when managed should include a costs consideration.[22] This means that if a judge is intent upon setting a part or whole of the budget at a particular level and will not shift from it, then the claimant lawyer may wish to consider whether they seek to persuade the judge to manage the case in a different way.

One of the challenges in the new world will be that whilst judges are likely to enthusiastically embrace the idea of reducing the amount of costs that can be spent in a case, it will be a challenge as to whether they are prepared to be more flexible and more modern in their management of the case. Are they prepared to take more robust case decisions? Will they permit more split trials where appropriate? Will they consider single or joint experts where previously it might not have done? They have been provided with greater management flexibility in terms of the orders that are given in relation to lay and expert evidence and disclosure. It is no longer assumed that the parties will simply have to produce disclosure at the levels that they did historically. For example the court now has powers to limit the witness evidence, it will permit to be called, both lay and expert.[23]

Consequently, if the claimant lawyer considers that the court is being unrealistic as to the level of costs then they will need a robust argument to justify managing the case in an alternative manner.

The court must have regard to budgets in its management of the case:[24]

> '(1) When making any case management decision, the court will have regard to any available budgets of the parties and will take into account the costs involved in each procedural step.

---

[22] CPR, r 3.17.
[23] CPR, r 32.1.
[24] CPR, r 3.17.

(2) Paragraph (1) applies whether or not the court has made a costs management order.'

If the court makes a costs management order under CPR, r 3.15, the following paragraphs apply:[25]

'2.2 Save in exceptional circumstances –
(1) the recoverable costs of initially completing Precedent H shall not exceed the higher of £1,000 or 1% of the approved budget;
(2) All other recoverable costs of the budgeting and costs management process shall not exceed 2% of the approved budget.

2.3 If the budgets or parts of the budgets are agreed between all parties, the court will record the extent of such agreement. In so far as the budgets are not agreed, the court will review them and, after making any appropriate revisions, record its approval of those budgets. The court's approval will relate only to the total figures for each phase of the proceedings, although in the course of its review the court may have regard to the constituent elements of each total figure. When reviewing budgets, the court will not undertake a detailed assessment in advance, but rather will consider whether the budgeted costs fall within the range of reasonable and proportionate costs.

2.4 As part of the costs management process the court may not approve costs incurred before the date of any budget. The court may, however, record its comments on those costs and should take those costs into account when considering the reasonableness and proportionality of all subsequent costs.

2.5 The court may set a timetable or give other directions for future reviews of budgets.

2.6 Each party shall revise its budget in respect of future costs upwards or downwards, if significant developments in the litigation warrant such revisions.

Such amended budgets shall be submitted to the other parties for agreement. In default of agreement, the amended budgets shall be submitted to the court, together with a note of (a) the changes made and the reasons for those changes and (b) the objections of any other party. The court may approve, vary or disapprove the revisions, having regard to any significant developments which have occurred since the date when the previous budget was approved or agreed.

---

[25] PD 3E.

2.7 After its budget has been approved, each party shall re-file and re-serve the budget in the form approved with re-cast figures, annexed to the order approving it.

2.8 A litigant in person, even though not required to prepare a budget, shall nevertheless be provided with a copy of the budget of any other party.

2.9 If interim applications are made which, reasonably, were not included in a budget, then the costs of such interim applications shall be treated as additional to the approved budgets.'

Assessing costs on the standard basis where a costs management order has been made:[26]

'In any case where a costs management order has been made, when assessing costs on the standard basis, the court will –
(a) have regard to the receiving party's last approved or agreed budget for each phase of the proceedings; and
(b) not depart from such approved or agreed budget unless satisfied that there is good reason to do so.'

The claimant will need to watch their opponent's case carefully. If any work is identified that was not anticipated and not provided for in the budget then the lawyer should make an assessment of the additional costs and revise their budget. The test is whether the work represents a 'significant development'. For example, responding to evidence of surveillance may be such a case in point. This amended budget should be submitted to the defendant for agreement. If it cannot be agreed then an application will need to be made to the court for the budget to be varied. In the absence of agreement the court will decide if the budget is to be varied and to what extent. Bearing in mind QOCS and the limited circumstances in which a defendant will recover costs, some wonder why the defendant will bother with a budget. The first answer is because the rules require it, the second is that whilst Part 36 provides for cost recovery, the defendant will need to have demonstrated what costs are being incurred so that a claimant may be pressured into accepting the Part 36 offer because of the pressure of seeing a good chance that their compensation may be extinguished.

Once a case is concluded the successful party will provide the opponent with a breakdown or bill of costs for possible agreement in the usual detailed assessment procedure (or follow the provisional assessment procedure). If the figures fall within the budget previously approved by

---

[26] CPR, r 3.18.

the court then the expectation is that the bill will be allowed as drafted subject to any specific arguments on the items claimed.

Early on in the pilot in the Commercial Court, His Honour Judge Simon Brown commented in a case that a detailed assessment would be an expensive and futile exercise and then allowed the amount of the budget by way of summary assessment.[27] However, easy though that is to suggest, the problem arises if the case does not go to trial. The budget is set for the whole case and all phases last from the outset of the case through to the trial itself. The result is that if the case settles before trial, then it is highly unlikely that the budget will have been completed for any particular phase by the time of any settlement. There is then likely to be an argument as to what proportion of the costs attributable to that phase should be awarded for the work done. Regretfully, therefore, that is likely to impact upon the ability for much short circuiting of the detailed assessment procedure and of course it does not remove the ability of the paying party to complain that even though work has been undertaken within the budget that it was not reasonably undertaken.

6.3 COSTS CAPPING

It is important to remember that budgeting is not the same as capping. Capping has been in the rules long before April 2013 and was used to limit costs in a way in which budgeting is likely to do in the majority of cases. Nevertheless the rule makers have specifically left cost capping rules in and therefore anticipate that there will be situations in which such an order is appropriate rather than simply relying upon a court approved budget.

> '(1) A costs capping order is an order limiting the amount of future costs (including disbursements) which a party may recover pursuant to an order for costs subsequently made.
>
> (2) In this rule, 'future costs' means costs incurred in respect of work done after the date of the costs capping order but excluding the amount of any additional liability.
>
> (3) This rule does not apply to protective costs orders.
>
> (4) A costs capping order may be in respect of –
> (a) the whole litigation; or
> (b) any issues which are ordered to be tried separately.

---

[27] *Safetynet Security Limited v Coppage* [2012] EWHC, Birmingham Civil Justice Centre, 15 August 2012.

(5) The court may at any stage of proceedings make a costs capping order against all or any of the parties, if –
(a) it is in the interests of justice to do so;
(b) there is a substantial risk that without such an order costs will be disproportionately incurred; and
(c) it is not satisfied that the risk in subparagraph (b) can be adequately controlled by –
  (i) case management directions or orders made under this Part; and
  (ii) detailed assessment of costs.

(6) In considering whether to exercise its discretion under this rule, the court will consider all the circumstances of the case, including –
(a) whether there is a substantial imbalance between the financial position of the parties;
(b) whether the costs of determining the amount of the cap are likely to be proportionate to the overall costs of the litigation;
(c) the stage which the proceedings have reached; and
(d) the costs which have been incurred to date and the future costs.

(7) A costs capping order, once made, will limit the costs recoverable by the party subject to the order unless a party successfully applies to vary the order. No such variation will be made unless –
(a) there has been a material and substantial change of circumstances since the date when the order was made; or
(b) there is some other compelling reason why a variation should be made.'

It is noteworthy that the justification for making such and order contained in CPR, r 3.19(5) are 'the interest of justice', a substantial risk that without such an order costs will be disproportionately incurred or that this risk cannot be adequately controlled by normal case management or ultimately the detailed assessment of costs.

There appears to be a two-stage process that the court will go through. The first is to see whether any of the three reasons set out in the rule arise and then (contrary to proportionality) where Sir Rupert took the view it was not necessary to have guidance, the rule makers have provided for four circumstances to be included:
(i) imbalance between the financial position of the parties;
(ii) whether the costs of working out whether there should be a cap are proportionate;
(iii) the stage of the proceedings; and
(iv) the costs have been incurred at that point.

It is perhaps these first and last elements that provide a clue as to whether the court would make such an order. If a financially dominant party ran up an inordinate amount of costs then it may be that the court would be persuaded that a cap is appropriate. The cap itself produces a level of finality that perhaps a budget does not.

It is of course important to remember CPR, r 3.19(7) that the capping order (as indeed is the case with the budget) is in relation to *recoverable* costs. Consequently, if one had a David v Goliath scenario with a large multinational or richly funded party for example, they could choose to spend whatever they want on the case, it is just that there is a limit on what they can recover from their opponent at the conclusion of the case.

Even when making the application, a budget will be required.[28] However, that being said CPR, r 3.21 provides for an application to vary a cost capping order. It will be interesting to see in what situations cost capping orders are made and whether in fact over time they are replaced completely by budgeting.

6.4 COSTS PROCESS

Practice Direction 3E provides that 'save in exceptional circumstances'[29] the recoverable costs of initially completing Precedent H shall not exceed the higher of £1,000 or 1% of the approved budget and all other recoverable costs of the budget in the costs management process shall not exceed 2% of the approved budget.[30] Therefore the work undertaken in preparing a costs budget must be proportionate to the potential savings. The direction, however, does make clear that this a process primarily about agreement and that the court has the power to review or approve budgets if there is a lack of agreement to some or all of the budget between the parties.[31] The court has the power to consider costs incurred before the date of the budget but are not in a position to approve it, which must be done at detailed or summary assessment. They can record their comments (presumably favourable as well as non-favourable; although it is unlikely that the former is going to merit comment) and those comments are to be taken into account on a subsequent assessment.[32]

---

[28] CPR, r 3.20(2)(b).
[29] CPR, r 2.2.
[30] PD 3E, para 2.2.
[31] PD 3E, para 2.3.
[32] CPR, r 2.4.

The judiciary has been issued with pre-CMC checklists to assist them in the costs and case management. In *Willis v MRJ Rundell & Associates Ltd*,[33] Coulson J offered several comments in a case's budget that may give clues to the future management of cases and the application of the budget. He declined to approve the parties' costs budgets in a professional negligence claim where he considered both parties' costs and budgets were disproportionate and unreasonable. The professional negligence claim related to building works and the total claim was for £1.1m which included the cost of rectifying defects, and overpayments. Each side produced a costs budget at a case management conference in December 2012. W's costs budget was £821,000 and R's costs budget was £616,000. Following mediation, the parties applied for an adjournment of the trial which had been due to start in October 2013. The judge ordered a costs management hearing due to his concerns as to the high figures stated. Both costs budgets had since increased to £897,369 and £703,130. Neither party had specific criticisms about the budgets save they were too high.

The total amount of the costs in the two costs budgets was £1.6m for a claim worth £1.1m. It would cost more to fight the claim than the claimant would ever recover. The judge considered on that basis alone, the costs budgets were disproportionate and unreasonable. It is unclear whether he suggests that the court should look at the combined budgets against the sums claimed in determining proportionality. It is difficult to see that as being workable.

Rightly the judge was critical of the failure to make clear which costs had been incurred and which were estimated. The parties had included large and unspecified contingencies and Coulson J ruled it was not appropriate to include a large lump sum for contingent costs and settlement costs without a breakdown by reference to each component part. It needed to be made very clear what each amount was for and how it had been calculated.[34]

Coulson J said that some were of the view that the absence of an approved costs budget meant that that party would recover no costs at all, but such a draconian approach was not in accordance with the letter and spirit of the new costs rules or PD 51G.[35]

The judge before the CMC may order the parties to prepare a comparison of the parties spends phase by phase and to include incurred and estimated costs.

---

[33] [2013] EWHC 2923 (TCC).
[34] Paras 18–23.
[35] Para 26.

Even if not ordered, this may be a useful tool. Page 1 gives an overview to the judge and the parties. They can see the spikes in their budget and in opponent's budget. This will be the focus of the case management.

How will the court approach the costs management exercise? Three models have emerged:
- directions and then budget;
- budget and then directions; and
- budget then directions then directions budget (a hybrid).

The latter approach is likely to be adopted by the court. Initial attempts at case management were made by the court in *Morrison v Buckinghamshire County Council & Another*[36] where it made directions in the case and then costed the directions.

The pure Jacksonian model is to decide the proportionate spend and then to give directions consistent with that budget. On this basis the court will briefly address the five factors underpinning proportionality and then fit the directions to the budget.

But a hybrid model seems to be the more practical approach. At the outset that court will address the issues of proportionality and decide a provisional budget figure. The parties should then construct directions that will meet this budget. At the end the court will review the cost of the directions given and review whether the figure is proportionate. It may well be that the court having heard submissions on the directions and having a better view of the issues will relax the budget slightly using the final figure as a cross-check.

The court approves phases, not the whole budget and not hourly rates for example – PD 3E, para 2.3:

> '2.3 If the budgets or parts of the budgets are agreed between all parties, the court will record the extent of such agreement. In so far as the budgets are not agreed, the court will review them and, after making any appropriate revisions, record its approval of those budgets. The court's approval will relate only to the total figures for each phase of the proceedings, although in the course of its review the court may have regard to the constituent elements of each total figure. When reviewing budgets, the court will not undertake a detailed assessment in advance, but rather will consider whether the budgeted costs fall within the range of reasonable and proportionate costs.'

---

[36] SCCO 20 January 2011, HQ09D05424.

To achieve proportionality, the court has extensive powers of case management:

- disclosure (CPR Part 31);
- witness statements (CPR Part 32); and
- experts (CPR Part 35).

Ramsay J in his introductory speech in May 2012 when explaining the process stated that the court's purpose was not to undertake a detailed assessment in advance but rather to 'consider whether the budgeted costs fall within the range of reasonable and proportionate costs'.

It is likely that judges will quickly become aware of the 'going rate' for certain types of case and will be prepared to agree budgets which are within striking distance of those rates. Where the case is particularly large or complex the budget might perhaps only relate to the initial phases of the case rather than seeking to budget for all eventualities. Whilst this might detract from the pure theory of costs management it is the sensible approach.

The indemnity principle applies. The budget is not a bill. But note the statement of truth.

At any stage the court may make a costs management order (CPR, r 3.15):

> '3.15.—(1) In addition to exercising its other powers, the court may manage the costs to be incurred by any party in any proceedings.
>
> (2) The court may at any time make a 'costs management order'. By such order the court will—
> (a) record the extent to which the budgets are agreed between the parties; or
> (b) in respect of budgets or parts of budgets which are not agreed, record the court's approval after making appropriate revisions.
>
> (3) If a costs management order has been made, the court will thereafter control the parties' budgets in respect of recoverable costs.'

The training of the judiciary suggested that it is very difficult to think of an example when the court will not costs manage – 'may' is getting close to 'must'. The reason for this is that the making of an order will control the budget. Judges are being taught that there is no escape unless there is good reason. However, much may depend upon the resources of individual courts and the appetite for budgeting of individual judges.

The recoverable cost of the budgeting and cost management process (after preparation of the initial budget) will be limited to 2% of the approved budget.

6.5 VARIATIONS

Budget can be revised 'upwards or downwards'[37] but as commented above, it is only if 'significant developments' warrant it. Simply underestimating the amounts involved will not be sufficient.

The practice direction provides that the application for costs capping must be made 'as soon as possible'.[38]

The court has retained something of the pre-April provisions in relation to the warning flag being applied where the receiving party on detailed assessment has costs that are 20% or more of those that have been previously filed in their budget and are required to provide a statement of reasons. The burden is then shifted onto the paying party to demonstrate that they 'reasonably relied' on the budget or wish to rely on the budget to dispute the *reasonableness* or *proportionality* and must set out a statement identifying the basis of these submissions.[39] If the court accepts the submission that the paying party had relied on it, then the court can limit what it awards to the budget.

The various budgeting pilots have begun to generate judicial guidance which is likely to follow through into the current regime. *Henry v News Group Newspapers Limited*,[40] was a decision of the Court of Appeal relating to such a budget made under the defamation pilot scheme and arrived just as the new rules were coming into force. The claimant was successful, but her claim for costs on assessment was much greater than had been set out in the claimant's budget. The Senior Costs Judge on assessment had disallowed much of these costs but to many people's surprise the Court of Appeal allowed the claimant's appeal from this decision and remitted the case back for assessment. The Court of Appeal held:

> '18. I do not think that it would be wise to attempt an exhaustive definition of the circumstances in which there may be good reason for departing from the approved budget. The words themselves are very broad and experience teaches that any attempt by an appellate court to provide assistance in a matter of this kind risks creating a set of rigid rules where

---

[37] PD 3E, para 2.6.
[38] PD 3F, para 1.2.
[39] CPR, r 3.3.
[40] [2013] EWCA Civ 19.

flexibility was intended. Circumstances are infinitely variable and it is vital that judges exercise their own judgment in each case. Having said that, the starting point must be that the approved budget is intended to provide the financial limits within which the proceedings are to be conducted and that the court will not allow costs in excess of the budget unless something unusual has occurred. Whether there is good reason to depart from the approved budget in any given case, therefore, is likely to depend on, among other things, how the proceedings have been managed, whether they have developed in a way that was not foreseen when the relevant case management orders were made, whether the costs incurred are proportionate to what is in issue and whether the parties have been on an equal footing.

19. In the present case the judge found himself in a difficult position. He thought that there was a strong argument that the costs incurred by the appellant were both reasonable and proportionate, but he was faced with the fact that the appellant had largely failed to comply with paragraph 5.5 of the practice direction, which obliges solicitors to communicate with each other regularly to ensure that the budgets are not being exceeded. Indeed, as he recorded it, the main plank of the respondent's argument was that the court cannot properly find that there is good reason to depart from the approved budget unless the parties have complied with the practice direction. The judge concluded that the failure of the appellant's solicitors to tell the respondent's solicitors that they were exceeding their budget prevented the parties from being on an equal footing and that because they had largely ignored the provisions of the practice direction there was no good reason for departing from the approved budget.

20. In my view the judge misunderstood the reference in paragraph 1.3 to the parties' being on an equal footing and took too narrow a view of what may amount to good reason under paragraph 5.6(2)(b). The object of the practice direction, as described in paragraph 1.3, is twofold: (i) to ensure that the costs incurred in connection with the proceedings are proportionate to what is at stake and (ii) to ensure that one party is unable to exploit superior financial resources by conducting the litigation in a way that puts the other at a significant disadvantage. The intention is that both these objects are to be achieved by management of the proceedings in a way that controls the costs being incurred. When paragraph 1.3 speaks of the parties' being on an equal footing it is concerned with the unfair exploitation of superior resources rather than with the provision of information about how expenditure is progressing. Paragraph 5.5 assumes that the parties will exchange information about expenditure at regular intervals, but a failure to do so does not of itself put the parties on an unequal footing in the sense in which that expression is used in paragraph 1.3. In this case neither party was financially embarrassed and in my view, whatever else may be said about the way in which the proceedings were conducted, there was no inequality of arms.'

However, the Court of Appeal points out that there are differences between the pilot scheme and the procedure set out in section II of CPR Part 3. Whilst it is welcome clarification that the budget regime will be enforced with flexibility the Court said:

> 'Those rules, which will become effective from 1st April 2013, differ in some important respects from the practice direction with which this appeal is concerned. In particular, they impose greater responsibility on the court for the management of the costs of proceedings and greater responsibility on the parties for keeping budgets under review as the proceedings progress. Read as a whole they lay greater emphasis on the importance of the approved or agreed budget as providing a prima facie limit on the amount of recoverable costs. In those circumstances, although the court will still have the power to depart from the approved or agreed budget if it is satisfied that there is good reason to do so, and may for that purpose take into consideration all the circumstances of the case, I should expect it to place particular emphasis on the function of the budget as imposing a limit on recoverable costs. The primary function of the budget is to ensure that the costs incurred are not only reasonable but proportionate to what is at stake in the proceedings. If, as is the intention of the rule, budgets are approved by the court and revised at regular intervals, the receiving party is unlikely to persuade the court that costs incurred in excess of the budget are reasonable and proportionate to what is at stake.'

In *Elvanite Full Circle Ltd v AMEC Earth and Environmental (UK) Ltd*,[41] Coulson J considered a case in the Mercantile Courts and Technology and Construction Courts – Pilot Scheme ('PD 51G'). In particular, Coulson J considered: (i) the impact of an order for costs on the indemnity basis; (ii) what a party needs to do to seek approval of a revised costs budget; (iii) when a party should make an application for such approval; and (iv) what test the court applies on such an application. The original approved budget was £264,708. However, around one month before trial the receiving party defendant served a revised budget of £531,946.18 and the paying party served a revised one of £372,179.53. No applications were made by either party to revise or vary the court approved budget. In the end the receiving party's bill was actually £497,593. The expert costs were £170,000 more than the £30,000 budget. The paying party's ATE indemnity limit was £250,000. The receiving party sought an order for indemnity costs which was refused. Nevertheless the court said that that even had such an order been made the budget would still be the starting point. A little odd as the rule should disapply proportionality and in many cases should steer away from the budget which may well be made with proportionality in mind.

---
[41] [2013] EWHC 1643.

The court considered whether simply serving the revised budget was enough. In other words the opponent was not kept in the dark as in *Henry*. The court said no, you have to apply to the court, 'immediately it becomes apparent that the original budget costs have been exceeded by a more than a minimal amount'.

The receiving party's next submission was to apply to vary post-judgment. The court said an application to amend an approved costs budget after judgment is a contradiction in terms.

As a matter of fact the court asked itself was there a 'good reason to depart'? – No: 'Everything went pretty much as it might have been expected to go.'

Strangely the judge said prejudice was not essential but if it was considered the paying party argued that it had suffered prejudice because its ATE cover of £250,000 was inadequate and there was some force to this.

6.6 COURT'S DISCRETION AS TO COSTS

In deciding what order to make about costs the court is required to have regard to all the circumstances including: the conduct of all the parties; whether a party's case has been successful in part, even if not wholly successful; and whether or not there has been an offer of settlement.[42] The court has complete discretion as to what order for costs to make but those orders may include an order that a party must pay:

(i) a proportion of another party's costs;

(ii) a stated amount in respect of another party's costs;

(iii) costs from or until a certain date;

(iv) costs incurred before proceedings have begun;

(v) costs relating to particular steps in the proceedings;

(vi) costs relating only to a distinct part of the proceedings; and

(vii) interest on costs from or until a certain date.[43]

Where the court orders a party to pay costs subject to detailed assessment it will order that party to pay a reasonable sum on account unless there is good reason not to do so.[44] This is a very useful addition

---

[42] CPR, r 44.2(4).
[43] CPR, r 44.2(6).
[44] CPR, r 44.2(8).

to the rules since April 2013. Previously it was often difficult to secure cost interim payments without court hearings.

PD 44, para 4.2 lists the more common costs orders which the court may make in proceedings before trial and explains their effect.

The court may order costs between the parties to be assessed on either the standard or the indemnity basis. The court will not allow costs which have been unreasonably incurred.

On the standard basis, the court will only allow costs which are proportionate to the matters in issue and will resolve any doubt which it may have as to whether costs were reasonably incurred or reasonable and proportionate in amount in favour of the paying party.[45]

Where the court assesses costs on the indemnity basis it will resolve any doubt which it may have as to whether costs were reasonably incurred or were reasonable in amount in favour of the receiving party.[46] Such an award disapplies the usual proportionality rules. Thus it becomes a substantial prize to a claimant's lawyer when, for example, they match or beat their own Part 36 offer.

In respect of costs payable to a solicitor by his client, the basis of assessment is the indemnity basis to which certain presumptions and limitations apply or which are unreasonable in amount.

6.7 SUMMARY ASSESSMENT

There are two ways in which courts will assess costs: detailed assessment and summary assessment. The former will inevitably be undertaken by a judge while detailed assessment may be undertaken by a costs officer.[47]

Guidance on this can be found in PD 44. There is an overriding requirement on the court to consider making a summary assessment of costs on each occasion that it makes an order about costs which does not involve fixed costs.[48] As with the situation before 1 April 2013, the general rule is that the court should make a summary assessment of costs at the conclusion of the trial of a case in the fast track and at the conclusion of any other hearing which has not lasted more than one day.[49]

---

[45] CPR, r 44.3(2).
[46] CPR, r 44.3(3).
[47] CPR, r 44.6.
[48] PD 44, para 9.1.
[49] PD 44, para 9.2.

CHAPTER 7

PART 36 AND OFFERS TO SETTLE

7.1 HISTORY

Prior to the introduction of the Civil Procedure Rules[1] (CPR) in 1999 it had been possible for a defendant to make an offer to settle a claim by paying money into court. If the payment was more than awarded at judgment the costs were reversed from the time of the payment in.

Claimants had always (like defendants) had the ability to make a without prejudice offer but this could not be referred to on costs so it was much less powerful than a payment into court. As claimants had no opportunity to make a formal offer that affected costs, various alternatives were developed. The main one of these was the Calderbank offer. This was a letter making an offer but stated to be without prejudice save as to costs. In other words it could not be referred to during the action but could be raised when costs were being considered. However, this still suffered from the disadvantage that the question of costs was entirely at the discretion of the court.

Lord Woolf when creating the CPR believed that the then existing system was useful but that the new system he was creating needed to include a formal opportunity for a claimant to attempt a settlement which would affect costs. As a result the payment in by the defendant was kept in the new rules and a form of claimant offer was added, both of these forming Part 36 of the CPR.

This situation remained until Part 36 was revised in 2007 when the payment into court was removed and either party could make an offer simply in writing. However, the offers continued to have sanctions in costs against a party that failed to accept a good offer. The pre-2007 regime applies to offers made before April 2007 but as there will be so few offers still in existence they will not be dealt with here.

---

[1] Civil Procedure Rules 1998, SI 1998/3132.

The sanction against a claimant who failed to accept a good offer from the defendant was to have to pay the defendant's costs from the time of the offer rather than get their own costs from the defendant.

The sanction against a defendant who failed to accept a good offer from the claimant was that the costs would be assessed on an indemnity basis (as opposed to a standard basis) and costs at up to 10% above base rate would be awarded on the damages and the costs.

In both cases the sanctions were to apply unless the court decided that it was unjust to do so.

Part 36 does not apply to claims allocated to the small claims track. It is, of course, possible to make without prejudice offers in such cases but in the absence of costs shifting between the parties any such offer is of limited value.

The system created in 2007 has continued, with minor amendments, until 2013 when the Jackson reforms made significant changes in a number of respects.

7.2 JACKSON REFORMS

Just as Lord Woolf felt that the pre-CPR rules were unfair to claimants, Jackson LJ felt that the CPR was still not properly balanced between the parties. As a result he proposed an increase in the sanctions against a defendant who failed to accept a good claimant offer. The sanction to be applied was an increase in the damages as well as the previous sanctions.

The effect of Part 36 on costs also had to be modified because of the effect of qualified one-way costs shifting (QOCS) (see Chapter 4). If the claimant would not in normal circumstances have to pay the defendant's costs if unsuccessful, what was the relationship between costs assessment and Part 36? In particular what should happen to the defendant's costs if the claimant was successful but failed to improve on a defendant's Part 36 offer? If the defendant's Part 36 offer has no effect on costs then fewer offers will be made and more claims will go to trial. This is not what either Lord Woolf or Jackson LJ wanted to achieve. The answer to this puzzle is that the claimant will still have to pay the defendant's costs from the time of the offer. However, to preserve the value of QOCS to the claimant the costs recovery for the defendant is limited to the amount of any damages awarded. In other words the claimant can lose their damages but cannot be required to lose anything that they had at the start of the action.

7.3 HOW TO DEAL WITH AN OFFER

CPR Part 36 is widely regarded as the greatest success of the Woolf reforms. However, that has not stopped there being significant amounts of satellite litigation on this Part so it is important to ensure that you comply with the rules.

If an offer is received, you must act promptly to notify the client. Explain to the client, both at interview and by letter, the consequences if the offer is rejected and they fail to beat it at trial. Notify the client's insurers, if any. Do not simply present the client with the facts and wait for them to make a decision – you must give them your advice as well.

If the client agrees to the offer, do not formally accept it until you have the client's consent in writing. It is risky to rely on verbal instructions on such an important matter. If the client changes his or her mind shortly after giving the verbal instructions it could result in a complaint from them if you have already accepted the offer.

Therefore send the client a letter confirming any telephone call or meeting, and ask them to sign a copy and return it. If time is short, it is always worth asking for an extension from the other party. If it's a genuine attempt to settle, then they are likely to agree. Even if they do not agree the sanction for late acceptance will be minimal if it is a very short delay.

If the matter is at a stage where you have insufficient information to form a complete view make sure that the defendant is fully aware of the situation and ask them to confirm an extension of the time for acceptance. If they refuse, you need to assemble the information that will allow you to argue against sanctions in due course.

Do you know why the client wants to accept when in your view they could get more? It may be that they are taking a pragmatic view and want to close the matter, but they could be suffering psychological trauma or stress connected with the injury. Beware the client who agrees settlement, and then claims that they were not capable of giving consent!

Remember that you can make offers at any time including pre-action but they need to be pitched carefully and to comply with Part 36 to get benefit of rules (but note the general discretion on costs in CPR Part 44 (see Chapter 9).

7.4 THE LAW

The rules for CPR Part 36 are divided into two sections. CPR, rr 36.1 to 36.15 cover all claims except those under the portals. CPR, rr 36.16 and 36.22 cover claims under the portals.

The rules use the terms 'offeree' and offeror' for the recipient and maker of an offer. These terms can be confusing and for greater clarity I shall use the terms 'recipient' and 'maker'.

Similarly the rules refer to the initial period given for acceptance of at least 21 days as the 'relevant period'. I will refer to this as the period for acceptance.

Where an application is required at any stage that application is to be made in accordance with CPR Part 23.

7.5 NON-PORTAL OFFERS

7.5.1 Formalities

CPR, r 36.1 states that to be effective, a Part 36 offer must comply with the specific requirements of the rules. These requirements are set out in CPR, r 36.2.

That rule states that a Part 36 offer must be in writing and must specifically state on the face of it that it is intended to have the consequences of the Part 36.

The defendant must give the claimant a period of not less than 21 days in which to accept the offer. If they do accept the offer within this period then the defendant will be liable for the claimant's costs.

The Part 36 offer must also state whether it is in respect of the whole claim or to part of it or a single issue. If it is in relation to only a part of the claim or a single issue, the offer must sufficiently identify which part or issue it relates to. The Part 36 offer must also state whether it takes into account any counterclaim in the matter.

However, the rule makes clear that offers can be made in any form but they will not attract the sanctions in Part 36.

A Part 36 offer can be made solely for an issue or on liability.

An example of the effect of a failure to comply with the rules is shown by the case of *Thewlis v Groupama*.[2] In that case the offer contained the wording that it was open for 21 days but 'thereafter it can only be accepted if we agree the liability for costs or the Court gives permission'. This is wording that was used in Part 36 before the amendment to the CPR in April 2007. The court decided that this requirement for agreement or the court's permission meant that the offer could not be freely accept after 21 days. Also the offer failed to comply with r 36.2(2)(b) in that it did not say on its face that it was intended to have the consequences of Part 36. Therefore for both those reasons it did not comply with the form of Part 36 and was not a valid Part 36 offer. Thus the sanctions in that Part do not apply and any costs consequences must be dealt with under the court's general discretion in CPR Part 44 (see Chapter 9).

In the case of *F & C Alternative Investments (Holdings) Ltd v Barthelemy*[3] the court found that Part 36 was highly prescriptive and could not be applied by analogy. Thus the general discretion could not be used in the normal course of events to give the same sanctions as would apply to a Part 36 offer.

But if the alleged failure to comply with the Part 36 requirements is ambiguous the courts have taken a pragmatic approach to the rule. Thus in *C v D*,[4] Stanley Burnton LJ said:

> 'Any ambiguity in an offer purporting to be a Part 36 offer should be construed so far as reasonably possible as complying with Part 36.'

Form N242A sets out the requirements for a Part 36 offer and can be used to make an offer which is compliant with the rules but is not mandatory.

7.5.2 Timing and clarification of an offer

CPR, r 36.7 deals with the timing of an offer which is made when the recipient actually receives the offer. Similarly when an offer is amended the new offer is made when the recipient receives the amended terms.

Where the terms of an offer are not clear to the recipient they can seek clarification under CPR, r 36.8. Any request for clarification must be made within 7 days of the receipt of it. No format for the request is

---

[2] [2012] EWHC 3 (TCC).
[3] [2012] EWCA Civ 843.
[4] [2011] EWCA Civ 646.

given and it can be by a simple letter so long as it is clear that the letter is a request under this rule and it sufficiently specifies the clarification required.

The maker of the offer must provide the clarification within 7 days of receipt of the request. If this is not done the recipient of the offer can make an application to the court for the clarification to be ordered. When making such an order the court will specify the date by which the clarification must be given. The only exception to this is that an application cannot be made once the trial has started.

7.5.3 Acceptance of an offer

Further provisions applicable to all Part 36 offers are set out in CPR, r 36.3. This rule gives definitions; confirms that an offer cannot be accepted once the trial starts; and that an offer made in the claim does not have effect in any appeal. However, a Part 36 offer can be renewed by being re-made in any appeal proceedings.

An offer must be accepted in writing (CPR, r 36.9). Again no format is specified for the acceptance and it will be valid so long as it is clear what offer is being accepted. The notice of acceptance must be served on the offer maker and filed with the court (PD 36 para 3.1). Once an offer is made it remains available for acceptance at any time until it is withdrawn in writing (see above CPR, r 36.3). This was confirmed in *Gibbon v Manchester City Council: LG Blower Specialist Bricklayer Ltd v Reeves*[5] in which the court confirmed that an offer once made remains available for acceptance unless it is withdrawn in writing. This was confirmed even in the position where the offer has been specifically rejected by the recipient or a further offer has been made by the maker of the initial offer. The *Gibbon* case also confirmed that a party may have several offers validly made at one time. The result of this is that a party should keep reviewing any offer that they have made as changing circumstances may mean that they would no longer want it to be accepted. Similarly any offers made by the other side should be regularly reviewed as they may now look acceptable.

7.5.4 When permission is needed to accept an offer

However, there are four circumstances where the normal rule that permission is not needed to accept an offer does not apply.

---

[5] [2010] EWCA Civ 726.

The first is where there are multiple defendants and the offer being accepted is not from all of them (see CPR, r 36.12).

The second is where there are deductible benefits and the amount of those benefits has changed since the offer was made (see CPR, r 36.15). In this case the application for permission must state:

(a) the net amount offered in the Part 36 offer;
(b) the deductible amounts that had accrued at the date the offer was made;
(c) the deductible amounts that have subsequently accrued; and
(d) be accompanied by a copy of the current certificate of deductible benefits.

The third is where an apportionment is needed under the Fatal Accidents Act 1976 or the Law Reform (Miscellaneous Provisions) Act 1934 (see CPR, r 41.3A).

The final circumstance is when the trial has started.

In all of the above situations the party wishing to accept must apply to the court for permission to accept. If the court makes an order in those terms it will also deal with costs unless the parties have agreed costs. If the court deals with costs it may implement the sanctions specified in Part 36.

Note, however, that an offer can only be accepted at the end of the trial but before judgment is given if all parties agree. The court cannot give permission in that situation.

The basis for acceptance of an offer made by some but not all of several defendants is set out in CPR, r 36.12. The claimant needs the permission of the court to accept such an offer except in limited circumstances.

The first exception is that the claimant can accept without permission if they discontinue against the remaining defendants and those defendants give written consent to the acceptance of the offer.

The claimant can also accept without permission if they allege that the defendants have several liability and he or she can continue against the remaining defendants if entitled.

In every other circumstance the claimant will need to apply to the court for permission to accept such an offer.

The Part 36 offer is regarded as a 'without prejudice' offer as a result of CPR, r 36.13. As a result the offer cannot be made known to the trial judge until judgment has been given.

Again there are exceptions in this case where the action has been stayed by acceptance or the parties have agreed in writing that this provision does not apply.

There is a further exception that should not be relevant to personal injury cases, namely that of a defence of 'tender before claim'. This is a defence that, before the claimant started proceedings, the defendant unconditionally offered to the claimant the amount due or, if no specified amount is claimed, an amount sufficient to satisfy the claim.

7.5.5 Amount as single sum, periodic payment, etc

An offer from a defendant to settle the claim must be in terms of a single payment (CPR, r 36.4) for most types of claim but for personal injury claims it can include an offer of periodical payments (CPR, r 36.5) or provisional damages (CPR, r 36.6). The rules create further requirements when there are future losses. In these circumstances the offer may include a sum for future losses as a lump sum; periodical payments or a combination of the two. This may be added to a lump sum offer in respect of other damages (general damages and past losses). The offer may be for the whole claim or part of it.

The offer must state the value of the offer as a single lump sum but then set out how that amount is split between future losses and other damages.

Then the amount relating to periodical payments (if any) must be specified giving the duration and amount of the periodical payments; the amount of any capital payments and the provisions for indexing both amounts. The periodical payments must also be funded by a secure method.

If the offer is made by the defendant it must also comply with CPR, r 36.4 (see above).

A split offer in this form must be accepted in total and a recipient cannot accept part and reject the other part.

If an offer including periodical payments is accepted then the claimant must apply to the court within 7 days for a periodical payments order.

Similarly CPR, r 36.6 sets out the special provisions where provisional damages are at issue. In such cases the Part 36 offer must state whether it includes an offer of provisional damages. If it does the offer must state that the offer is made on the basis that the claimant will not suffer a specified disease or deterioration.

It must also specify that provisional damages will only be available if the claimant makes a further claim in respect of the specified disease or deterioration within a specified period and what that period is.

If an offer including provisional damages is accepted then the claimant must apply to the court within 7 days for an order awarding provisional damages on the basis of the offer.

7.5.6 Interest on amount offered

CPR, r 36.3 also makes provision for interest in respect of the offer. The amount offer includes all interest until the end of the period (at least 21 days) given for acceptance of the offer. If the offer is made within 21 days of the trial starting then the interest included is up to the end of 21 days from the date of the offer.

7.5.7 Deductible benefits

Part 36 offers have to take account of deductible benefits and this is covered in CPR, r 36.15. If an offer is made by a defendant they have to state whether it takes into account any deductible benefits.

If it does take account of deductible benefits the defendant must apply for a certificate of deductible benefits before making the offer. If the certificate is received before the offer is made then the defendant must state the gross amount of the offer; the names and amounts of benefits to be deducted and the net amount offered.

If the certificate is not available at the time of the offer the gross sum must be stated and the deductions and net amount notified to the claimant within 7 days of receipt of the certificate.

For the purpose of testing whether the claimant has received more than a defendant's offer (see above CPR, r 36.14) is whether the net amount is greater than the damages awarded less deductible benefits identified by the court.

Where permission is required to accept a Part 36 offer because further benefits are deductible (see above CPR, r 36.9) the court may reduce the amount that can be accepted by deductible benefits that have been paid to the claimant since the date of the offer.

All these rules and sanctions make Part 36 offers very powerful incentives to settle a claim. Offers made as soon as the claim can be properly valued will place significant pressure on the other party. The Court of Appeal has recently confirmed that 'the legislative purpose of Part 36 is to motivate parties to make, and to accept, appropriate offers of settlement' (*Walsh v Singh*).[6]

7.5.8 Costs consequences of accepting an offer within the period for acceptance

CPR, r 36.10 specifies the position on costs when an offer is accepted. Where the offer is for the settlement of the entire claim and it is accepted within the period given for acceptance (at least 21 days) the claimant is entitled to their costs up until the date the acceptance is received by the offer maker. The costs will be assessed on the standard basis if not agreed between the parties.

If the offer is only in respect of part of the claim and on acceptance with the period the claimant abandons the remainder of the claim then he or she is also entitled to the costs of the claim on the standard basis or as agreed.

The rules refer to the costs of the proceedings being payable which raises the question of what the position is when the offer is made and accepted pre-proceedings. This was considered in the case of *Thompson v Bruce*.[7] Rule 36.3(2)(a) states that an offer 'may be made at any time, including before the commencement of proceedings'. Rule 36.10(1) states that 'where a Part 36 offer is accepted within the relevant period the claimant will be entitled to the costs of the proceedings up to the date on which notice of acceptance was served on the offeror'. The problem is that where the matter is settled by way of an offer and acceptance before proceedings are issued there are no 'costs of the proceedings' to be recovered. The court took a pragmatic view and decided that it must have been the intention of the creators of the rule that the costs consequences applied in all cases and therefore that the wording in Part 36 covered this situation.

---

[6] [2011] EWCA Civ 87.
[7] *Thompson & Thompson (By Their Father & Litigation Friend Christopher Thompson & Maureen Williams (Administrators of the Estate of Tracy Ann Williams, Deceased)) v Bruce* [2011] EWHC 2228 QB.

A similar conclusion was reached by the Court of Appeal in the case of *Solomon v Cromwell*.[8]

7.5.9 Late acceptance of an offer outside the period for acceptance

Different provisions apply where either the offer was made less than 21 days before the trial or the acceptance was given outside the period for acceptance (of at least 21 days). In those cases the court will make an order for costs. The presumption in the rules is that the claimant will get their costs up to the end of the period for acceptance regardless of who made the offer. For the period after the period of acceptance then the recipient will normally have to pay the costs of the maker of the offer. Thus if the claimant made the offer they get all of their costs. If the defendant made the offer then the claimant has to pay the defendant's costs from the end of the period for acceptance until the date of the actual acceptance.

Note that where the defendant raised a counterclaim the costs of the claimant dealing with that are part of the claimant's costs recoverable from the defendant.

It must also be noted that the split payment of costs set out above is a presumption and that the court can rule otherwise. Three cases over the last couple of years have considered the question of what should happen in relation to costs when a claimant accepts a defendant's Part 36 offer after the 21-day period. The issue in all the recent cases is when the court should rule otherwise and what the court can do.

The first case is *Kunaka v Barclays Bank plc*.[9] As the claimant accepted the Part 36 offer after expiry of the 21-day period, the default position was as under CPR, r 36.10. But the claimant was a litigant in person and the defendant had sent an email reminding the claimant that the offer was open but did not state the consequence of a late acceptance. The court considered what was fair in this situation and as it was an exceptional case the court ordered the defendant to pay all of the claimant's costs. However, the fact that the claimant was a litigant in person and the defendant had not been entirely honest with them were crucial to this decision.

The second case is *Lumb v Hampsey*[10] in which the court considered what factors it should take into account when making this decision. Neither the Rules nor the Practice Direction provide any guidance on

---

[8] *Solomon v Cromwell Group and Oliver v Doughty* [2011] EWCA Civ 1584.
[9] [2010] EWCA Civ 1035.
[10] [2011] EWHC 2808 (QB).

how the court should exercise its discretion under CPR, r 36.10 regarding the payment of costs following a late acceptance of a Part 36 offer. The court decided that the test in deciding the issue under CPR, r 36.10 is similar to that in CPR, r 36.14 (whether to apply sanctions following failure to beat an offer). The test is whether the usual costs order would be unjust in the particular circumstances of the case. Such a finding would be the exception rather than the rule.

CPR, r 36.14 gives some guidance as to matters that the court should take into account in considering whether the usual order as to costs would be unjust. These include:

(a) the terms of any Part 36 offer;

(b) the stage in the proceedings when any Part 36 offer was made, including in particular how long before the trial started the offer was made;

(c) the information available to the parties at the time when the Part 36 offer was made; and

(d) the conduct of the parties with regard to the giving or refusing to give information for the purposes of enabling the offer to be made or evaluated.

These are likely to be relevant factors under CPR, r 36.10 also. Considering the particular case CPR, r 36.14 requires the court to take into account that:

(a) the offer was made at an appropriate stage of the proceedings;

(b) proceedings had been served;

(c) medical and care evidence had been exchanged; and

(d) the offer was made well in advance of the trial.

The court concluded that in this case the parties had sufficient evidence to value the claim and this was not a case where criticisms can be made of the defendant's conduct. For all these reasons the usual order was made under CPR, r 36.10.

The third case is *SG v Hewitt*[11] in which the claimant was child who was involved in a road traffic accident in March 2003 in which he suffered a serious brain injury. The medical experts stated that they could not predict the outcome of the claimant's injuries until he had reached adolescence. Following service of the initial medical reports the defendant made an offer to settle the claim for £500,000. The offer was

---

[11] [2012] EWCA Civ 1053.

accepted 2 years later and the defendant then sought the normal Part 36 costs rule. At first instance the Court awarded the defendant its costs but the claimant appealed.

The claimant stated that it was only nearly 2 years after the offer was made that his clinical psychologists stated that it was possible to confirm with increased confidence what the claimant's future prognosis may be. Following that the claimant's neurosurgeon agreed that the acceptance of the offer would be to the claimant's advantage. It was at this point that the offer was accepted.

When the offer was made the claimant's solicitors had obtained counsel's advice. He said that given the uncertainties he could not advise a court to approve a settlement at that stage. He could not put a definitive value on the claim. Following the counsel's advice, the claimant's solicitors told the defendant's solicitors of the position. The defendant did not withdraw the offer and knew that the claimant was in fact getting more reports to assist with whether or not the offer would be acceptable.

Following the late acceptance of the offer, the defendant said that there were good reasons not to depart from the normal Part 36 rules. The claimant could have accepted the offer which had a built-in substantial contingency for if the claimant's future prognosis was much poorer than anticipated. The defendant stated that the claimant did in fact receive a windfall when the settlement was reached and he could have requested an extension of time to accept the offer or alternatively agreed a provisional damages settlement.

Having considered Part 36, the court held that the perceived windfall was not relevant to the issue of costs. The defendant could have withdrawn the offer and it was likely that had the claimant requested an extension of time to accept the offer, the defendant would have refused because they would not have been able to withdraw the offer at a later stage.

The court held that the claimant could not have accepted the offer at the time that it was made because counsel could not advise the court to approve the settlement.

The court therefore found that the claimant had acted reasonably and that all the costs incurred after the offer was made were in respect of whether or not it would be reasonable to accept the offer so that the court could approve a settlement.

The court therefore found that it was unjust to follow the normal costs rule and the appeal was allowed and the claimant received their full costs.

However, this case was decided on its very specific facts and should not be regarded as a general exception to the costs presumption. However, in the type of case in question (eg clinical negligence or accident causing very serious injuries to a very young child) it is a significant decision.

Although the rule provides that the costs on acceptance within the period for acceptance will be on the standard basis there is no similar provision where the acceptance is outside that period. This was considered by the court in the case of *Fitzpatrick Contractors Ltd v Tyco Fire & Integrated Solutions (UK) Ltd*.[12] The claimant had made a Part 36 offer which the accepted outside the period for acceptance. The claimant argued that had there been a trial and damages were recovered in the same amount as the Part 36 offer it would have been entitled to indemnity costs, unless the court concluded that it was unjust to make such an order, because of the express words of CPR, r 36.14. The defendant argued that there was no difference between a claimant who had recovered a sum equivalent to his offer after trial and a claimant who had recovered a sum equivalent to his offer before trial. The claimant submitted that by analogy with CPR, r 36.14 there was a presumption that a claimant was entitled to indemnity costs under CPR, r 36.10 or that it was entitled to seek indemnity costs which did not depend on the ordinary test (see CPR, r 44.3).

The court decided that the starting point was CPR, r 36.10. There was no reference in that rule to a presumption that, unless it was unjust to do so, the court would order a late-accepting defendant to pay a claimant's costs on an indemnity basis. The usual basis for the assessment of costs was the standard basis and if there was an entitlement to seek indemnity costs then it had to be expressly spelled out in the CPR. A party could seek indemnity costs in one of two ways, either because there was a presumption that such costs would apply, for example under CPR, r 36.14 (see below) or because it could demonstrate the necessary evidence of conduct under CPR, r 44.3. There was no basis under the CPR which would allow the court to order indemnity costs for any other reason or on any other basis. Accordingly, the claimant's claim for indemnity costs failed as a matter of principle. Thus the sanction against a defendant for late acceptance of a claimant's offer is effectively zero as they will only be ordered to pay the costs that they would have to pay in any event.

---

[12] [2009] EWHC 274 (TCC).

7.5.10 Procedure following acceptance of offer

When a Part 36 offer is accepted the claim is stayed under CPR, r 36.11. If the offer deals with the entire claim then that is stayed except for the purposes of enforcement and costs.

If the offer deals only with a part of the claim then that part is stayed but the rest of the claim can continue (unless abandoned) with costs being decided by the court or agreed between the parties.

Where the settlement needs the approval of the court (eg because the claimant is a child or protected party) the stay does not come into effect until the approval is given. Thus even when an offer has been accepted it is necessary for the claimant to apply for a settlement approval hearing to confirm the deal.

Where the maker of the offer is the defendant and it includes the payment of a single sum, then that amount must be paid within 14 days of the acceptance or the making of a court order for periodical payments or provisional damages where appropriate (see above CPR, rr 36.5 and 36.6). If the money is not paid within that period then the claimant can enter judgment for the amount and enforce it. But if the terms of the offer are such that whole payment is not to be made within 14 days then the offer is not a Part 36 offer for the purposes of sanctions.

In any other case (such as an offer by the claimant or the periodic payment element of an offer) the claimant can enforce the agreement without starting a separate claim if the terms of the offer are not complied with.

7.5.11 Costs consequences following trial

CPR, r 36.14 specifies the detail of the costs sanctions that have been mentioned several times above. These sanctions apply when, at trial, the maker of an offer gets a judgment that is more advantageous than the offer in question. Note that the sanctions only apply where there has been a trial and judgment and they do not apply where there has been summary judgment (*Petrotrade Inc v Texaco Ltd*)[13] and costs must be dealt with under CPR, r 44.3.

For the purposes of this rule a money judgment is more advantageous when the amount awarded is larger than the offer no matter how small is the difference. Thus a judgment that exceeds an offer by 1p is

---

[13] [2000] EWCA Civ 512.

sufficient for the offer to have been beaten (CPR, r 36.14(1A)). It is not relevant that the costs of obtaining the extra amount are disproportionate. Thus in *McGinty v Pipe*,[14] a clinical negligence case, the defendant had made an offer of £350,000 and 2 years later the claimant obtained judgment for £365,267.17. The defendant argued that the additional sum of £15,260.10 was not justified by the effort taken and costs incurred over the 2 intervening years. This argument was not accepted and no costs sanctions were applied to the successful claimant as they had obtained a more advantageous judgment.

The issue of the effect of deductible benefits arose in the case of *Fox v Foundation Piling Ltd*[15] where the defendant had made a Part 36 offer amounting to £16,050.79 being a gross amount of £63,000 with deductible benefits of £39,449.21. Subsequently the parties agreed damages, less deductible benefits at £31,705.53 based on a gross figure of only £37,500 less reduced benefits of £5,797.47. This issue for the court was whether the test based on the gross figures or the net figures. If the gross figure was used then the claimant had failed to get a more advantageous judgment, but they had done so if the net figures were used. The Court of Appeal confirmed that the net figures were to be used and the claimant was the successful party in this case.

A similar situation applies in relation to the test against the claimant's own offer. In the case of *Acre 1127 Ltd v De Montford Fine Art*[16] the claimant made a Part 36 offer to accept £500,000. At trial they obtained judgment for £1,032.364.81, but this was reduced on appeal to £442,442.04. The costs between the parties had to be considered on the basis of the appeal judgment. The court stated that the comparison was to be between the offer and the judgment plus interest until the end of the period for acceptance. This is because the Part 36 offer includes interest until that point. When the court included the relevant interest the sum awarded became £510,113.44.

Where a claimant fails to get a more advantageous judgment than a defendant's offer, they will have to pay the defendant's costs from the end of the period for acceptance and interest on those costs.

Where a defendant fails to get a judgment which is more advantageous than a claimant's offer then the court will make additional costs orders unless it is 'unjust to do so'. Those additional costs orders will be:

---

[14] [2012] EWHC 506 (QB).
[15] [2001] EWCA Civ 797.
[16] *Acre 1127 Ltd (In Liquidation) (formerly Castle Galleries Ltd) v De Monford Fine Art Ltd* [2011] EWCA Civ 137.

(a) interest on some or all of the damages (excluding interest) at up to 10% above base rate for some or all of the time since the end of the period for acceptance;
(b) costs on an indemnity basis;
(c) interest at up to 10% above base rate on those costs; and
(d) an additional amount of damages being 10% on the first £500,000 and 5% on damages above that figure with a cap of £75,000.

Note that the interest at up to 10% above base rate must include all interest awarded and is not additional to ordinary interest. But in the case of *Little v George Little Sebire & Co*[17] the court said that the starting point was for the maximum sanctions to apply and it was for the paying party to show that justice required the sanctions not to be applied.

Also note that the costs payable by the successful claimant are to be assessed on the standard basis as there is no provision in these rules for the costs to be on the indemnity basis (*Excelsior Commercial and Industrial Holdings Ltd v Salisbury Hamer Aspden and Johnson (a firm)*).[18] See also the analogy with the case of *Fitzpatrick Contractors Ltd v Tyco Fire & Integrated Solutions (UK) Ltd*[19] (see above).

In considering whether it is 'unjust' to apply the sanctions the court should look at:
(a) the terms of any Part 36 offer;
(b) the stage in the proceedings when any Part 36 offer was made, including in particular how long before the trial started the offer was made;
(c) the information available to the parties at the time when the Part 36 offer was made; and
(d) the conduct of the parties with regard to the giving or refusing to give information for the purposes of enabling the offer to be made or evaluated (CPR, r 36.14(4)).

See the application of the above factors in different circumstances in the case of *SG v Hewitt*[20] (see above).

---

[17] [2001] EWCA Civ 894.
[18] [2002] EWCA Civ 879.
[19] [2009] EWHC 274 (TCC).
[20] [2012] EWCA Civ 1053.

The fact of the award of indemnity costs and additional interest do not imply any misconduct on the part of the defendant and therefore it is not necessary to show misbehaviour to get those sanctions (*McPhilemy v Times Newspapers Ltd*).[21]

The presumption is that the sanctions are 'just' thus the court rejected the view that the need for a precedent overrode the question of justice. (*Hemming v Westminster City Council*).[22]

The sanctions do not apply where:

(a) the offer has been withdrawn;

(b) the offer has been reduced and the claimant has beaten the reduced offer even though they have not beaten the original offer; or

(c) the offer was made less than 21 days before the start of the trial unless the court shortens the period for acceptance.

7.5.12 Costs following a trial on liability or a preliminary issue

The question of the costs order that should be made following a trial on liability or a preliminary issue has been considered in a number of cases. In *AB v CD*,[23] the court said that it was 'on the balance preferable ... to reserve the costs ... so that the court can review the whole question of costs with a free hand at the conclusion of the litigation'.

A similar decision was reached in the case of *Beasley v Alexander*[24] where the court said that if a claimant makes an offer on liability and gets a better result costs cannot be determined until quantum is dealt with.

7.5.13 Withdrawal of an offer

CPR, r 36.3 also sets out the requirements for withdrawal of an offer. Any Part 36 offer can be withdrawn with a simple written notice. Within the period for acceptance (at least 21 days) the permission of the court is needed to withdraw the offer. After the period for acceptance the offer can be withdrawn without permission so long as it has not been accepted.

---

[21] [2001] EWCA Civ 933.
[22] *Hemming (t/a Simply Pleasure Ltd) v Westminster City Council* [2012] EWHC 1582 (Admin).
[23] *AB v CD* [2011] EWHC 602 (Ch).
[24] [2012] EWHC 2715 (QB).

No format is given for the notice of withdrawal and in the case of *Gibbon v Manchester City Council: LG Blower Specialist Bricklayer Ltd v Reeves*,[25] in the Court of Appeal Moore-Bick LJ said:

> 'Rule 36.3(7) provides that an offer is withdrawn by serving written notice on the offeree. In my view that leaves no room for the concept of implied withdrawal; it requires express notice in writing in terms which bring home to the offeree that the offer has been withdrawn.'

Therefore the notice of withdrawal must be explicit and clear to the recipient that the offer is withdrawn. Anything less would not be effective.

7.5.14 Tactical Part 36 offer

The High Court considered the issue of 'tactical' offers in the case of *Wharton v Bancroft*.[26] The claimant succeeded at trial in proving the will of her deceased partner. Her Part 36 offer had been rejected and at trial she beat that offer. The question was whether the costs sanctions should be granted. It was argued that the offer was merely tactical, that it is designed only to get the costs benefits of Part 36 and not a genuine offer to settle. The judge took account of the costs that the Part 36 offer would have included. Although the offer had been to pay £5,000 to each of the two defendants the costs took that value to £100,000 to each. On that basis the Part 36 offer was not derisory and there were no facts to warrant not ordering indemnity costs to the claimant.

The judge said of tactical offers:

> 'The concept is not an easy one to apply. All Part 36 offers are tactical in the sense that they are designed to take advantage of the incentives provided by Part 36. A low offer in a case where the offeror considers that the offeree's position has no merit cannot be written off as self evidently merely a tactical step.'

Therefore the argument that a Part 36 offer should be ignored as a low offer and merely 'tactical' is not one that a court is likely to quickly follow.

---

[25] [2010] EWCA Civ 726.
[26] [2012] EWHC 91 (Ch).

7.5.15 Defendant failing to make a Part 36 offer

A useful case in considering Part 36 overall and it links to CPR, r 44.3 (general discretion on costs) is *Fox v Foundation Piling Ltd*,[27] in which Jackson LJ considered a number of the recent Part 36 authorities, and decided that:

(a) Parties who choose to use Part 36 need to have a clear understanding of the legal effects of making, accepting and rejecting Part 36 offers, given that CPR, r 36.14 modifies the court's general discretion on costs.

(b) Parties can choose to make Calderbank offers outside the framework of Part 36. If a party does so, and then achieves a better result, the court's discretion is wider, although it may still be appropriate to order the party which rejected the offer to pay all costs after the date when the offer expired.

(c) Where a claimant recovers more than a defendant's Part 36 offer but less than the claimant's Part 36 offer, the claimant is normally 'the successful party' under CPR, r 44.3(2). The starting point is that the successful party should recover its costs from the other side, subject to any adjustment to reflect issues which the successful party has lost or other circumstances, eg to compensate the unsuccessful party for costs incurred because of the unreasonable conduct of the successful party.

(d) In a personal injury action, the fact that a claimant has deliberately exaggerated his claim may or may not be a good reason for depriving him of part of his costs, depending on the circumstances. If the claimant has a strong case on liability, the defendant's remedy is to make a modest Part 36 offer. If he does not do that at the first opportunity, he cannot expect to secure costs protection. Different considerations may arise where the claimant has been dishonest.

(e) The fact that the successful party has failed on certain issues may mean it is appropriate to adjust the normal costs order to reflect that failure.

7.6 PORTAL OFFERS

CPR, r 36.16 states that different rules apply to a claim that has followed the protocol procedure and then had proceedings started for stage 3. The rules are significantly different in both the procedure and the effect from those explained above.

---

[27] [2011] EWCA Civ 797.

An offer within the Protocol must be set out in the Court Proceedings Pack (Part B) Form; and contain the final total amount of the offer from both parties (CPR, r 36.17). It therefore differs substantially from the above form of Part 36 offer in that it must be produced by the claimant and must show offers from both sides.

The offer is made on the day after the Court Proceedings Pack (A and B) is sent electronically to the defendant (CPR, r 36.18).

CPR, r 36.19 provides that the offer is exclusive of interest (unlike non-portal offers) and that costs sanctions apply only in respect of stage 3 of the portal and not in respect of any appeal from the decision.

The amounts in the portal offer must not be disclosed to the court until after the final decision. At that point the court will consider the offers in relation to costs (CPR, r 36.20).

CPR, r 36.21 sets out the cost sanctions that apply following judgment based on the portal offer.

Where the claimant's award is less than or equal to the defendant's offer the claimant will have to pay the defendant's fixed costs for stage 3 together with interest from the business day after the date of the offer (see above CPR, r 36.18). Thus interest runs from the second business day after it is sent to the defendant.

Where the claimant's award is more than the defendant's offer but less than the claimant's offer the defendant will be ordered to pay the claimant the fixed costs.

Where the claimant's award is equal to or more than the claimant's offer then the defendant must pay the claimant:

(a) interest on the damages at 10% above base rate for all or part of the time from the date of the offer;
(b) fixed costs; and
(c) interest on the fixed costs at up to 10% above base rates.

In judging whether the award is less than or equal to the defendant's offer the damages awarded are reduced by the deductible benefits identified in the judgment (CPR, r 36.22).

CHAPTER 8

TRIAL

8.1 INTRODUCTION

The White Book Cumulative Second Supplement to the 2013 edition records:[1]

> 'before the subcommittee could turn its attention to revising the Costs Practice Direction it was first necessary to go through the existing costs rules to remove *all the rules relating to funding arrangements which became redundant with the abolition of the right to recover success fees and after the event insurance premiums* by virtue of ss 44 and 46 of the Legal Aid Sentencing and Punishment of Offenders Act (LASPOA) 2012. The result of this exercise was that the remaining rules had large gaps, and it was therefore necessary to consolidate, and to a certain extent re-number the rules before the Practice Direction could be dealt with in detail.' (Emphasis added)

The result therefore is an anomaly as there will continue to be cases run for at least 2, if not 3 years or more, on pre-April 2013 basis where claimants will seek to recover both success fees and after the event insurance premiums. With this in mind Costs Practice Direction PD 48 states:

> '1.3 The provisions in the CPR relating to funding arrangements have accordingly been revoked (either in whole or in part as they relate to funding arrangements) with effect from 1 April 2013; but they will remain relevant, and will continue to have effect notwithstanding the revocations, after that date for those cases covered by the saving provisions.
>
> 1.4 The provisions in the CPR are enforced prior to 1 April 2013 related to funding arrangements include:
> (a) CPR 43.2(1)(a), (k), (l), (m), (n), (o), 43.2(3) and 43.2(4);
> (b) CPR 44.3A, 44.3B, 44.12B, 44.15 and 44.16;
> (c) CPR 45.8, 45.10, 45.12, 45.13, Sections iii to iv (45.15 to 45.19, 45.20 to 45.22 and 45.23 to 45.26) 45.28 and 45.31 to 45.40;

---

[1] 43N.01.

(d) CPR 46.3;
(e) CPR 48.8.'

Unfortunately the official online version of the CPR (www.justice.gov.uk/courts/procedure-rules/civil) does not make this clear; it is silent as to the changes save for PD 48. The print version makes this both clearer and easier to follow and extra care will need to be taken in relation to pre-April 2013 cases.

8.2 SUMMARY ASSESSMENT

In respect of any interim hearing at which the claimant intends to seek payment of the costs of the hearing (by the defendant) you should complete form N260 (the statement of costs) and file it at court no later than 24 hours before the hearing.[2]

The judge will have the option of dealing with the costs by way of a summary assessment, or adjourning for a detailed assessment. However, the court will not deal with the additional liability (assuming it is a pre-April 2013 retainer) until the conclusion of the claim, or the conclusion of the part of the proceedings to which the CFA relates (if the CFA was limited to a particular part of the proceedings).[3]

8.3 FINAL HEARING SUMMARY ASSESSMENT

For fast track cases, or other cases which conclude with a hearing lasting less than one day (including infant approval applications, but subject to the solicitor agreeing to waive any claim for solicitor and own client costs and appeals) the rule prior to April, the Costs Practice Direction, para 14.9 required any party seeking the recovery of an additional liability to be filed at court a bundle containing:

- copies of any form N251 filed in the proceedings;
- copies of any estimates and statement of costs filed in the proceedings; and
- copies of the risk assessments used at the time the CFA was entered into.

It is presumed that the same should still arise now in relation to cases with pre-April CFAs containing additional liabilities, although the rule itself has been removed from the CPR.

---

[2] PD Costs, para 44 9.5(4).
[3] PD Costs, para 44.3A.

In addition the same process as set out above in relation to serving details of the costs claimed will apply save that the time for filing the statement is 2 days before the hearing.[4] It is clearly important that the trial advocate has had the opportunity to consider the bundle and the implications of the information within it before the hearing. As well as understanding the risk assessment and being able to defend the additional liability, the advocate will need to be able to defend any substantial difference between the costs claimed now and those originally estimated.[5]

The brief will need to deal with the following matters:
- amount of base costs being claimed and reasons for them;
- any issues on proportionality;
- an explanation if the costs have exceeded the last filed estimate by 20%;
- the basis for the calculation of the success fees (if relevant);
- the basis for the calculation of the ATE premium (if relevant); and
- arguments to oppose the defendant's claim for costs in the event of losing a contested hearing.

It is open to the court to adjourn the summary assessment and give directions for a detailed assessment if the defendant's objections to the costs are substantial or there is insufficient time for the assessment to take place at that date.[6]

The judiciary has been encouraged to complete the summary assessment, and in order to avoid cash flow problems, the claimant should continue to request the judiciary to do so.

If any part of the success fee on (pre-1 April CFAs) is disallowed, and there is an application from the case handler or counsel to require the claimant to pay it, the court will, in the absence of the case handler and/or the counsel whose success fee may have been reduced, give directions to bring the application back before it at a later date.[7]

For cases that conclude through proceedings, detailed assessment (and indeed, summary assessment) will require a good deal of attention to ensure a proper result and maximum costs award. The order or judgment will set in motion the 3-month timetable to commence the

---

[4] PD Costs, para 44 9.5(4).
[5] PD Costs, para 6.
[6] PD Costs, para 13.2.
[7] PD Costs, para 20.3(1).

detailed assessment procedure, by service of the bill upon the defendants. The order for costs does not need to specify recovery of additional liability.[8]

8.4 MULTITRACK

Whilst there will be no requirement to have costs prepared for any form of assessment at the conclusion of a multitrack trial, the brief to counsel should be no less detailed in relation to the potential costs orders open to the judge. This of course separates into two parts: an order which finds the claimant succeeding and one in which the defendant succeeds. As far as the claimant's costs are concerned, the advocate should be fully briefed as to the costs order that is being sought and whether there are any particular elements of the case that should be flagged up to the judge for special comment. This is particularly the case if it is anticipated that the budget may have been exceeded either generally on any particular aspect and it can be argued that this is a result of an obvious piece of behaviour by the defendant where it would be helpful to have the trial judge comment upon it in their judgment rather than leaving it to fresh argument before a costs officer or costs judge when it may be too late to have the same impact. So in simple terms if the judge is dismissive about a particular strand of the defendant's case or evidence they have called and if it is felt that it will affect costs recovery then it is important that this is drawn to the judge's attention.

Clearly the advocate should be properly briefed as to Part 36 offers that have been made by the claimant so that in the event that the judge finds in the claimant's favour and awards the same or more than the claimant's Part 36 then immediate submissions are made by the claimant's advocate to ensure that full sanctions are made by the judge on the order. This begins with the awarding of additional compensation to the claimant.[9]

But then the advocate should strive to obtain an order for indemnity costs in addition and this is particularly the case if there is any risk of the claimant's costs being held to be disproportionate. The award of indemnity costs immediately removes the proportionality issue.[10] The advocate should have been briefed to deal with the risk of any split costs orders, for example issue based orders or otherwise.[11]

---

[8] CPR, r 43.3. PD Costs, para 2.1 because this is included unless otherwise ordered.
[9] CPR, r 36.14
[10] CPR, r 44.5.
[11] See p 157.

The advocate should seek an order for an interim payment of costs. The rule which required the court to consider ordering an interim payment of costs when an order has been made was strengthened in April 2013 to impress the requirement that there should be a presumption for interim costs payments whenever an order for costs is made:

> 'Where the court orders a party to pay costs subject to detailed assessment, it will order that party to pay a reasonable sum on account of costs, unless there is good reason not to do so.'[12]

This follows a long line of first instance decisions quoted in the White Book, which have seen disputes over whether interim payments should be made and at what level.[13]

> 'The principle is that the Claimant is entitled to something by way of costs and he should be paid it without delay. The fact that there may be difficulties of assessment – large sums involved and greater disputes – does not absolve the Judge from the need to consider whether the justice that comes from not keeping someone out of the money to which he is entitled, can only be achieved at too high a price to a Defendant, putting him in a position where he has paid more than due.'[14]

So the burden will shift to the defendant to show the good reason by which the order for the payment on account of costs should not be made. The issue then turns to how much one could secure. In *Dyson v Hoover*[15] the court said:

> 'a better test is to make a reasonable assessment of what is likely to awarded.'

In *United Airlines Inc v United Airways Limited*[16] 'on the facts, it was difficult to see how an order for 95% of the costs claimed could be a reasonable assessment'.

The amount of the payment was reduced to approximately 70%. Realistically one should be comfortable in seeking at least 50% on an interim payment. This will be based upon base costs as under the pre-April 2013 CPR, r 44.3A the court will not assess any additional liability until the conclusion of the proceedings, or the part of proceedings, to which the funding agreement relates.

---

[12] CPR, r 44.2(8).
[13] *Mars UK Ltd v Teknowledge Ltd (No. 2)* 1999 2 Costs LR44; *Soliman v London Borough of Islington* 2001 LTL16/10/01.
[14] *Ryan Beach v Dimitri Smirnov (1) and Service Point (UK) Limited (2)* (unreported).
[15] [2003] EWHC 624.
[16] [2011] EWHC 2411 (Ch).

CHAPTER 9

DETAILED ASSESSMENT

9.1 GENERAL

Detailed assessment takes place where costs are awarded in a case that does not fall within the fixed costs[1] or summary assessment[2] rules.

An overriding limit on the amount of costs that a successful party can recover is the Indemnity Principle. This states that a party cannot recover as costs a sum which is in excess of his liability to pay his own legal representatives (*Gundry v Sainsbury*).[3]

A further limit on the costs that can be recovered is contained in the overriding objective.[4] This states that the overriding objective of the civil procedure system is for cases to be dealt with 'justly and at proportional cost'. Thus the question of proportionality in costs is key to the assessment process.

9.2 TIME FOR DETAILED ASSESSMENT OF COSTS

Normally costs will not be assessed until the case is concluded. This means until the court has finally concluded the matters in issue in the case.[5] However, the court can order assessment of costs at an earlier stage if appropriate or the parties can agree in writing for an earlier costs assessment.[6] Also a costs judge or district judge can order an assessment of the costs if he or she believes that the case is unlikely to continue.[7]

---

[1] See Chapter 5.
[2] See Chapter 8.
[3] [1910] 1 KB 645.
[4] CPR, r 1.1.
[5] CPR, r 47.1 and PD 47, para 1.1.
[6] PD 47, para 1.2.
[7] PD 47, para 1.4.

If the paying party wishes to argue that the assessment has been started prematurely it can make an application to a costs judge or district judge to halt the assessment. At the hearing of such an application the court can order that the assessment continues or that the notice of commencement be set aside.[8]

9.3 EFFECT OF AN APPEAL

The fact that the judgment in the claim is subject to an appeal does not suspend the process for assessment of costs.[9] If the paying party wishes the assessment to be suspended it must make an application to the court which made the original judgment or the court which will hear the appeal.[10]

9.4 AUTHORISED COURT OFFICER

Except where the costs are to be assessed provisionally, authorised court officers in the costs office at the Royal Courts of Justice (RCJ) have the power to assess costs at a detailed assessment.[11] These authorised costs officers can assess costs in cases where the base costs (excluding VAT) are no more than £35,000 (senior executive officers) or £110,000 (principal officers).[12]

If all the parties involved in a detailed assessment object to the costs being assessed by an authorised costs officer, then the receiving party should notify the court of this fact and the matter will be listed before a costs judge.[13]

If one or more (but not all) of the parties object to the costs being assessed by an authorised costs officer they may make an application to the costs judge or district judge. The application must be made in accordance with the General Rules of Applications for Court Orders[14] and set out the reasons for the application.[15]

---

[8] PD 47, para 1.3.
[9] CPR, r 47.2 and PD 47, para 2.
[10] PD 47, para 2.
[11] CPR, r 47.3 and PD 47, para 47.3.
[12] PD 47, para 3.1.
[13] PD 47, para 3.2.
[14] CPR, r 23.
[15] PD 47, para 3.3.

9.5 COSTS DISCLOSURE

When costs are being assessed, one of the subjects that arises from time to time is the amount of disclosure of documentation that a paying party is entitled to see. One of the cases that sets down the main principles is that of *Bailey v IBC Vehicles Limited*[16] in which the judge said that the taxing officer (as costs judges were then called) was exercising a judicial function in undertaking a taxation (as a costs assessment was then called) in circumstances that had substantial consequences for the parties. The court concluded that in order for the judge to perform that function, he had to be trusted to look at material which would normally be protected from disclosure under the rules of legal professional privilege. It was perfectly proper, indeed necessary, for the judge to see that material. When the judge saw that material it in most circumstances would give him all the information that he required. However, if after reflecting on the material available to him, some feature of the case alerts him to the need to make further investigations, or causes him to wonder if the information which is being provided is full and accurate, then the judge is entitled to seek further information. The court said that they expected that the judge would begin the process of seeking that further information by asking for a letter or some other form of written confirmation or explanation of the matter that he wished to investigate. Again, the court concluded that on receipt of such letter or written confirmation or explanation, in the vast majority of cases the judge would have all the information that they needed. However, it might be that the judge was still dissatisfied in that he may feel that the written information or explanation was inadequate. In those circumstances, the judge could make orders for discovery or require a witness statement to provide the necessary information. Finally, the court concluded that if all else fails, then at least in theory the judge could order the relevant party to answer a Part 18 questionnaire.

Since the advent of the Civil Procedure Rules (CPR),[17] the position is:

> 'The court may direct the receiving party to produce any document which in the opinion of the court is necessary to enable it to reach its decision. These documents will in the first instance be produced to the court, but the court may ask the receiving party to elect whether to disclose the particular document to the paying party in order to rely on the contents of the document, or whether to decline disclosure and instead rely on other evidence.'

---

[16] [1998] 3 All ER 570.
[17] PD 47, para 13.13.

It is clear from the wording of that order that the Practice Direction accepts that there is no power under the rules to insist that a party discloses a privileged document to the other party even in the course of a costs assessment following judgment in the case. The appropriate route, therefore, is for the court to put the receiving party to an election as to disclose or provide alternative evidence. This position was confirmed in the case of *Vinayak v Lovegrove and Eliot*.[18] Furthermore, the powers of the court as described in the Practice Direction to Part 47 above only come into play when the detailed assessment hearing has been applied for.

Thus if there is any significant issue that needs to be explored in respect of a privileged document, the receiving party can deal with the issue by way of witness statements, and possibly oral evidence, on behalf of the firm or the client in question.

The question of disclosure of documents sometimes arises in the reverse form, in that it is argued that disclosure of information by the paying party will assist the costs judge in dealing with the bill on behalf of the receiving party. This point was considered in the case of *Simpson's Motor Sales (London) Limited v Hendon Corporation (No 2) (1965)*.[19] In that case, the court said that it was plain that the judge dealing with costs is likely to be assisted in assessing the reasonableness of a fee claimed by counsel for a receiving party by knowing the fee charged by counsel for a paying party. The court said that such information is 'certainly a factor of weight but not ... by any means conclusive'. However, this is very different from the suggestion that a paying party can be forced to disclose information. If the situation envisaged by the judge in this case, was one where the paying party had voluntarily given information to the costs judge in order to assist him in his assessment. Clearly, this is likely to happen where the fee charged by the counsel for the paying party is significantly lower that the fee charged by counsel for a receiving party.

9.6 VENUE FOR ASSESSMENT

The court may direct the assessment to be done at the costs office at the Royal Courts of Justice or at a county court other than that at which the case was heard.[20] Normally the procedure must be started at the county court or the district registry where the matter was dealt with. Otherwise

---

[18] [2007] EWHC 10 July SCCO.
[19] 1 WLR 112.
[20] CPR, r 47.4(1).

it is to be started at the costs office at the RCJ.[21] However, any assessment can be directed to the costs office by the originating court.[22]

Also, a county court can direct that the assessment is dealt with at another county court.[23]

If the case was heard at any London county court then the assessment must be started at the costs office. For this purpose London county courts includes Barnet, Bow, Brentford, Bromley, Central London, Clerkenwell and Shoreditch, Croydon, Edmonton, Ilford, Kingston, Lambeth, Mayors and City of London, Romford, Uxbridge, Wandsworth, West London, Willesden and Woolwich.[24] In those cases an appeal is to the Designated Civil Judge for the London Group of County Courts and it is to be lodged at the London Civil Justice Centre.[25]

9.7 TIME FOR ASSESSMENT PROCEDURE

The receiving party has to start the detailed assessment procedure within 3 months of the trigger event. The trigger event is:

(1) judgment, direction, order, award or other determination;
(2) the order lifting the stay because of an appeal;
(3) discontinuance under Part 38;
(4) the dismissal of application to set the notice of discontinuance aside under r 38.4; or
(5) acceptance of an offer to settle under Part 36.[26]

But the time for commencing the detailed assessment proceedings may be extended or shortened either by agreement[27] or by the court.[28] Any application to extend the time must be made to the office which would do the detailed assessment.

If the receiving party does not start the assessment procedure within the specified time, the paying party can require them to start the procedure

---

[21] PD 47, para 4.1.
[22] CPR, r 47.4(2).
[23] CPR, r 47.4(3).
[24] PD 47, para 4.2(1).
[25] PD 47, para 4.2(2)(B).
[26] CPR, r 47.7.
[27] CPR, r 2.11.
[28] CPR, r 3.1(2)(a).

within a specified time.[29] If the receiving party does not start the procedure within the specified time then some or all of the claimed costs may be disallowed.[30]

If the receiving party starts the assessment process out of time when the paying party has not made an application as above, then the court can disallow some or all of the interest due on the costs but cannot make any further deduction except in accordance with the rules on costs deduction for conduct issues.[31]

9.8 ASSESSMENT PROCEDURE – PARTY AND PARTY COSTS

Detailed assessment proceedings are started by the receiving party serving on the paying party a notice of commencement (Form N252); a copy of the bill of costs; copies of the fee notes of counsel and of any expert in respect of fees claimed in the bill; written evidence as to any other disbursement which is claimed and which exceeds £500; and a statement giving the name and address for service of any person upon whom the receiving party intends to serve the notice of commencement.[32]

A paying party can request an electronic copy of the bill.[33]

The same papers must also be served on any person who has taken part in the proceedings which gave rise to the assessment and who is directly liable under an order for costs; any person who has given to the receiving party written notice that they have a financial interest in the assessment and wish to be a party; and any other person whom the court orders to be served.[34]

If the receiving party is not sure whether they need to serve a person then they must apply to the court concerned for directions.[35]

Any non-party who wishes to play a part in the assessment would normally have to apply to be made a party to the action.[36]

---

[29] CPR, r 47.8(1).
[30] CPR, r 47.8(2).
[31] CPR, r 44.11.
[32] CPR, r 47.6 and PD 47, para 5.2.
[33] PD 47, para 5.6.
[34] PD 47, para 5.5(1).
[35] PD 47, para 5.5(2).
[36] PD 47, para 5.5(3).

9.9 FORM OF BILL OF COSTS

The bill of costs will normally contain a series of sections to explain the nature of the action and the costs incurred. The sections to be included are:

(1) title page;

(2) background information;

(3) items of costs claimed under the relevant headings;

(4) summary showing the total costs claimed on each page of the bill;

(5) schedules of time spent on non-routine attendances; and

(6) the relevant solicitor's certificates.[37]

But if the only dispute between the parties concerns disbursements, the bill of costs only needs the title page and background information together with a list of the disbursements in issue and brief written submissions in respect of those disbursements.

The bill of costs should be split into different sections where for different parts of the case:

- the client acted in person;
- the work was done pro bono or was legally aided;
- different solicitors acted for the client;
- there are different paying parties; or
- different interest is claimed.[38]

There are precedents for the various types of bill of costs set out in the Schedule to the Practice Direction to CPR Part 47.

The title page of the bill of costs must include the full title of the proceedings; the name of the party whose bill it is and details of the order or other document giving the right to assessment; where relevant the VAT number of the legal representative or other person in respect of whom VAT is claimed; and details of any relevant legal aid documents.[39]

The background information section of the bill of costs must include a brief description of the proceedings; a statement of the status of the legal representatives' employees in respect of whom costs are claimed and the

---

[37] PD 47, para 5.7.
[38] PD 47, para 5.8.
[39] PD 47, para 5.10.

hourly rates claimed for each; and a brief explanation of the retainer between the receiving party and his legal representatives.[40]

The costs section of the bill of costs should separate out the costs in the categories of:

- attendances at court and on counsel;
- attendances on and communications with the client;
- attendances on and communications with witnesses including expert witness;
- attendances to inspect any property or place for the purposes of the proceedings;
- attendances on and communications with other persons;
- communications with the court and with counsel;
- work done on documents;
- work done in negotiations with a view to settlement not covered above;
- attendances on and communications with agents and work done by them; and
- other work not covered above done relating to the proceedings.[41]

For this purpose 'communications' means letters or emails sent and any telephone calls. Non-routine communications are listed chronologically whilst routine communications are included en bloc at the end of the relevant section.[42] Routine communications are normally charged at 6 minutes of the relevant hourly rate and include dealing with the incoming communications.[43]

Travelling expenses will not normally be allowed within 10 miles of the solicitor's office. Travelling and waiting time is charged at the rate agreed with the client or the hourly rate whichever is lower.[44]

Postage, couriers, fax, telephone charges and photocopying are all overheads for the solicitor and not separately claimable.[45]

---

[40] PD 47, para 5.11.
[41] PD 47, para 5.12.
[42] PD 47, paras 5.13 and 5.14.
[43] PD 47, para 5.22(1).
[44] PD 47, para 5.22(3).
[45] PD 47, paras 5.22(4) and (5).

In respect of attendances at court or on counsel, the bill of costs must include all relevant events and any orders for costs which the court made (whether or not a claim is made in respect of those items in this assessment).[46]

In respect of all other categories of costs if the number of attendances and communications (other than routine communications) is 20 or more, the claim for the costs of those items in that section of the bill of costs should be for the total only and should refer to a schedule in which the full record of dates and details is set out. If the bill of costs contains more than one schedule each schedule should be numbered consecutively.[47]

Agency charges are to be included as part of the solicitor's costs in the relevant section. Agents at court or with counsel are included in the first section of the bill of costs and all other agency costs in the last but one (agency) section.[48]

The only costs of the assessment to be included in the bill of costs are those of preparing and checking it.[49]

Each item in the bill of costs should be numbered separately.[50]

9.10 POINTS OF DISPUTE

The paying party (and any other party to the detailed assessment) may dispute any item in the bill of costs by serving points of dispute on the receiving party and every other party to the detailed assessment with 21 days of being served with the notice of commencement. Any party not serving points of dispute within that period cannot take any further part in the assessment process unless the receiving party agrees or the court permits. An application for permission must be made in accordance with CPR Part 23 to the court at which the assessment will take place.

Points in dispute must be in the format given in Precedent G[51] and be brief.[52] The paying party must state in an open letter with the points of

---

[46] PD 47, para 5.16.
[47] PD 47, para 5.18.
[48] PD 47, para 5.22(6).
[49] PD 47, para 5.19.
[50] PD 47, para 5.15.
[51] PD 47, Schedule of Costs Precedents.
[52] PD 47, para 8.2.

dispute what sum, if any, they offer to pay in settlement of the total costs claimed. The paying party may also make an offer under Part 36.[53]

The receiving party may file a request for a default costs certificate (see below) if points of dispute have not been served within 21 days but the certificate cannot be issued if points of dispute are served beforehand.[54]

Where points of dispute have been served, the receiving party may serve, within 21 days, a reply on the other parties to the assessment.[55]

9.11 COSTS AGREED

Where the parties have agreed costs they should apply for a consent order for the issue of a certificate for the agreed costs. If the paying party will not consent to the order then the receiving party can make an application under CPR Part 23.

If the receiving party discontinues the detailed assessment before a detailed assessment hearing has been requested, the paying party may apply for an order about the costs of the detailed assessment proceedings. Where a detailed assessment hearing has been requested the receiving party may not discontinue unless the court gives permission. But a bill of costs may be withdrawn by consent whether or not a detailed assessment hearing has been requested.[56]

9.12 DEFAULT COSTS CERTIFICATE

A request for a default costs certificate must be made in Form N254 signed by the receiving party or his legal representative together with a copy of the order or other document giving the right to assessment. A default costs certificate will be in Form N255. The issue of a default costs certificate does not affect any detailed assessment of any related legal aid costs.

An application for an order staying enforcement of a default costs certificate may be made either to a costs judge or district judge of the court office which issued the certificate; or to the court (if different)

---

[53] PD 47, para 8.3.
[54] CPR, r 47.9.
[55] CPR, r 47.13.
[56] PD 47, para 9.

which has general jurisdiction to enforce the certificate. But proceedings for enforcement of default costs certificates may not be issued in the costs office.[57]

Unless the case falls within the small claims track fixed costs regime or the court orders otherwise, the fixed costs for the default costs certificate are £80 plus the court fee on the issue of the certificate[58] but must be no more than that given in the notice of commencement.

The court will set aside a default costs certificate if the receiving party was not entitled to it. In any other case, the court may set aside or vary a default costs certificate if it appears to the court that there is some good reason why the detailed assessment proceedings should continue.[59]

A court officer may set aside a default costs certificate at the request of the receiving party. A costs judge or a district judge will make any other order or give any directions under this rule. An application for an order to set aside or vary a default costs certificate must be supported by evidence. As a general rule a default costs certificate will be set aside only if the applicant shows a good reason for the court to do so and if the applicant files with the application a copy of the bill, a copy of the default costs certificate and a draft of the points of dispute the applicant proposes to serve if the application is granted.[60]

9.13 REQUESTING AN ASSESSMENT HEARING

Where points of dispute have been served the receiving party must file a request for a detailed assessment hearing within 6 months of the event ordering the costs to be paid but the court can extend this time.[61]

If the receiving party does not request in that period the paying party may apply for an order requiring the receiving party to file the request within such time as the court may specify. On such an application the court may direct that, unless the receiving party requests a detailed assessment hearing within a time specified by the court, all or part of the costs to which the receiving party would otherwise be entitled will be disallowed.[62]

---

[57] PD 47, para 10(1)–(6).
[58] PD 47, para 10.7.
[59] CPR, r 47.12.
[60] PD 47, para 11.
[61] CPR, r 47.14(1).
[62] CPR, r 47.14(2) and (3).

If the receiving party starts the assessment process out of time when the paying party has not made an application as above, then the court can disallow some or all of the interest due on the costs but cannot make any further deduction except in accordance with the rules on costs deduction for conduct issues.[63]

9.14 PROVISIONAL COSTS ASSESSMENT

Provisional assessment of costs is the standard process for all cases where the total costs are £75,000[64] or less and it applies whether the case was heard in the High Court or the county court.[65]

The overall procedure is similar to that where there is a detailed assessment hearing but with some modifications.[66]

The court will undertake a provisional assessment of the receiving party's costs on receipt of Form N258[67] together with:

(a) a copy of the notice of commencement of detailed assessment proceedings;

(b) a copy of the bill of costs;

(c) the order or other document giving the right to detailed assessment;

(d) a copy of the points of dispute, annotated as necessary in order to show which items have been agreed and their value and to show which items remain in dispute and their value;

(e) a copy of the annotated points of dispute for each person to be served;

(f) a copy of any replies served;

(g) copies of all orders made by the court relating to the costs to be assessed;

(h) copies of the fee notes and other written evidence as served on the paying party;

(i) where there is a dispute as to the receiving party's liability to pay costs to their legal representatives, any explaining how the charges are to be calculated;

---

[63] CPR, r 44.14(4).
[64] PD 47, para 14.1.
[65] CPR, r 47.15(1).
[66] CPR, r 47.15(2) and PD 47 para 14.2.
[67] CPR, r 47.15(3).

(j) a statement signed by the receiving party or the legal representative giving the name, address for service, reference and telephone number and fax number, if any, of:
 (i) the receiving party;
 (ii) the paying party;
 (iii) any other person who has served points of dispute or given notice to be involved in the assessment;
 and giving an estimate of the length of time the detailed assessment hearing will take;

(k) where the application for a detailed assessment hearing is made by a party other than the receiving party, such of the above as are in the possession of that party;

(l) where the court is to assess the costs of an assisted person or LSC[68] funded client:
 (i) the legal aid certificate, LSC certificate and relevant amendment certificates, any authorities and any certificates of discharge or revocation;
 (ii) a certificate, in Precedent F(3) of the Schedule of Costs Precedents;
 (iii) if the assisted person has a financial interest in the detailed assessment hearing and wishes to attend, the postal address of that person to which the court will send notice of any hearing;
 (iv) if the rates payable out of the LSC fund are prescribed rates, a schedule to the bill of costs setting out all the items in the bill which are claimed against other parties calculated at the legal aid prescribed rates with or without any claim for enhancement;
 (v) a copy of any default costs certificate in respect of costs claimed in the bill of costs.[69]

(m) the paying party must state in an open letter accompanying the points of dispute what sum, if any, that party offers to pay in settlement of the total costs claimed. The paying party may also make an offer under Part 36;

(n) an additional copy of the bill, including a statement of the costs claimed in respect of the detailed assessment drawn on the assumption that there will not be an oral hearing following the provisional assessment;

---

[68] Now the Legal Aid Agency.
[69] PD 47, para 13.2.

(o) the offers made (those marked 'without prejudice save as to costs' or made under Part 36 must be contained in a sealed envelope, marked 'Part 36 or similar offers', but not indicating which party or parties have made them); and

(p) completed Precedent G (points of dispute and any reply).[70]

The court may at any time decide that the matter is unsuitable for a provisional assessment and give directions for the matter to be listed for a detail assessment hearing (see below).[71]

The provisional assessment will be based on the information contained in the bill and supporting papers and the contentions set out in Precedent G (the points of dispute and any reply).[72] The court will not award more than £1,500 to any party in respect of the costs of the provisional assessment.[73]

On receipt of the request for detailed assessment and the supporting papers, the court will use its best endeavours to undertake a provisional assessment within 6 weeks. No party will be permitted to attend the provisional assessment.[74]

Once the provisional assessment has been carried out the court will return Precedent G (the points of dispute and any reply) with the court's decisions noted upon it. Within 14 days of receipt of Precedent G the parties must agree the total sum due to the receiving party on the basis of the court's decisions. If the parties are unable to agree the arithmetic, they must refer the dispute back to the court for a decision on the basis of written submissions.[75]

When a provisional assessment has been carried out, the court will send a copy of the bill, as provisionally assessed, to each party with a notice stating that any party who wishes to challenge any aspect of the provisional assessment must, within 21 days of the receipt of the notice, file and serve on all other parties a written request for an oral hearing identifying the item or items in the court's provisional assessment which are to be reviewed and providing a time estimate for the hearing. If no

---

[70] PD 47, para 8.3.
[71] CPR, r 47.15(6).
[72] CPR, r 47.15(4).
[73] CPR, r 47.15(5).
[74] PD 47, para 14.4.
[75] PD 47, para 14.4.

such request is filed and served within that period, the provisional assessment shall be binding upon the parties, save in exceptional circumstances.[76]

On receipt of a notice requiring a review the court will fix a date for the hearing and give at least 14 days' notice of the time and place of the hearing to all parties.[77]

Any party which has requested an oral hearing, will pay the costs of and incidental to that hearing unless:

(a) it achieves an adjustment in its own favour by 20% or more of the sum provisionally assessed; or
(b) the court otherwise orders.[78]

9.15 DETAILED ASSESSMENT HEARING

The request for a detailed assessment hearing must be in Form N258. The request must be accompanied by:

(a) a copy of the notice of commencement of detailed assessment proceedings;
(b) a copy of the bill of costs;
(c) the order or other document giving the right to detailed assessment;
(d) a copy of the points of dispute, annotated to show which items have been agreed and their value and which items remain in dispute and their value;
(e) a copy of the annotated points of dispute for each person to be served;
(f) a copy of any replies served;
(g) copies of all orders made by the court relating to the costs to be assessed;
(h) copies of the fee notes and other written evidence as served on the paying party;
(i) where there is a dispute as to the receiving party's liability to pay costs to their legal representatives, any retainer explaining how the charges are to be calculated;

---

[76] CPR, r 47.15(7) and (8).
[77] CPR, r 47.15(9).
[78] CPR, r 47.15(10).

(j) a statement signed by the receiving party or the legal representative giving the name, address for service, reference and telephone number and fax number, if any, of:
   (i) the receiving party;
   (ii) the paying party;
   (iii) any other person who has served points of dispute or given notice to be involved in the assessment;
   and giving an estimate of the length of time the detailed assessment hearing will take;

(k) where the application for a detailed assessment hearing is made by a party other than the receiving party, such of the documents above as are in their possession;

(l) where the court is to assess the costs of an assisted person or LSC funded client or person to whom civil legal services (within the meaning of Part 1 of the Legal Aid, Sentencing and Punishment of Offenders Act 2012) are provided under arrangement made for the purposes of that Part of that Act:
   (i) the legal aid certificate, LSC certificate, the certificate recording the determination of the Director of Legal Aid Casework and relevant amendment certificates, any authorities and any certificates of discharge or revocation or withdrawal;
   (ii) a certificate, in Precedent F(3) of the Schedule of Costs Precedents;
   (iii) if that person has a financial interest in the detailed assessment hearing and wishes to attend, the postal address of that person to which the court will send notice of any hearing;
   (iv) if the rates payable out of the LSC fund or by the Lord Chancellor under Part 1 of the Legal Aid, Sentencing and Punishment of Offenders Act 2012 are prescribed rates, a schedule to the bill of costs setting out all the items in the bill which are claimed against other parties calculated at the legal aid prescribed rates with or without any claim for enhancement (further information as to this schedule is set out in para 17 of this Practice Direction); and
   (v) a copy of any default costs certificate in respect of costs claimed in the bill of costs.[79]

On receipt of the request for a detailed assessment hearing the court will fix a date for the hearing, or, if the costs officer so decides, will give directions or fix a date for a preliminary appointment. The court will

---

[79] PD 47, para 13.2.

give at least 14 days' notice of the time and place of the detailed assessment hearing to every person named in the statement referred to above.[80]

Unless the court otherwise orders, if the only dispute between the parties concerns disbursements, the hearing shall take place in the absence of the parties on the basis of the documents and the court will issue its decision in writing.[81]

No party other than:
(a) the receiving party;
(b) the paying party; and
(c) any party who has served points of dispute;

may be heard at the detailed assessment hearing unless the court gives permission.

Also only items specified in the points of dispute may be raised at the hearing, unless the court gives permission.[82]

If an assessment is carried out at more than one hearing, then the time for appealing does not start to run until the conclusion of the final hearing, unless the court orders otherwise.[83]

The assessment itself is a normal adversarial hearing and should be prepared for in the same way as a trial.

9.16 DETAILED ASSESSMENT – TACTICS

It must be remembered that there are two aspects to assessment, the first is what costs are reasonable and the second is proportionate costs.

What reasonable fees are will depend upon the grade of fee earner it was reasonable to employ and the hourly rate it is reasonable to claim for that fee earner. As a general rule solicitors' work should be delegated to the lowest grade of fee earner reasonable.

Work which is fit only for a trainee includes collating documents and preparing court bundles (not photocopying) and sitting behind counsel in court in all interlocutory hearings except the most important.

---

[80] PD 47, para 13(4) and (6).
[81] PD 47, para 13(5).
[82] CPR, r 47.14(5) and (6).
[83] CPR, r 47.14(7).

Work which justifies the employment of a senior solicitor includes interviewing the client as to strategy, attending a first consultation with leading counsel and negotiations with the opponents or their solicitors.

Hourly rates for each grade of fee earner depend upon the locality in which the work is done. As a starting point the guideline rates in the Guide to the Summary Assessment of Costs should be considered.

The fact that a firm based in a cheaper locality could have undertaken the work just as efficiently is not necessarily conclusive. The question to be asked is whether it was reasonable to employ a firm in a more expensive area. The court must consider all the factors. Thus in two reported cases *Truscott v Truscott; Wraith v Sheffield Forgemasters Ltd*[84] and *Sullivan v Co-operative Insurance Society*[85] trade union funded claimants had appointed London solicitors in cases which were pre-eminently provincial cases. In both, the claimants were awarded provincial rates only.

In respect of each fee earner routine letters and emails out and routine telephone calls should be claimed at one-tenth of the hourly rate. Dealing with incoming letters and emails is included in the costs allowed for the related outgoing letter.

Reasonable time spent travelling and waiting is recoverable at the full hourly rate unless the client has agreed a lower rate.

Counsel's fees depend upon the seniority of counsel which it was reasonable to instruct and the market price for the item of work in question. The factors relevant when calculating a brief fee include:
- the difficulty and complexity of the subject matter;
- the urgency with which the work had to be done;
- the time likely to be spent out of chambers (ie the inability to do other work);
- the financial value of the claim; and
- the likelihood of media attention.

The paying party may wish to attack your costs and the areas which arise most frequently are:
- the work does not fall within the scope of the order for costs made;
- the grade of fee earner employed was too high;

---

[84] [1998] 1 WLR 132.
[85] (1999) *The Times*, May 13.

- the hourly rates claimed are excessive;
- too much time was spent with the client;
- too much time was spent perusing documents;
- too much time was spent on travel and waiting;
- local travelling expenses have been claimed;
- the cost of making copies of documents (not allowed unless exceptional);
- VAT that is not recoverable from the loser (eg where the winner is based overseas, or is registered for VAT and can claim it back from his output tax, or is a solicitor representing himself ('self supply')); and
- the work done was disproportionate to the matters in issue.

Justify your challenges by reference to your client's statement of costs; the Guide to the Summary Assessment of Costs; and your own knowledge of the judge's likely view as to what costs are reasonable.

Once the reasonable costs have been assessed the court must then consider whether those costs are proportionate to:

- the value of the claim;
- the complexity of the claim;
- the extra work caused by the behaviour of the defendant; and
- wider factors such as representation.

This means that for personal injury cases the sole factor is likely to be value. This does not mean that there is a formula for setting the ratio between damages and costs as each case is to be judged on its own merits.

9.17 CONDITIONAL FEE AGREEMENTS SIGNED BEFORE 1 APRIL 2013

9.17.1 Costs disclosure

The success fee for a CFA signed before 1 April 2013 or in relation to a mesothelioma claim is recoverable from the opponent. In most cases this will be the fixed success fee in the CPR Part 45 that applied prior to that date. For all other cases the detailed assessment rules that applied before April 2013 apply.

Similarly an ATE insurance premium for policies taken out before 1 April 2013 and certain policies in respect of clinical negligence claims is recoverable from the opponent. Again as a result the pre-April 2013 rules for detailed assessment apply.

These pre-April 2013 rules include additional requirements for disclosure in these circumstances.

The relevant details are:

(1) In the case of a conditional fee agreement with a success fee:
(a) a statement showing the amount of costs which have been summarily assessed or agreed; and the percentage increase which has been claimed in respect of those costs;
(b) where the conditional fee agreement was entered into before 1 November 2005, a statement of the reasons for the percentage increase given in accordance with reg 3(1)(a) of the Conditional Fee Agreements Regulations 2000 or reg 5(1)(c) of the Collective Conditional Fee Agreements Regulations 2000 (Both sets of regulations were revoked by the Conditional Fee Agreements (Revocation) Regulations 2005 but continue to have effect in relation to conditional fee agreements and collective conditional fee agreements entered into before 1 November 2005.];
(c) where the conditional fee agreement was entered into on or after 1 November 2005 (except in cases where the percentage increase is fixed by CPR Part 45, sections II to V), either a statement of the reasons for the percentage increase or a copy of the risk assessment prepared at the time that the conditional fee agreement was entered into;
(d) if the conditional fee agreement is not disclosed (and the Court of Appeal has indicated that it should be the usual practice for a conditional fee agreement, redacted where appropriate, to be disclosed for the purpose of costs proceedings in which a success fee is claimed), a statement setting out the following information contained in the conditional fee agreement so as to enable the paying party and the court to determine the level of risk undertaken by the solicitor:
  (i) the definition of 'win' and, if applicable, 'lose';
  (ii) details of the receiving party's liability to pay costs if that party wins or loses; and
  (iii) details of the receiving party's liability to pay costs if that party fails to obtain a judgment more advantageous than a Part 36 offer.

(2) If the additional liability is an insurance premium, a copy of the insurance certificate showing:

(a) whether the policy covers:
- (i) the receiving party's own costs;
- (ii) the receiving party's opponent's costs;
- (iii) the receiving party's own costs and opponent's costs; and

(b) the maximum extent of that cover; and

(c) the amount of the premium paid or payable.

(3) If the receiving party claims an additional amount under s 30 of the Access to Justice Act 1999, a statement setting out the basis upon which the receiving party's liability for the additional amount is calculated.

This information is vital as was shown in the case of *Long v Value Properties Ltd & Another*[86] where the claimant failed to serve the paying parties' solicitors with copies of her conditional fee agreements and a statement setting out the details of the success fees. When the issue was raised in the defendants' points of dispute the claimant's solicitor said this was an 'inadvertent omission' and sent the documents.

Master Rowley said that throughout the hearing he had been troubled by the 'one strike and you're out' nature of the default – having failed to serve the documents, 'unless the claimant's solicitor recognised his error before the points of dispute were served (and even then it may have been too late), he had breached the rule and oversight would not be sufficient to bring him back into play however promptly an application was made'.

Nonetheless, he ruled that the non-compliance was not trivial as defined by *Mitchell v News Group Newspapers Limited*[87] and the claimant was not able to provide a good reason for it now that 'oversight or human error is no longer to be regarded as a good reason'.

He distinguished the case of *Forstater v Python (Monty) Pictures Ltd*[88] which allowed recovery of a success fee despite the failure to serve Form N251. In that case Norris J drew a distinction between a failure, through human error, to comply with a rule of general application – as in this case – and 'a conscious failure to comply with a specific order made in the action itself'. In the *Long* case Master Rowley said that he was not bound by that case and the decision in *Durrant v Chief*

---

[86] [2014] EWHC SCCO JR1306057 (13 January).
[87] [2013] EWCA Civ 1537.
[88] [2013] EWHC 3759.

Constable of Avon & Somerset Constabulary[89] 'makes it clear that the Court of Appeal's general view is clear on applications of this sort'.

He concluded:

> 'Therefore, whilst I may have qualms about the nature of the sanction imposed for a breach of this particular provision of the CPR, I am clear that I need to take that as being the correct sanction and simply concentrate on whether the breach was trivial and if not whether there is good reason for granting relief. Both of those questions are to be answered in the negative in this case.'

Hutchings v British Transport Police[90] was a case to which the CFA Regulations applied but it did not specifically concern breach of the Regulations. It dealt instead with the issue of what questions about funding the defendant could legitimately ask by way of Part 18 request. At first instance before a deputy district judge their very lengthy interrogation was dismissed as a fishing expedition but by the time of the appeal before Senior Costs Judge Hurst they had whittled down their questions to the more pertinent '*Myatt*' questions about BTE enquiries.

Senior Costs Judge Hurst concluded that it was legitimate for defendants to enquire about funding, even for cases to post-November 2005 cases, by way of Part 18 questions. However, those questions are limited to:

(1) Does the claimant have insurance?
(2) With whom?
(3) Does the claimant have any LEI?

Given that in this case the defendant believed the claimant had access to LEI via his mortgage it is likely that the Part 18 request would create a 'genuine issue' to allow them to challenge Regulation 4 compliance.

I would suggest that it is also relevant to ask about compliance with the Consumer Contracts Signed at Home or the Distance Selling Regulations.

---

[89] [2013] EWCA Civ 1624.
[90] [2006] EWHC 900064 (Costs).

APPENDIX 1

THE DAMAGES-BASED AGREEMENTS REGULATIONS 2013, SI 2013/609

Made   *13th March 2013*
Coming into force   *1st April 2013*

The Lord Chancellor in exercise of the powers conferred by sections 58AA(4) and (5) and 120(3) of the Courts and Legal Services Act 1990[1], having consulted in accordance with section 58AA(6) of that Act, makes the following Regulations, a draft of which has been laid before and approved by resolution of each House of Parliament in accordance with section 120(4)[2] of that Act.

Citation, commencement, interpretation and application

1.(1) These Regulations may be cited as the Damages-Based Agreements Regulations 2013 and come into force on 1st April 2013.

(2) In these Regulations—

> "the Act" means the Courts and Legal Services Act 1990;
> "claim for personal injuries" has the same meaning as in Rule 2.3 of the Civil Procedure Rules 1998[3];
> "client" means the person who has instructed the representative to provide advocacy services, litigation services (within section 119 of the Act) or claims management services (within the meaning of section 4(2)(b) of the Compensation Act 2006[4] and is liable to make a payment for those services;
> "costs" means the total of the representative's time reasonably spent, in respect of the claim or proceedings, multiplied by the reasonable hourly rate of remuneration of the representative;

---

[1] 1990 c.41. Section 58AA was inserted by section 154 of the Coroners and Justices Act 2009 (c.25) and was amended by section 45 of the Legal Aid, Sentencing and Punishment of Offenders Act 2012 (c.10).
[2] Section 120(4) was amended by section 154(3) of the Coroners and Justice Act 2009 and sections 44(5) and 45(12) of the Legal Aid, Sentencing and Punishment of Offenders Act 2012.
[3] SI 1998/3132, to which there have been amendments not relevant to these Regulations.
[4] 2006 c.29

"employment matter" means a matter that is, or could become, the subject of proceedings before an employment tribunal;

"expenses" means disbursements incurred by the representative, including the expense of obtaining an expert's report and, in an employment matter only, counsel's fees;

"payment" means that part of the sum recovered in respect of the claim or damages awarded that the client agrees to pay the representative, and excludes expenses but includes, in respect of any claim or proceedings to which these regulations apply other than an employment matter, any disbursements incurred by the representative in respect of counsel's fees;

"representative" means the person providing the advocacy services, litigation services or claims management services to which the damages-based agreement relates.

(3) Subject to paragraphs (4), (5) and (6), these Regulations shall apply to all damages-based agreements entered into on or after the date on which these Regulations come into force.

(4) Subject to paragraph (6), these Regulations shall not apply to any damages-based agreement to which section 57 of the Solicitors Act 1974[5] (non-contentious business agreements between solicitor and client) applies.

(5) In these Regulations—
   (a) regulation 4 does not apply; and
   (b) regulations 5, 6, 7 and 8 only apply,
to any damages-based agreement in respect of an employment matter.

(6) Where these Regulations relate to an employment matter, they apply to all damages-based agreements signed on or after the date on which these Regulations come into force.

Revocation of 2010 Regulations and transitional provision

2.(1) Subject to paragraph (2), the Damages-Based Agreements Regulations 2010[6](b) ("the 2010 Regulations") are revoked.

(2) The 2010 Regulations shall continue to have effect in respect of any damages-based agreement to which those Regulations applied and which was signed before the date on which these Regulations come into force.

---

[5] 1974 c.47. Section 57 has been amended by section 98 of the 1990 Act and sections 117 and 221 of, and Schedule 16 to, the Legal Services Act 2007 (c.29).
[6] SI 2010/1206.

Requirements of an agreement in respect of all damages-based agreements

3. The requirements prescribed for the purposes of section 58AA(4)(c) of the Act are that the terms and conditions of a damages-based agreement must specify—
   (a) the claim or proceedings or parts of them to which the agreement relates;
   (b) the circumstances in which the representative's payment, expenses and costs, or part of them, are payable; and
   (c) the reason for setting the amount of the payment at the level agreed, which, in an employment matter, shall include having regard to, where appropriate, whether the claim or proceedings is one of several similar claims or proceedings.

Payment in respect of claims or proceedings other than an employment matter

4.(1) In respect of any claim or proceedings, other than an employment matter, to which these Regulations apply, a damages-based agreement must not require an amount to be paid by the client other than—
   (a) the payment, net of—
      (i) any costs (including fixed costs under Part 45 of the Civil Procedure Rules 1998); and
      (ii) where relevant, any sum in respect of disbursements incurred by the representative in respect of counsel's fees,
      that have been paid or are payable by another party to the proceedings by agreement or order; and
   (b) any expenses incurred by the representative, net of any amount which has been paid or is payable by another party to the proceedings by agreement or order.

(2) In a claim for personal injuries—
   (a) the only sums recovered by the client from which the payment shall be met are—
      (i) general damages for pain, suffering and loss of amenity; and
      (ii) damages for pecuniary loss other than future pecuniary loss,
      net of any sums recoverable by the Compensation Recovery Unit of the Department for Work and Pensions; and
   (b) subject to paragraph (4), a damages-based agreement must not provide for a payment above an amount which, including VAT, is equal to 25% of the combined sums in paragraph (2)(a)(i) and (ii) which are ultimately recovered by the client.

(3) Subject to paragraph (4), in any other claim or proceedings to which this regulation applies, a damages-based agreement must not provide for a payment above an amount which, including VAT, is equal to 50% of the sums ultimately recovered by the client.

(4) The amounts prescribed in paragraphs (2)(b) and (3) shall only apply to claims or proceedings at first instance.

Information required to be given before an agreement is made in an employment matter

5.(1) In an employment matter, the requirements prescribed for the purposes of section 58AA(4)(d) of the Act are to provide—
   (a) information to the client in writing about the matters in paragraph (2); and
   (b) such further explanation, advice or other information about any of those matters as the client may request.

(2) Those matters are—
   (a) the circumstances in which the client may seek a review of costs and expenses of the representative and the procedure for doing so;
   (b) the dispute resolution service provided by the Advisory, Conciliation and Arbitration Service (ACAS) in regard to actual and potential claims;
   (c) whether other methods of pursuing the claim or financing the proceedings, including—
      (i) advice under the Community Legal Service,
      (ii) legal expenses insurance,
      (iii) pro bono representation, or (iv) trade union representation,
      are available, and, if so, how they apply to the client and the claim or proceedings in question; and
   (d) the point at which expenses become payable; and
   (e) a reasonable estimate of the amount that is likely to be spent upon expenses, inclusive of VAT.

Additional causes of action in an employment matter

6. In an employment matter, any amendment to a damages-based agreement to cover additional causes of action must be in writing and signed by the client and the representative.

Payment in an employment matter

7. In an employment matter, a damages-based agreement must not provide for a payment above an amount which, including VAT, is equal to 35% of the sums ultimately recovered by the client in the claim or proceedings.

Terms and conditions of termination in an employment matter

8.(1) In an employment matter, the additional requirements prescribed for the purposes of section 58AA(4)(c) of the Act are that the terms and conditions of a damages-based agreement must be in accordance with paragraphs (2), (3) and (4).

(2) If the agreement is terminated, the representatives may not charge the client more than the representative's costs and expenses for the work undertaken in respect of the client's claim or proceedings.

(3) The client may not terminate the agreement—
   (a) after settlement has been agreed; or
   (b) within seven days before the start of the tribunal hearing.

(4) The representative may not terminate the agreement and charge costs unless the client has behaved or is behaving unreasonably.

(5) Paragraphs (3) and (4) are without prejudice to any right of either party under general law of contract to terminate the agreement.

Signed by authority of the Helen Grant
Lord Chancellor
13th March 2013 Parliamentary Under Secretary of State
  Ministry of Justice

EXPLANATORY NOTE

(This note is not part of the Order)

These Regulations prescribe the requirements with which a damages-based agreement ("DBA") must comply in order to be enforceable under section 58AA of the Courts and Legal Services Act 1990 (c.41) ("the Act").

DBAs are a type of 'no win, no fee' agreement under which a representative (defined in these Regulations as a person providing the advocacy services, litigation services or claims management services to which the DBA relates) can recover an agreed percentage of a client's damages if the case is won ("the payment"), but will receive nothing if the case is lost.

Prior to amendment by the Legal Aid, Sentencing and Punishment of Offenders Act 2012 (c.10), section 58AA of the Act only provided for the regulation of DBAs used in employment matters. The effect of the amendment, subject to exceptions, is to permit and regulate the use of DBAs in all civil litigation.

These Regulations apply to all DBAs, including those which relate to employment matters, entered into or signed on or after the date on which they come into force. However, section 58AA(9) of the Act provides that, where section 57 of the Solicitors Act 1974 (c.47) applies to a DBA (other than one relating to an employment matter), it is not unenforceable only because it does not satisfy the conditions in section 58AA(4), under which these Regulations are made. Accordingly, article 1(4) excludes those DBAs to which section 57 of the Solicitors Act 1974 applies from the scope of these Regulations. Further, the effect of regulation 4 is limited to all DBAs other than those which relate to employment matters, whereas regulations 5, 6, 7 and 8 only apply to DBAs in respect of employment matters.

Regulation 2 revokes the Damages-Based Agreements Regulations 2010 (SI 2010/1206), which applied only to employment matters and which will continue to have effect in respect of any DBA relating to an employment matter signed before the date on which these Regulations come into force. However, these Regulations make similar separate provision in respect of employment matters. Regulation 3 applies to all DBAs and specifies the requirements of a DBA.

Regulation 4, which applies to all DBAs other than those which relate to employment matters, provides that the payment from a client's damages shall be the sum agreed to be paid (which, where relevant, will include any disbursements incurred by the representative in respect of counsel's fees) net of any costs (including fixed costs), or sum in respect of counsel's fees, payable to the representative by another party to the proceedings.

Regulation 4 also provides that:
— in a claim for personal injuries, the amount to be paid by a client, including VAT, must not be greater than 25% of the combined total of the damages recovered by the client in the proceedings for pain, suffering and loss of amenity and pecuniary loss (other than future pecuniary loss), net of any sums recoverable by the Compensation Recovery Unit. The 25% cap will only apply to claims or proceedings at first instance; and

— in any other claim or proceedings to which these Regulations apply, the amount of the payment, including VAT, must not be greater than 50% of the sums ultimately recovered by the client. The 50% cap will only apply to claims or proceedings at first instance.

Regulations 5, 6, 7 and 8 apply only to DBAs in respect of employment matters.

Regulation 5 specifies the information that a representative must provide before a DBA is made. Regulation 6 specifies that additional causes of action can be added to the agreement by written and signed amendment.

Regulation 7 provides for the maximum amount that is payable to the representative from a client's damages under a DBA in respect of an employment matter, so that the amount of the payment, including VAT, must not be greater than 35% of the sums ultimately recovered by the client in the claim or proceedings.

Regulation 8 states that the terms and conditions of an agreement that provide for the termination of the DBA in an employment matter must comply with the following requirements: if the agreement is ended then the representative cannot charge more than his or her costs and expenses for the work done in respect of the client's claim or proceedings; the client may not end the agreement at particular stages; the representative may not end the agreement unless the client has been or is being unreasonable; nothing in regulation 8 prevents a party from exercising a right under the general law of contract to terminate the agreement, for example for misrepresentation or fundamental breach.

APPENDIX 2

LAW SOCIETY MODEL AGREEMENT (FOR USE IN CASES AFTER 1 APRIL 2013)

© 2013 The Law Society.

DISCLAIMER

This model agreement is not a precedent for use with all clients and it will need to be adapted/modified depending on the individual clients' circumstances and solicitors' business models. In all cases solicitors must therefore ensure that any agreement with a client is made in compliance with their professional duties, the requirements of the SRA and any statutory requirements. The Law Society does not accept any responsibility for any breaches of such requirements in respect of this model agreement which is intended for guidance only.

Conditional Fee Agreement ('CFA')

For use in personal injury and clinical negligence cases only.

This agreement is a binding legal contract between you and your solicitor/s. Before you sign, please read everything carefully. This agreement must be read in conjunction with the Schedules and the Law Society Conditions attached.

I/We, [..] the solicitor/s

You [..] of [..], the client

What is covered by this agreement

- Your claim for damages for personal injury suffered on or about the [.................................] of [.................................] as a result of [.................................].

- Any application for pre-action or non-party disclosure.
- Any appeal by your opponent.
- Any appeal you make against an interim order or an assessment of costs.
- Any proceedings you take to enforce a judgment, order or agreement.
- Negotiations about and/or a court assessment of the costs of this claim.

What is not covered by this agreement

- Any counterclaim against you.
- Any appeal you make against the final judgment order.

Paying us if you win

If you win your claim, you pay our basic charges, our expenses and disbursements and a success fee together with the premium for any insurance you take out. You are entitled to seek recovery from your opponent of part or all of our basic charges and our expenses and disbursements, but not the success fee or (save for clinical negligence cases) any insurance premium. If your claim is for clinical negligence and you have taken out a costs insurance policy, then, if you win, you may be able to recover from your opponent that part of the insurance premium which relates to the risk of having to pay for expert reports.

[The overall amount we will charge you for our basic charges, success fees, expenses and disbursements is limited as set out in Schedule 2 below.]

It may be that your opponent makes a formal offer to settle your claim which you reject on our advice, and your claim for damages goes ahead to trial where you recover damages that are less than that offer. If this happens, we will *[not add our success fee to the basic charges] [not claim any costs]* for the work done after we received notice of the offer or payment. In these circumstances, you may be ordered to pay your opponent's costs, but (unless you are found to have been fundamentally dishonest in the claim) any order will normally only be up to the amount of damages and interest awarded to you.

Expenses and Disbursements

If you receive interim damages, we may require you to pay our expenses and disbursements at that point and a reasonable amount for our future expenses and disbursements.

If you receive provisional damages, we are entitled to payment of our basic charges, our expenses and disbursements and success fee at that point.

If you win overall but on the way lose an interim hearing, you may be required to pay your opponent's charges of that hearing, but usually only up to the amount of damages awarded to you.

If on the way to winning or losing you are awarded any costs, by agreement or court order, then we are entitled to payment of those costs, together with a success fee on those charges if you win overall.

What do I pay if I lose?

If you lose, you do not pay [us anything] [any base costs or success fee but we may require you to pay our expenses and disbursements].

If you lose you may be liable to pay some or all of your opponents costs. However you will normally have the benefit of Qualified One-Way Cost Shifting so the court will not usually enforce an order for costs against you, unless:

- the proceedings have been struck out; or
- the claim is fundamentally dishonest; or
- the claim includes a claim for the financial benefit of someone else.

The Success Fee

The success fee is set out in Schedule 1.

Basic Charges

Details of our basis charges are set out in Schedule 2.

Ending this agreement

If you have a right to cancel this agreement under Schedule 3 (see below) and do so within the 7 day time limit, you will pay nothing. Otherwise if you end this agreement before you win or lose, you pay our basic charges and expenses and disbursements. If you go on to win, you also pay a success fee.

We may end this agreement before you win or lose, with the consequences set out in the Law Society Conditions.

Other points

Definitions of words used in this CFA are explained in the Law Society Conditions.

You have the right to cancel this agreement in the circumstances set out in Schedule 3.

We add VAT, at the rate that applies when the work is done, to the total of the basic charges and success fee. Our VAT Registration Number is *[Insert]*.

[You may be able to take out an insurance policy against the risk of paying expenses and disbursements (but not our charges) if you lose, or some or all of your opponent's costs even if you win. You will be responsible for paying the insurance premium for this if you win unless your claim is for clinical negligence in which case you may be able to recover part of the premium. If you lose the premium [is still/is not] payable. Full details are contained in the insurance policy documents. We will give further information about insurance policies to you so that you can decide whether you wish to take one out].

The parties acknowledge and agree that this agreement is not a Contentious Business Agreement within the terms of the Solicitors Act 1974.

Signatures	
Signed by the solicitor(s):	....
Signed by the client: Dated:	....

Note: We are not bound to act on a conditional fee basis until both you and we have signed this agreement.

Schedule 1

Success Fee

Law Society Model Agreement (For Use in Cases after 1 April 2013) 219

The success fee is set at [.....]% of our basic charges, where the claim concludes at trial; or [.....]% of our basic charges where the claim concludes before a trial has commenced.

The success fee percentage reflects the following:

(a)   the fact that if you lose, we will not earn anything;

(b)   our assessment of the risks of your case;

(c)   any other appropriate matters;

(d)   the fact that if you win we will not be paid our basic charges until the end of the claim;

(e)   our arrangements with you about paying expenses and disbursements;

(f)   the arrangements about payment of our costs if your opponent makes a Part 36 offer or payment which you reject on our advice, and your claim for damages goes ahead to trial where you recover damages that are less than that offer or payment.

The Success Fee cannot be more than 100% of the basic charges in total.

Cap on the amount of Success Fee which you will pay us in the event of Success in proceedings

In addition, there is a maximum limit on the amount of the success fee which we can recover from you.

In proceedings at first instance, that maximum limit is 25% of the total amount of any:

(i)   general damages for pain suffering and loss of amenity; and

(ii) damages for pecuniary loss, other than future pecuniary loss;

which are awarded to you in the proceedings covered by this agreement. The maximum limit is applicable to these damages net of any sums recoverable by the Compensation Recovery Unit of the Department of Work and Pensions.

However, this maximum limit applies only to a success fee for proceedings at first instance and not to a success fee in other proceedings (such as, for example, an appeal against a final judgment or order). In proceedings other than proceedings at first instance the maximum limit is 100% of the types of damages set out in (i) and (ii) above. Again this maximum limit is also applicable to these damages net of any sums recoverable by the Compensation Recovery Unit of the Department of Work and Pensions.

These maximum limits are inclusive of any VAT which is chargeable.

[These maximum limits include any success fee payable to a barrister who has a CFA with us.]

We will provide you with a copy of any relevant judgment or of our calculation of any settlement showing how much of your damages should be attributed to General Damages and Past Pecuniary Loss, net of any sums recoverable by the Compensation Recovery Unit. [If you do not agree our calculation and this makes a difference to the amount of the Success Fee payable you, then we will put the matter for determination by an independent barrister of at least 10 years call, to be appointed by agreement between us or, in default of agreement, by the President of the Law Society of England and Wales, such barrister to act as expert and not as arbitrator and his decision shall be binding. The barrister's costs for assessing this issue *are* to be paid by you if the barrister agrees with us, but otherwise *are to be* paid by us.]

You also have the right to apply to the court for assessment of our costs, including our success fee.

Schedule 2

Basic charges

These are for work done from now until this agreement ends. These are subject to review.

How we calculate our basic charges

These are calculated for each hour engaged on your matter. Routine letters and telephone calls will be charged as units of one tenth of an hour. Other letters and telephone calls will be charged on a time basis. The hourly rates are:

Grade of Fee Earner	Hourly Rate
1. Solicitors with over eight years post-qualification experience including at least eight years litigation experience.	

Grade of Fee Earner	Hourly Rate
2. Solicitors and legal executives with over four years post-qualification experience including at least four years litigation experience.	
3. Other solicitors and legal executives and fee earners of equivalent experience.	
4. Trainee solicitors, para legals and other fee earners.	

We review the hourly rate in [month] each year and we will notify you of any change in the rate in writing.

[Fixed Fee]

Instead of calculating our Basic Charges by reference to the hours spent on you claim multiplied by an hourly rate, we have agreed with you that, if you become liable to pay our Basic Charges, then you will pay us the fixed amount of £[ ]. We will be entitled to this sum no matter how many hours we spend working on your claim. References in this CFA to Basic Charges or base costs are references to this fixed amount. If you become liable to pay our Success Fee, then this will be calculated as the [relevant] percentage set out in Schedule 1 of this sum.]

[Overall cap on your liability for costs]

[We will limit the total amount of charges, success fees, expenses and disbursements (inclusive of **VAT**) payable by you (net of any contribution to your costs paid by your opponent) to a maximum of [25%] of the damages you receive].

Schedule 3

Notice of the Right to Cancel

This only applies if you sign the Conditional Fee Agreement:

(i) At your home, workplace or at someone else's home; or

(ii) At our offices but following a visit by us (or by someone acting on our behalf) to your home, workplace or someone else's home; or

(iii) At our offices but following a meeting between us away from our offices.

You have the right to cancel this contract if you wish and can do so by delivering, sending (including electronic mail) a cancellation notice to the person mentioned below at any time within 7 days starting with the day of receipt of this Notice.

The person to whom a cancellation notice may be given is [..................................] of [*Name of Firm*] at [*Address of Firm* ....] [*Case Reference*]

Notice of cancellation is deemed to be served as soon as it is posted or sent to us.

You can use the cancellation form provided below if you wish.

Signed on behalf of [*Name of Firm*]: ....

Dated: ....

If you wish to cancel the contract, you **must do so in writing** and deliver personally or send (which [*may*] [*may not*] be by electronic mail) this to the person named below. You may use this form if you want to but you do not have to.

....

(Complete, detach and return this form ONLY IF YOU WISH TO CANCEL THE CONTRACT)

To: [..................................] of [*Name of Firm*]

at [*Address of Firm*]

Case Reference No: [..................................]

I hereby give notice that I wish to cancel my Conditional Fee Agreement with your firm.

Signed: ....

Name (please print): ....

Address: ....

Date: ....

Law Society Conditions

The Law Society Conditions below are part of this agreement. Any amendments or additions to them will apply to you. You should read the conditions carefully and ask us about anything you find unclear.

OUR RESPONSIBILITIES

We must:

- always act in your best interests, subject to our duty to the court;
- explain to you the risks and benefits of taking legal action;
- give you our best advice about whether to accept any offer of settlement;
- give you the best information possible about the likely costs of your claim for damages.

YOUR RESPONSIBILITIES

You must:

- give us instructions that allow us to do our work properly;
- not ask us to work in an improper or unreasonable way;
- not deliberately mislead us;
- co-operate with us;
- go to any medical or expert examination or court hearing.

DEALING WITH COSTS IF YOU WIN

- **[Subject to any overall cap agreed with you]** you are liable to pay all our basic charges, our expenses and disbursements and the success fee (up to the maximum limit) **[together with the premium of any insurance policy you take out]**.

- Normally, you can claim part or all of our basic charges and our expenses and disbursements from your opponent,. You provide us with your irrevocable agreement to pursue such a claim on your behalf. However, you cannot claim from your opponent the success fees **[or the premium of any insurance policy you take out (unless your claim is for clinical negligence in which case you may be able to recover part of the premium)]**.

- If we and your opponent cannot agree the amount, the court will decide how much you can recover. If the amount agreed or allowed by the court does not cover all our basic charges and our expenses and disbursements, then you pay the difference [**up to any maximum agreed with you**].

- You, not your opponent, pay our success fee [**and any insurance premium**].

- You agree that after winning, the reasons for setting the success fee at the amount stated may be disclosed to the court and any other person required by the court.

- If your opponent is receiving Community Legal Service funding, we are unlikely to get any money from him or her. So if this happens, you have to pay us our basic charges, expenses and disbursements and success fee.

We are allowed to keep any interest your opponent pays on the charges.

You agree to pay into a designated account any cheque received by you or by us from your opponent and made payable to you. Out of the money, you agree to let us take the balance of the basic charges; success fee; [**insurance premium**]; our remaining expenses and disbursements; and VAT.

You take the rest.

If your opponent fails to pay monies due to you

If your opponent does not pay any damages or charges owed to you, we have the right to take recovery action in your name to enforce a judgment, order or agreement. The charges of this action become part of the basic charges.

PAYMENT FOR ADVOCACY

The cost of advocacy and any other work by us, or by any solicitor agent on our behalf, forms part of our basic charges. We shall discuss with you the identity of any barrister instructed, and the arrangements made for payment.

Barristers who have a conditional fee agreement with us

If you win, you are normally entitled to recover their fee from your opponent, but not their success fee. The barrister's success fee is shown in the separate conditional fee agreement we make with the barrister. You must pay the barrister's success fee shown in the separate conditional fee

Law Society Model Agreement (For Use in Cases after 1 April 2013) 225

agreement we make with the barrister. We will discuss the barrister's success fee with you before we instruct him or her. If you lose, you pay the barrister nothing.

[The barrister's success fee is included within the maximum limit to the recoverable success fee in proceedings at first instance as explained in Schedule 1].

Barristers who do not have a conditional fee agreement with us

If you win, then you will normally be entitled to recover all or part of their fee from your opponent. If you lose, then you must pay their fee.

WHAT HAPPENS WHEN THIS AGREEMENT ENDS BEFORE YOUR CLAIM FOR DAMAGES ENDS?

(a) Paying us if you end this agreement

You can end the agreement at any time. Unless you have a right to cancel this agreement under Schedule 3 and do so within the 7 day time limit we then have the right to decide whether you must:

- pay our basic charges and our expenses and disbursements including barristers' fees but not the success fee when we ask for them; or

- pay our basic charges, and our expenses and disbursements including barristers' fees and success fees if you go on to win your claim for damages.

(b) Paying us if we end this agreement

(i) We can end this agreement if you do not keep to your responsibilities. We then have the right to decide whether you must:

- pay our basic charges and our expenses and disbursements including barristers' fees but not the success fee when we ask for them; or

- pay our basic charges and our expenses and disbursements including barristers' fees and success fees if you go on to win your claim for damages.

(ii) We can end this agreement if we believe you are unlikely to win. If this happens, you will [pay us nothing] [only have to pay our expenses and disbursements]. [These will include barristers' fees if the barrister does not have a conditional fee agreement with us.]

(iii) We can end this agreement if you reject our opinion about making a settlement with your opponent. You must then:

- pay the basic charges and our expenses and disbursements, including barristers' fees;

- pay the success fee if you go on to win your claim for damages.

In these circumstances, if your opponent has made a formal offer to settle your claim which you have rejected and the damages you have recovered are less than that offer, you may be ordered to pay your opponent's costs but only up to the amount of damages and interest awarded to you.

If you ask us to get a second opinion from a specialist solicitor outside our firm, we will do so. You pay the cost of a second opinion.

[(iv) We can end this agreement if you do not pay your insurance premium when asked to do so.]

(c) Death

This agreement automatically ends if you die before your claim for damages is concluded. We will be entitled to recover our basic charges up to the date of your death from your estate.

If your personal representatives wish to continue your claim for damages, we may offer them a new conditional fee agreement, as long as they agree to pay the success fee on our basic charges from the beginning of the agreement with you.

WHAT HAPPENS AFTER THIS AGREEMENT ENDS?

After this agreement ends, we may apply to have our name removed from the record of any court proceedings in which we are acting unless you have another form of funding and ask us to work for you.

We have the right to preserve our lien unless another solicitor working for you undertakes to pay us what we are owed including a success fee if you win.

CESSATION OF BUSINESS

If we stop carrying on business then you must pay us or any successor to our business (or to that part of our business which takes over the conduct of your claim) our basic charges and our expenses and disbursements including barristers' fees and success fees if you go on to win your claim for damages.

EXPLANATION OF WORDS USED

(a) *Advocacy*

Appearing for you at court hearings.

(b) *Basic charges*

Our charges for the legal work we do on your claim for damages as set out in Schedule 2.

(c) *Claim*

Your demand for damages for personal injury whether or not court proceedings are issued.

(d) *Counterclaim*

A claim that your opponent makes against you in response to your claim.

(e) *Damages*

Money that you win whether by a court decision or settlement.

(f) *Our expenses and disbursements*

Payments we make on your behalf such as:

- court fees;
- experts' fees;
- accident report fees;
- travelling expenses;
- the fees of barristers who do not have a Conditional Fee Agreement with us.

(g) *Interim damages*

Money that a court says your opponent must pay or your opponent agrees to pay while waiting for a settlement or the court's final decision.

(h) *Interim hearing*

A court hearing that is not final.

(i) *Lien*

Our right to keep all papers, documents, money or other property held on your behalf until all money due to us is paid. A lien may be applied after this agreement ends.

(j) *Lose*

The court has dismissed your claim or you have stopped it on our advice.

(k) *Formal Offer to Settle*

An offer to settle your claim made in accordance with Part 36 of the Civil Procedure Rules.

(l) *Provisional damages*

Money that a court says your opponent must pay or your opponent agrees to pay, on the basis that you will be able to go back to court at a future date for further damages if:

- you develop a serious disease; or

- your condition deteriorates;

in a way that has been proved or admitted to be linked to your personal injury claim.

(m) *Qualified One-Way Cost Shifting*

The rules in respect of costs payable if you lose a personal injury claim set out in [Part 44 Section II] of the Civil Procedure Rules.

(n) *Success fee*

The percentage of basic charges that we add to your bill if you win your claim for damages.

(o) *Trial*

The final contested hearing or the contested hearing of any issue to be tried separately and a reference to a claim concluding at trial includes a claim settled after the trial has commenced or a judgment.

(p) *Win*

Your claim for damages is finally decided in your favour, whether by a court decision or an agreement to pay you damages or in any way that you derive benefit from pursuing the claim.

'Finally' means that your opponent:

- is not allowed to appeal against the court decision; or
- has not appealed in time; or
- has lost any appeal.

APPENDIX 3

PRECEDENT H – COSTS BUDGETS

PRECEDENT H

Costs budget of [Claimant / Defendant] dated [ ]

In the: [to be completed]
Parties: [to be completed]
Claim number: [to be completed]

Work done / to be done	Assumptions	Incurred			Estimated		
		Disbursements (£)	Time costs (£)	Disbursements (£)	Time costs (£)	Total (£)
Pre-action costs		£0.00	£0.00	£0.00	£0.00	£0.00
Issue /statements of case		£0.00	£0.00	£0.00	£0.00	£0.00
CMC		£0.00	£0.00	£0.00	£0.00	£0.00
Disclosure		£0.00	£0.00	£0.00	£0.00	£0.00
Witness statements		£0.00	£0.00	£0.00	£0.00	£0.00
Expert reports		£0.00	£0.00	£0.00	£0.00	£0.00
PTR		£0.00	£0.00	£0.00	£0.00	£0.00
Trial preparation		£0.00	£0.00	£0.00	£0.00	£0.00
Trial		£0.00	£0.00	£0.00	£0.00	£0.00
ADR / Settlement discussions		£0.00	£0.00	£0.00	£0.00	£0.00
Contingent cost A: [explanation]		£0.00	£0.00	£0.00	£0.00	£0.00
Contingent cost B: [explanation]		£0.00	£0.00	£0.00	£0.00	£0.00
GRAND TOTAL (including both incurred costs and estimated costs)		£0.00		£0.00	£0.00	£0.00

This estimate excludes VAT (if applicable), success fees and ATE insurance premiums (if applicable), costs of detailed assessment, costs of enforcing any judgment and [complete as appropriate]

[Statement of truth]

Signed

Position   Date

		RATE (per hour)	PRE-ACTION COSTS					ISSUE / STATEMENTS OF CASE					CMC		
			Incurred costs	Estimated costs		TOTAL		Incurred costs	Estimated costs		TOTAL		Estimated costs		TOTAL
			£	Hours	£	£		£	Hours	£	£		Hours	£	£
	Fee earners' time costs (fee earner description)															
1		£0.00			£0.00	£0.00				£0.00	£0.00			£0.00	£0.00
2		£0.00			£0.00	£0.00				£0.00	£0.00			£0.00	£0.00
3		£0.00			£0.00	£0.00				£0.00	£0.00			£0.00	£0.00
4		£0.00			£0.00	£0.00				£0.00	£0.00			£0.00	£0.00
5	**Total Profit Costs (1 to 4)**		£0.00		£0.00	£0.00		£0.00		£0.00	£0.00				
	Expert's costs															
6	Fees					£0.00					£0.00				£0.00
7	Disbursements					£0.00					£0.00				£0.00
	Counsel's fees [indicate seniority]															
8	Leading counsel					£0.00					£0.00				£0.00
9	Junior counsel					£0.00					£0.00				£0.00
10	Court fees					£0.00					£0.00				£0.00
11	**Other Disbursements**					£0.00					£0.00				
12	Explanation of disbursements [details to be completed]														
13	**Total Disbursements (6 to 11)**		£0.00		£0.00	£0.00		£0.00		£0.00	£0.00			£0.00	£0.00
14	**Total (5 + 13)**		0		£0.00	£0.00		0		£0.00	£0.00			0	£0.00

In the: [to be completed]
Parties: [to be completed]
Claim number: [to be completed]

In the: [to be completed]
Parties: [to be completed]
Claim number: [to be completed]

	RATE (per hour)	DISCLOSURE			WITNESS STATEMENTS			EXPERT REPORTS		
		Incurred costs	Estimated costs		Incurred costs	Estimated costs		Incurred costs	Estimated costs	
	£	£	Hours	£	TOTAL £	£	Hours	£	TOTAL £	£	Hours	£	TOTAL £
Fee earners' time costs (fee earner description)													
1	£0.00			£0.00	£0.00			£0.00	£0.00			£0.00	£0.00
2	£0.00			£0.00	£0.00			£0.00	£0.00			£0.00	£0.00
3	£0.00			£0.00	£0.00			£0.00	£0.00			£0.00	£0.00
4	£0.00			£0.00	£0.00			£0.00	£0.00			£0.00	£0.00
5 **Total Profit Costs (1 to 4)**		£0.00	0	£0.00	£0.00	£0.00		£0.00	£0.00	£0.00		£0.00	£0.00
Expert's costs													
6 Fees	£0.00				£0.00				£0.00				£0.00
7 Disbursements					£0.00				£0.00				£0.00
Counsel's fees [indicate seniority]													
8 Leading counsel					£0.00				£0.00				£0.00
9 Junior counsel					£0.00				£0.00				£0.00
10 Court fees					£0.00				£0.00				
11 Other Disbursements					£0.00				£0.00				£0.00
12 Explanation of disbursements [details to be completed]													
13 **Total Disbursements (6 to 11)**					£0.00	£0.00			£0.00	£0.00			£0.00
14 Total (5 + 13)		£0.00	0		£0.00	£0.00	0		£0.00	£0.00	0		£0.00

In the: [to be completed]
Parties: [to be completed]
Claim number: [to be completed]

		RATE (per hour)	PTR				TRIAL PREPARATION				TRIAL		
			Incurred costs	Estimated costs		TOTAL	Incurred costs	Estimated costs		TOTAL	Incurred costs	Estimated costs		TOTAL
			£	Hours	£		£	Hours	£		£	Hours	£	
	Fee earners' time costs (fee earner description)													
1		£0.00			£0.00	£0.00			£0.00	£0.00			£0.00	£0.00
2		£0.00			£0.00	£0.00			£0.00	£0.00			£0.00	£0.00
3		£0.00			£0.00	£0.00			£0.00	£0.00			£0.00	£0.00
4		£0.00			£0.00	£0.00			£0.00	£0.00			£0.00	£0.00
5	Total Profit Costs (1 to 4)		£0.00	0	£0.00	£0.00	£0.00		£0.00	£0.00	£0.00		£0.00	£0.00
	Expert's costs													
6	Fees	£0.00				£0.00				£0.00				£0.00
7	Disbursements					£0.00				£0.00				£0.00
	Counsel's fees [indicate seniority]													
8	Leading counsel					£0.00				£0.00				£0.00
9	Junior counsel					£0.00				£0.00				£0.00
10	Court fees					£0.00				£0.00				£0.00
11	Other Disbursements					£0.00				£0.00				£0.00
12	Explanation of disbursements [details to be completed]													
13	Total Disbursements (6 to 11)		£0.00			£0.00	£0.00			£0.00	£0.00			£0.00
14	Total (5 + 13)		0			£0.00	0			£0.00	0			£0.00

Precedent H – Costs Budgets

In the: [to be completed]
Parties: [to be completed]
Claim number: [to be completed]

			SETTLEMENT / ADR			CONTINGENT COST A: [EXPLAIN]				CONTINGENT COST B: [EXPLAIN]			
	RATE (per hour)	Incurred costs	Estimated costs		TOTAL	Incurred costs	Estimated costs		TOTAL	Incurred costs	Estimated costs		TOTAL
		£	Hours	£	£	£	Hours	£	£	£	Hours	£	£
	Fee earners' time costs (fee earner description)												
1	£0.00			£0.00	£0.00			£0.00	£0.00			£0.00	£0.00
2	£0.00			£0.00	£0.00			£0.00	£0.00			£0.00	£0.00
3	£0.00			£0.00	£0.00			£0.00	£0.00			£0.00	£0.00
4	£0.00			£0.00	£0.00			£0.00	£0.00			£0.00	£0.00
5	**Total Profit Costs (1 to 4)**	£0.00		£0.00	£0.00	£0.00		£0.00	£0.00	£0.00		£0.00	£0.00
	Expert's costs												
6	Fees	£0.00			£0.00				£0.00				
7	Disbursements				£0.00				£0.00				
	Counsel's fees [indicate seniority]												
8	Leading counsel				£0.00				£0.00				
9	Junior counsel				£0.00				£0.00				
10	**Court fees**				£0.00				£0.00				
11	**Other Disbursements**				£0.00				£0.00				
12	Explanation of disbursements [details to be completed]												
13	**Total Disbursements (6 to 11)**	£0.00			£0.00	£0.00			£0.00	£0.00			£0.00
14	**Total (5 + 13)**	0			£0.00	0			£0.00	0			£0.00

235

Guidance notes on Precedent H

1. This is the form on which you should set out your budget of anticipated costs in accordance with CPR Part 3 and Practice Directions 3E and 3F.

2. This table identifies where within the budget form the various items of work, **in so far as they are required by the circumstances of your case,** should be included. Allowance must be made in each phase for advising the client, taking instructions and corresponding with the other party/parties and the court in respect of matters falling within that phase.

Phase	Includes	Does NOT include
Pre-action	• Pre-Action Protocol correspondence • Investigating the merits of the claim and advising client • Considering ADR, advising on settlement and Part 36 offers • All other steps taken and advice given pre-action	• Any work already incurred in relation to any other phase of the budget
Statements of case	• Preparation of Claim Form	• Amendments to statements of case (see below)
	• Issue and service of proceedings • Preparation of Particulars of Claim, Defence, Reply, including taking instructions, instructing counsel and any necessary investigation • Considering opposing statements of case and advising client • Part 18 requests (request and answer) • Any conferences with counsel primarily relating to statements of case	
CMC	• Completion of AQs • Arranging a CMC • Preparation of costs budget for first CMC and reviewing opponent's budget	Subsequent CMCs

Phase	Includes	Does NOT include
	• Correspondence with opponents to agree directions and budgets, where possible • Preparation for, and attendance at, the CMC • Finalising the order	
Disclosure	• Obtaining documents from client and advising on disclosure obligations • Reviewing documents for disclosure, preparing disclosure report or questionnaire response and list • Inspection • Reviewing opponent's list and documents, undertaking any appropriate investigations • Correspondence between parties about the scope of disclosure and queries arising • Consulting counsel, so far as appropriate, in relation to disclosure	• Applications for specific disclosure • Applications and requests for third party disclosure
Witness Statements	• Identifying witnesses • Obtaining statements • Preparing witness summaries • Consulting counsel, so far as appropriate, about witness statements • Reviewing opponent's statements and undertaking any appropriate investigations • Applications for witness summaries	• Arranging for witnesses to attend trial (include in trial preparation)
Expert Reports	• Identifying and engaging suitable expert(s) • Reviewing draft and approving report(s)	• Obtaining permission to adduce expert evidence (include in CMC or as separate application) • Arranging for experts to attend trial (include in trial preparation)

Phase	Includes	Does NOT include
	• Dealing with follow-up questions of experts • Considering opposing experts' reports • Meetings of experts (preparing agenda etc)	
PTR	• Bundle • Preparation of updated costs budgets and reviewing opponent's budget • Preparing and agreeing chronology, case summary and dramatis personae (if ordered and not already prepared earlier in case) • Completing and filing pre-trial checklists • Correspondence with opponents to agree directions and costs budgets, if possible • Attendance at the PTR	• Assembling and/or copying the bundle (this is not fee earners' work)
Trial Preparation	• Trial bundles • Witness summonses, and arranging for witnesses to attend trial • Any final factual investigations • Supplemental disclosure and statements (if required) • Agreeing brief fee • Any pre trial conferences and advice from Counsel • Pre-trial liaison with witnesses	• Assembling and/or copying the trial bundle (this is not fee earners' work) • Counsel's brief fee and any refreshers
Trial	• Solicitors' attendance at trial • All conferences and other activity outside court hours during the trial • Attendance on witnesses during the trial	• Preparation for trial • Agreeing brief fee

Phase	Includes	Does NOT include
	• Counsel's brief fee and any refreshers • Dealing with draft judgment and related applications	
Settlement	• Settlement negotiations, including Part 36 and other offers and advising the client • Drafting settlement agreement or Tomlin order • Advice to the client on settlement (excluding advice included in the pre-action phase).	• Mediation (should be included as a contingency)

3. The 'contingent cost' sections of this form should be used for **anticipated costs** which do not fall within the main categories set out in this form. Examples might be the trial of preliminary issues, a mediation, applications to amend, applications for disclosure against third parties or (in libel cases) applications re meaning. **Costs which are not anticipated** but which become necessary later are dealt with in paragraph 4.7 of the Practice Direction.

4. Any party may apply to the court if it considers that another party is behaving oppressively in seeking to cause the applicant to spend money disproportionately on costs and the court will grant such relief as may be appropriate.

APPENDIX 4

ANDREW MITCHELL MP V NEWS GROUP NEWSPAPERS LIMITED [2013] EWCA CIV 1537

Court of Appeal

Master of The Rolls, Elias LJ

27 November 2013

Simon Browne QC and *Richard Wilkinson* for the appellant
Nicholas Bacon QC and *Roger Mallalieu* for the respondent

Cur adv vult

JUDGMENT:

Master of the Rolls: this is the judgment of the court.

[1] This is an appeal from two decisions of Master McCloud in relation to the recently introduced rules for costs budgeting in civil litigation. The first was her decision of 18 June 2013 that, because the appellant had failed to file his costs budget in time, he was to be treated as having filed a costs budget comprising only the applicable court fees. The costs budget actually filed by his solicitors was in the sum of £506,425. The second decision was her refusal on 25 July to grant relief under CPR 3.9 from her first decision. This is the first time that the Court of Appeal has been called upon to decide on the correct approach to the revised version of CPR 3.9 which came into force on 1 April 2013 to give effect to the reforms recommended by Sir Rupert Jackson. The question at the heart of the appeal is: how strictly should the courts now enforce compliance with rules, practice directions and court orders? The traditional approach of our civil courts on the whole was to excuse non-compliance if any prejudice caused to the other party could be remedied (usually by an appropriate order for costs). The *Woolf* reforms attempted to encourage the courts to adopt a less indulgent approach. In his *Review of Civil Litigation Costs, Sir* Rupert concluded that a still tougher and less forgiving approach was required. His recommendations were incorporated into the Civil Procedure Rules.

The procedural history

[2] On 21 September 2012, the Sun Newspaper reported that the claimant, then the Chief Whip of the Conservative Party, had raged against police officers at the entrance to Downing Street in a foul mouthed rant shouting "you're f...ing plebs". The incident, which received wide coverage, has since become known as "plebgate".

[3] On 7 March 2013, he issued these proceedings alleging defamation. A defence was filed on 17 May pleading justification and a *Reynolds* defence, i.e. that the story was one of strong public interest which had been reported responsibly.

[4] It is common ground that CPR PD51D Defamation Proceedings Costs Management Scheme applied to the proceedings. This was a pilot scheme which was in force until 31 March 2013. Para 4 of the practice direction provided:

> "4.1 During the preparation of costs budgets the parties should discuss the assumptions and the timetable upon which their respective costs budgets are based.
> 4.2 The parties must exchange and lodge with the court their costs budgets in the form of Precedent HA not less than 7 days before the date of the hearing for which the costs budgets are required."

[5] On 5 June 2013, the court issued an order (which was delivered to the claimant's solicitors on 6 June) that there would be a case management and costs budget hearing on Monday 10 June. As a result of the late notification of the date to the parties, the hearing was relisted for 18 June. The defendant used outside costs lawyers to prepare its costs budget which it filed on 11 June. Its budget figure was £589,558. The claimant's solicitors prepared their costs budget in-house. At 12.14 pm on 17 June, Master McCloud sent an email to the parties' solicitors noting that there was no budget from the claimant on the court file and asking whether the parties' budgets were agreed. The defendant's solicitor replied at 12.27 pm the same day saying: "… despite a number of written promptings from me to exchange costs budgets the Claimant's solicitors have not replied or provided us with a copy of their Costs Budget". At 12.44 pm, the claimant's solicitors emailed the Master saying:

> "Apologies, we have yet to be able to finalise the Claimant's Precedent H budget as we have been delayed in receiving Counsel's figures despite chasing for these daily since the middle of last week. We aim to file the document in the next two hours and exchange with the Defendant."

[6] In the event, the claimant's solicitors filed their budget during the afternoon of 17 June.

[7] The parties attended before the Master on 18 June. The claimant was represented by counsel and the defendant by its solicitor. The defendant's

solicitor said that there had not been sufficient time to consider the claimant's budget. The Master had to decide what to do in view of the fact that the claimant's costs budget had not been lodged with the court at least 7 days before 18 June. She was told by the claimant's counsel on instructions that the reason why the budget had not been filed until the previous day was "to do with pressure of litigation elsewhere in the firm on another case". She noted that this explanation was at odds with what she had been told in the email. At para 9 of her judgment, she said:

> "So what we have here is a position where a defendant has attempted to comply with the rules and has produced a budget and has engaged with the process and the claimant has not produced a budget and has not engaged until the very last minute in response to prompting from myself dealing with the costs management in the afternoon of the day before. On any basis that is a breach of the Practice Direction 51D and of the overriding objective in my judgment."

[8] She said that there were "really no adequate excuses for this breach" (para 12). There needed to be a case plan agreed if possible by the parties as to how the litigation would proceed and how it would be costed throughout. She then said: "… that process has simply died in this case. It has simply failed notwithstanding the defendant's compliance, and attempts by it to engage the claimant in budget discussion and exchange" (para 14). She continued:

> "15. The new rules have provisions in them which are essentially in identical terms to the rules under which I am proceeding today with one exception and that is the new rules provide a mandatory sanction and that is that where a party fails to file a cost budget within seven days prior to the date of the first hearing, the party is deemed to have filed a budget which is limited to court fees. I must act proportionately but I must also manage cases in accordance with the new overriding objective.
> 16. What I consider to be the best guide to as to what is considered proportionate (subject to the power to grant relief from sanctions) is what the Rules Committee has decided it should be in the new rules given that the circumstances of the breach in this case are identical to that envisaged in the new rules and the wording of the requirement to file a budget no less than seven days before a hearing and the requirement to discuss assumptions and so on is also practically identical.
> 17. All that is missing in Practice Direction 51D is a stipulation as to the nature of any sanction. It is simply left at large to the court, but I consider that professionals have now had ample warning for many months that the court would adopt a strict approach to the interpretation of application and rules and orders and it should come as no surprise that, subject to any powers I have to grant relief from sanctions, the sanction I should impose is that the claimant's budget will be limited to the court fees. The claimant has the right to apply

for relief from sanctions and I will adjourn the costs budgeting hearing, and matters can resume either to deal with any applications supported by evidence or to deal with costs budgeting, or both as appropriate in due course.

[9] Accordingly, she made an order in the following terms:

"1. The Claimant shall be treated as having filed a budget comprising only the applicable court fees.
2. The Claimant shall be entitled to apply for relief from sanctions, the hearing of the application to be heard at 2 pm on 25 July 2013, alongside the adjourned Case management and Cost Budget Hearing…."

[10] As the Master subsequently explained, in imposing this sanction, she had regard to the new CPR 3.14 by analogy (although it was not applicable to this case) because it was "an indication as to what may be an appropriate sanction for breach of the requirement to lodge a budget no later than 7 days before a case management conference" (para 2 of her judgment of 25 July).

Judgment of 25 July

[11] On 25 July, the Master heard the claimant's application for relief from the sanction imposed on 18 June that he should be treated as having filed a budget comprising only the applicable court fees. It was submitted on behalf of the claimant that she had been wrong to apply CPR 3.14 even if only by analogy. Reliance was placed on the decision in *F and C Alternative Investments Ltd (No 3)* [2012] EWCA Civ 843, [2013] 1 WLR 548. But the Master distinguished that authority. She said that she was entitled to look at CPR 3.14 as a guide to what may be regarded as a "proportionate sanction in a closely analogous situation of a failure to file a budget on time" (para 19). In any event, she said that she was not satisfied that she was entitled to review the correctness of her original decision (para 23).

[12] She then turned to the claimant's application for relief from the sanction. At paras 25 to 64 of her impressive judgment, the Master carefully considered the impact of the rule changes and the *Jackson* report. She drew attention to the "new overriding objective"(para 27), noting that as part of dealing with cases "justly", the court must now ensure that cases are dealt with at proportionate cost and so as to ensure compliance with rules, orders and practice directions. She drew attention to the fact that, in order to find time in her diary to list the application for relief within a reasonable time, she needed to vacate a half day appointment which had been allocated to deal with claims by persons affected by asbestos-related diseases. She identified the claimant's breaches as being (i) the failure to engage in discussion with the defendant as to budgets and budgetary assumptions in accordance with para 4.1 of PD51D and (ii) the failure to file a budget 7 days before the case management conference in accordance with para 4.2 of the practice direction.

[13] She noted (para 34) that there had been an "absolute failure" to engage in discussion of budget assumptions "when asked" and no attempt to apply for extra time or to ask the court informally for relief before "running into time difficulties". The budget was filed at the last minute and only as a result of prompting by the court after it had reviewed the file by chance the day before the hearing. There had been an abortive budgeting exercise and now time had been taken on a relief from sanctions application at a separate hearing. This was because the claimant had not been in a position to produce evidence at the earlier hearing in support of such an application.

[14] The Master was informed of the difficulties which had beset the claimant's solicitors. They were a small firm; two of their trainee solicitors were on maternity leave; the senior associate who was used to dealing with costs budgeting had recently left the firm; and the firm was engaged on work on other heavy litigation. As the Master put it at para 40, the firm was "stretched very thin in terms of resources". She noted at para 43 that none of these difficulties was notified to her on 18 June nor was an application for relief made at that time.

[15] It was submitted on behalf of the claimant that relief should be granted. It was said that the defendant had suffered no prejudice as a result of the claimant's defaults; and that, if relief were refused, the defendant would receive a windfall in the form of cost protection. It was submitted that post *Jackson* the rules were not about "no tolerance", but about "low tolerance". The new regime should be administered justly and the sanction imposed in this case was far too high.

[16] The Master explained her reasons for refusing relief at paras 53 to 62 of her judgment. She said (para 53) that the explanations put forward by the claimant's solicitors were not unusual: "pressure of work, a small firm, unexpected delays with counsel and so on". Such explanations carry even less weight in the post-*Jackson* era than they did before. She recognised, however, that she was not bound to dismiss an application for relief merely because there had been no good excuse for the default (para 55). At para 56, she said:

> "There is no evidence before me of particular prejudice to Mr Mitchell arising from my order: it would be for him to demonstrate that and it would be wrong of me to make assumptions about the wording of his CFA agreement with his solicitors which may or may not mean that my sanction affects him financially or in terms of legal representation. Even if it did affect him financially and as to representation, there are many claimants who manage without lawyers and it could not be said that he would be denied access to a court more than is the case for others if they have to represent themselves. Art 6 rights are engaged but a proportionate sanction can be a legitimate interference with Art 6 and in this instance Mr Mitchell is not driven from the court."

[17] At para 57, she recognised that it was obvious that the sanction was "something of a windfall" for the defendant, but "that is the way with sanctions". She then said:

> "58. This is a claim about reputation and about freedom of the press to report news stories. It is important to Mr Mitchell and it is important to the Defendants too. Cases are usually important to the parties but if such considerations weighed too heavily one would be unable to implement the objectives of the new rules. One would be unable to prevent some claims from taking unfair amounts of judicial resources away from other claims at the very moment when it is common knowledge that budgetary constraints may lead to fewer judges in the courts, and to reduced non-judicial resources to operate those courts.
> 59. Judicial time is thinly spread, and the emphasis must, if I understand the *Jackson* reforms correctly, be upon allocating a fair share of time to all as far as possible and requiring strict compliance with rules and orders even if that means that justice can be done in the majority of case but not all. Per the Master of the Rolls in the 18th Lecture quoted above:
>
> *"The tougher, more robust approach to rule-compliance and relief from sanctions is intended to ensure that justice can be done in the majority of cases. This requires an acknowledgment that the achievement of justice means something different now."*
>
> 60. I have given close consideration to the amount of time which the Claimant had to produce his budget. Was there procedural unfairness? On the face of it 4 days is short and even shorter when one considers that two days were weekend days. But having considered this carefully, because it was a point which troubled me, the view I have taken is that the parties were well aware that this was a case for which budgeting would be required from the start and that the mere fact that a date is set for CMC is not supposed to be the starting gun for proper consideration of budgeting.
> 61. Budgeting is something which all solicitors by now ought to know is intended to be integral to the process from the start, and it ought not to be especially onerous to prepare a final budget for a CMC even at relatively short notice if proper planning has been done. The very fact that the Defendants, using cost lawyers, were well able to deal with this in the time allotted highlights that there is no question of the time being plainly too short or unfairly so.
> 62. I have also given close consideration as to the stated objective of PD 51D and notably the concept of equality of arms referred to there but my conclusion is that the objective stated there relates to decisions made as part of cost budgeting, rather than sanctions for failure to engage with the process at all. Moreover the new

overriding objective and the identical wording in rule 3.9 highlight the emphasis to be placed, now, on rule compliance and one has to give effect to that."

[18] Finally, at para 65 she said:

"The stricter approach under the *Jackson* reforms has been central to this judgment. It would have been far more likely that prior to 1/4/13 I would have granted relief on terms, and in view of the absence of authority on precisely how strict the courts should be and in what circumstances, I shall grant permission to appeal to the claimant of my own motion."

The appeal lay to a High Court Judge, but was transferred to the Court of Appeal pursuant to CPR 52.14(1). The grant of permission to appeal was subsequently extended to cover the Master's original decision of 18 June as well as her refusal of relief from sanction.

The relevant provisions of the Civil Procedure Rules

[19] Rule 22(12) of the Civil Procedure (Amendment) Rules 2013 expressly continued the application of CPR PD51D to defamation proceedings issued before 1 April 2013. The requirement for parties to prepare, discuss and exchange costs budgets in advance of any case management conference was set out in paras 4.1 and 4.2 (which we have quoted at para 4 above). For cases commenced after 1 April 2013, new costs budgeting provisions are provided by CPR 3.12 to 3.18. These did not apply directly to the present case, but they are central to the issues that arise on this appeal.

[20] CPR 3.12(2) provides that "the purpose of costs management is that the court should manage both the steps to be taken and the costs to be incurred by the parties to any proceedings so as to further the overriding objective". CPR 3.13 provides:

"Unless the court otherwise orders, all parties except litigants in person must file and exchange budgets as required by the rules or as the court otherwise directs. Each party must do so by the date specified in the notice served under rule 26.3(1) or, if no such date is specified, seven days before the first case management conference."

[21] CPR 3.14 provides:

"Unless the court otherwise orders, any party which fails to file a budget despite being required to do so will be treated as having filed a budget comprising only the applicable court fees."

[22] CPR 3.17(1) provides:

"When making any case management decision, the court will have regard to any available budgets of the parties and will take into account the costs involved in each procedural step."

[23] CPR 3.9(1) provides:

"On an application for relief from any sanction imposed for a failure to comply with any rule, practice direction or court order, the court will consider all the circumstances of the case, so as to enable it to deal justly with the application, including the need—

(a) for litigation to be conducted efficiently and at proportionate cost; and
(b) to enforce compliance with rules, practice directions and orders."

[24] This should be contrasted with the previous version of CPR 3.9(1) which was in these terms:

"On an application for relief from any sanction imposed for failure to comply with any rule, practice direction or court order the court will consider all the circumstances including—

(a) the interests of the administration of justice;
(b) whether the application for relief has been made promptly;
(c) whether the failure to comply was intentional;
(d) whether there is a good explanation for the failure;
(e) the extent to which the party in default has complied with other rules, practice directions, court orders and any relevant preaction protocol;
(f) whether the failure to comply was caused by the party or his legal representatives;
(g) whether the trial date or the likely trial date can still be met if relief is granted;
(h) the effect which the failure to comply had on each party; and
(i) the effect which the granting of relief would have on each party."

[25] Finally, it is always necessary to have regard to CPR 1.1 and the "overriding objective" of enabling the court to deal with cases "justly and at proportionate cost". CPR 1.1(2) states that this includes, so far as is practicable:

"(a) ensuring that the parties are on an equal footing;
(b) saving expense;
...
(d) ensuring that it is dealt with expeditiously and fairly;
(e) allotting to it an appropriate share of the court's resources, while taking into account the need to allot resources to other cases; and
(f) enforcing compliance with rules, practice directions and orders"

The grounds of appeal

Challenge to the order of 18 June 2013

[26] Mr Browne QC submits that the decision of 18 June was wrong because (i) CPR 3.14 should not have been applied by analogy when it had not yet come into force; (ii) if it was appropriate to apply CPR 3.14 by analogy, the Master was wrong to interpret it as referring to a failure to file a budget *within the time prescribed by CPR 3.13* rather than a failure to file a costs budget *at all*; and (iii) the decision imposed a sanction that was disproportionate and contrary to the overriding objective.

Discussion

[27] As regards the first question, we consider that the Master was entitled to apply CPR 3.14 by analogy. She correctly understood that it did not apply directly because the proceedings continued to be governed by PD 51D (see para 19 above). Mr Browne accepts that the Master was entitled in the exercise of her discretion to impose such sanction as she considered appropriate to satisfy the overriding objective. In our judgment, she was entitled to be guided by CPR 3.14 since this represented the considered view of the Civil Procedure Rule Committee as to what constituted a proportionate sanction for failure to file a costs budget in time unless the court otherwise ordered.

[28] Mr Browne says that the Master's approach was unfair since the parties did not know that they were at risk of the sanction of the new scheme being applied to their case. But they knew that they were at risk that some sanction would be imposed even if they did not know what sanction would actually be imposed. Moreover, CPR 3.14 did not come as a bolt out of the blue. There had been a good deal of publicity of the new reforms, including CPR 3.14.

[29] We do not consider that the decision in *F & C* compels a different conclusion. In that case, the judge had awarded indemnity costs to a party which had made an offer which did not comply with the relevant provisions of CPR Part 36. His reasoning was that CPR 36.14 should be applied by analogy. The Court of Appeal said that the analogy was wrong in principle. CPR 36.14 represents a departure from otherwise established costs practice. It imposes a draconian costs sanction on a claimant who fails at trial to beat a defendant's Part 36 offer. There is no justification for indirectly extending Part 36 beyond its expressed ambit. As Mr Bacon QC points out, in the present case there was no question of a codified regime providing unusual benefits in return for a party acting in a distinct way. Rather, the court was considering what sanction to impose for breach of particular rules. The Master was not, therefore, applying a distinct regime by analogy. Instead, she was having regard to how the regime had been revised and how a breach would be addressed in the light of the new regime as to rule compliance. She was right to distinguish *F & C*.

[30] The second question is whether the Master was wrong to construe CPR 3.14 as referring to a failure to file a budget within the time prescribed by CPR 3.13 (in the present case, seven days). Mr Browne says that it is significant that the words "within the time prescribed by CPR 3.13" are absent from CPR 3.14 and that CPR 3.14 is directed to the case of a party who does not file a budget *at all*. In our judgment, this is not a sensible interpretation and it cannot have been intended. If it were right, it would mean that CPR 3.14 would not apply to a party who filed a budget just before the hearing of the first case management conference, but would apply to a party who had filed the budget immediately after the conclusion of the hearing. The mischief at which CPR 3.13 and 3.14 are directed is the last-minute filing of cost budgets. As CPR 3.12(2) makes clear, the purpose of costs management (including costs budgets) is to enable the court to manage the litigation and the costs to be incurred so as to further the overriding objective. This cannot be achieved unless costs budgets are filed in good time before the first case management conference. No less important is the requirement that parties should discuss with each other the assumptions and timetable on which their respective costs budgets are based. This is to enable the hearing for which the costs budgets are required to be conducted efficiently and in accordance with the overriding objective. The history of what happened in the present case shows how important it was to comply with *both* of the obligations in PD 51D. As a result of the defaults of the claimant's solicitors, no costs budgeting or case management was possible on 18 June 2013. Having imposed the CPR 3.14 sanction, the Master was unable to do anything other than adjourn the hearing.

[31] The third question is whether the Master's decision to impose the CPR 3.14 sanction by analogy was in accordance with the overriding objective. Mr Browne says that it did not give effect to the overriding objective, because it was not a proportionate decision. That is because (i) it did not reflect the fact that the breach of PD 51D was easily remedied; (ii) the breaches caused no prejudice to the defendant; (iii) they had no lasting effect on the conduct of the litigation; (iv) the breaches were minor; (v) the claimant had no history of default; and (vi) the order caused prejudice to the claimant.

[32] As we have said, the costs management hearing of 18 June proved to be abortive. The claimant was not in a position to invoke the saving provision in CPR 3.14 ("unless the court otherwise orders") and ask the Master to make an order relieving him from the sanction imposed by the rule itself. That is because his solicitors had not produced evidence which might have persuaded the court to adopt that course. We should add that in our view the considerations to which the court should have regard when deciding whether it should "otherwise order" are likely to be the same as those which are relevant to a decision whether to grant relief under CPR 3.9. In each case, in deciding whether to "otherwise order", the court must give effect to the overriding objective: see rule 1.2(a).

[33] We have concluded that the Master was entitled to make the order that she made on 18 June. She did so in the knowledge that the claimant would have

the opportunity to apply for relief at the adjourned hearing and that she would then be able to decide what response the court should give to the claimant's defaults so as to give effect to the overriding objective.

Challenge to the order of 25 July 2013

General comments on CPR 3.9

[34] Much has been said about the *Jackson* reforms and in particular on the question whether the court is now required to adopt a more "robust" approach to granting relief to defaulting parties from the consequences of their defaults. The amendment to CPR 3.9 followed the recommendations made in Sir Rupert Jackson's Final Report Ch 39. At para 6.5, he said:

> "First, the courts should set realistic timetables for cases and not impossibly tough timetables in order to give an impression of firmness. Secondly, courts at all levels have become too tolerant of delays and non-compliance with orders. In doing so, they have lost sight of the damage which the culture of delay and non-compliance is inflicting upon the civil justice system. The balance therefore needs to be redressed. However, I do not advocate the extreme course which was canvassed as one possibility in [the Preliminary Report] paragraph 43.4.21 or any approach of that nature".

[35] The "extreme course" to which he was referring was that non-compliance would no longer be tolerated, save in "exceptional circumstances". Instead, he recommended that sub-paragraphs (a) to (i) of CPR 3.9 be repealed and replaced by the wording that is to be found in the current version of the rule. He said that the new form of words

> "does not preclude the court taking into account all of the matters listed in the current paragraphs (a) to (i). However, it simplifies the rule and avoids the need for judges to embark upon a lengthy recitation of factors. It also signals the change of balance which I am advocating."

[36] As Sir Rupert made clear, the explicit mention in his recommendation for the version of CPR 3.9 of the obligation to consider the need (i) for litigation to be conducted efficiently and at proportionate cost and (ii) to enforce compliance with rules, practice directions and court orders reflected a deliberate shift of emphasis. These considerations should now be regarded as of paramount importance and be given great weight. It is significant that they are the only considerations which have been singled out for specific mention in the rule.

[37] We recognise that CPR 3.9 requires the court to consider "all the circumstances of the case, so as to enable it to deal justly with the application". The reference to dealing with the application "justly" is a reference back to the

definition of the "overriding objective". This definition includes ensuring that the parties are on an equal footing and that a case is dealt with expeditiously and fairly as well as enforcing compliance with rules, practice directions and orders. The reference to "all the circumstances of the case" in CPR 3.9 might suggest that a broad approach should be adopted. We accept that regard should be had to all the circumstances of the case. That is what the rule says. But (subject to the guidance that we give below) the other circumstances should be given less weight than the two considerations which are specifically mentioned.

[38] In the 18th implementation lecture on the Jackson reforms delivered on 22 March 2013, the Master of the Rolls said in relation to CPR 3.9 that there was now to be a shift away from exclusively focusing on doing justice in the individual case. He said:

> "25. In order to achieve this, the Woolf reforms and now the Jackson reforms were and are not intended to render the overriding objective, or rule 3.9, subject to an overarching consideration of securing justice in the individual case. If that had been the intention, a tough application to compliance would have been difficult to justify and even more problematic to apply in practice. The fact that since 1999 the tough rules to which Brooke LJ referred have not been applied with sufficient rigour is testament to a failure to understand that that was not the intention.
> 26. The revisions to the overriding objective and to rule 3.9, and particularly the fact that rule 3.9 now expressly refers back to the revised overriding objective, are intended to make clear that the relationship between justice and procedure has changed. It has changed not by transforming rules and rule compliance into trip wires. Nor has it changed it by turning the rules and rule compliance into the mistress rather than the handmaid of justice. If that were the case then we would have, quite impermissibly, rendered compliance an end in itself and one superior to doing justice in any case. It has changed because doing justice is not something distinct from, and superior to, the overriding objective. Doing justice in each set of proceedings is to ensure that proceedings are dealt with justly and at proportionate cost. Justice in the individual case is now only achievable through the proper application of the CPR consistently with the overriding objective.
> 27. The tougher, more robust approach to rule-compliance and relief from sanctions is intended to ensure that justice can be done in the majority of cases. This requires an acknowledgement that the achievement of justice means something different now. Parties can no longer expect indulgence if they fail to comply with their procedural obligations. Those obligations not only serve the purpose of ensuring that they conduct the litigation proportionately in order to ensure their own costs are kept within proportionate bounds. But more importantly they serve the wider public interest of ensuring that

other litigants can obtain justice efficiently and proportionately, and that the court enables them to do so."

[39] We endorse this approach. The importance of the court having regard to the needs and interests of all court users when case managing in an individual case is well illustrated by what occurred in the present case. If the claimant had complied with para 4 of PD 51D, the Master would have given case management and costs budgeting directions on 18 June and the case would have proceeded in accordance with those directions. Instead, an adjournment was necessary and the hearing was abortive. In order to accommodate the adjourned hearing within a reasonable time, the Master vacated a half day appointment which had been allocated to deal with claims by persons who had been affected by asbestos-related diseases.

[40] We hope that it may be useful to give some guidance as to how the new approach should be applied in practice. It will usually be appropriate to start by considering the nature of the non-compliance with the relevant rule, practice direction or court order. If this can properly be regarded as trivial, the court will usually grant relief provided that an application is made promptly. The principle "*de minimis non curat lex*" (the law is not concerned with trivial things) applies here as it applies in most areas of the law. Thus, the court will usually grant relief if there has been no more than an insignificant failure to comply with an order: for example, where there has been a failure of form rather than substance; or where the party has narrowly missed the deadline imposed by the order, but has otherwise fully complied with its terms. We acknowledge that even the question of whether a default is insignificant may give rise to dispute and therefore to contested applications. But that possibility cannot be entirely excluded from any regime which does not impose rigid rules from which no departure, however minor, is permitted.

[41] If the non-compliance cannot be characterised as trivial, then the burden is on the defaulting party to persuade the court to grant relief. The court will want to consider why the default occurred. If there is a good reason for it, the court will be likely to decide that relief should be granted. For example, if the reason why a document was not filed with the court was that the party or his solicitor suffered from a debilitating illness or was involved in an accident, then, depending on the circumstances, that may constitute a good reason. Later developments in the course of the litigation process are likely to be a good reason if they show that the period for compliance originally imposed was unreasonable, although the period seemed to be reasonable at the time and could not realistically have been the subject of an appeal. But mere overlooking a deadline, whether on account of overwork or otherwise, is unlikely to be a good reason. We understand that solicitors may be under pressure and have too much work. It may be that this is what occurred in the present case. But that will rarely be a good reason. Solicitors cannot take on too much work and expect to be able to persuade a court that this is a good reason for their failure to meet deadlines. They should either delegate the work to others in their firm or, if they are unable to do this, they should not take on the work at all. This

may seem harsh especially at a time when some solicitors are facing serious financial pressures. But the need to comply with rules, practice directions and court orders is essential if litigation is to be conducted in an efficient manner. If departures are tolerated, then the relaxed approach to civil litigation which the *Jackson* reforms were intended to change will continue. We should add that applications for an extension of time made before time has expired will be looked upon more favourably than applications for relief from sanction made after the event.

[42] A similar approach to that which we have just described has been adopted in relation to applications for an extension to the period of validity of a claim form under CPR 7.6. In *Hashtroodi v Hancock* [2004] EWCA Civ 652, [2004] 1 WLR 3206, this court said that (i) the discretion to extend time should be exercised in accordance with the overriding objective and (ii) the reason for the failure to serve the claim form in time is highly material. At para 19, the court said:

> "If there is a very good reason for the failure to serve the claim form within the specified period, then an extension of time will usually be granted….The weaker the reason, the more likely the court will be to refuse to grant the extension."

[43] This approach should also be adopted in relation to CPR 3.9. In short, good reasons are likely to arise from circumstances outside the control of the party in default: see the useful discussion in *Blackstone's Guide to The Civil Reforms J 2013* (Stuart Syme and Derek French, OUP 2013) at paras 5.85 to 5.91 and the article by Professor Zuckerman *"The revised CPR 3.9: a coded message demanding articulation"* in Civil Quarterly J 2013 at pp 9 to 11.

[44] Mr Browne sought to rely on certain factors which, he contended, showed that the sanction should not have been imposed by the Master in the first place. That was in our view a misguided submission. An application for relief from a sanction presupposes that the sanction has in principle been properly imposed. If a party wishes to contend that it was not appropriate to make the order, that should be by way of appeal or, exceptionally, by asking the court which imposed the order to vary or revoke it under CPR 3.1(7). The circumstances in which the latter discretion can be exercised were considered by this court in *Tibbles v SIG Plc (trading as Asphaltic Roofing Supplies)* [2012] EWCA Civ 518, [2012] 1 WLR 2591. The court held that considerations of finality, the undesirability of allowing litigants to have two bites at the cherry and the need to avoid undermining the concept of appeal all required a principled curtailment of an otherwise apparently open discretion. The discretion might be appropriately exercised normally only (i) where there had been a material change of circumstances since the order was made; (ii) where the facts on which the original decision was made had been misstated; or (iii) where there had been a manifest mistake on the part of the judge in formulating

the order. Moreover, as the court emphasised, the application must be made promptly. This reasoning has equal validity in the context of an application under CPR 3.9.

[45] On an application for relief from a sanction, therefore, the starting point should be that the sanction has been properly imposed and complies with the overriding objective. If the application for relief is combined with an application to vary or revoke under CPR 3.1(7), then that should be considered first and the *Tibbles* criteria applied. But if no application is made, it is not open to him to complain that the order should not have been made, whether on the grounds that it did not comply with the overriding objective or for any other reason. In the present case, the sanction is stated in CPR 3.14 itself: unless the court otherwise orders, the defaulting party will be treated as having filed a budget comprising only the applicable court fees. It is not open to that party to complain that the sanction does not comply with the overriding objective or is otherwise unfair. The words "unless the court otherwise orders" are intended to ensure that the sanction is imposed to give effect to the overriding objective. As we have said, the principles by which the court should decide whether to order "otherwise" are likely to be the same as the principles by which an application under CPR 3.9 is determined. In most cases, the question whether to relieve a party who has failed to file a costs budget in accordance with CPR 3.13 from the CPR 3.14 sanction will therefore be dealt with under CPR 3.14. That did not happen in the present case. That is why the question of relief from sanctions was dealt with under CPR 3.9.

[46] The new more robust approach that we have outlined above will mean that from now on relief from sanctions should be granted more sparingly than previously. There will be some lawyers who have conducted litigation in the belief that what Sir Rupert Jackson described as "the culture of delay and non-compliance" will continue despite the introduction of the *Jackson* reforms. But the Implementation Lectures given well before 1 April 2013 were widely publicised. No lawyer should have been in any doubt as to what was coming. We accept that changes in litigation culture will not occur overnight. But we believe that the wide publicity that is likely to be given to this judgment should ensure that the necessary changes will take place before long.

[47] We recognise that there are those who will find this new approach unattractive. There may be signs that it is not being applied by some judges. In *Ian Wyche v Careforce Group Plc* [2013] EWHC 3282, the defendant had failed to comply in all respects with an "unless" order. Walker J acceded to an application for relief under CPR 3.9 for two failures which he described as "material in the sense that they were more than trivial". But he said that they were "unintentional and minor failings in the course of diligently seeking to comply with the order". At para 61 of his judgment, Walker J said:

> "The culture which the court seeks to foster is a culture in which both sides take a common sense and practical approach, minimising interlocutory disputes and working in an orderly and mutually efficient

manner towards the date fixed for trial. It would be the antithesis of that culture if substantial amounts of time and money are wasted on preparation for and conduct of satellite litigation about the consequences of truly minor failings when diligently seeking to comply with an 'unless' order."

[48] We have earlier said that the court should usually grant relief for trivial breaches. We are not sure in what sense the judge was using the word "unintentional". In line with the guidance we have already given, we consider that well-intentioned incompetence, for which there is no good reason, should not usually attract relief from a sanction unless the default is trivial. We share the judge's desire to discourage satellite litigation, but that is not a good reason for adopting a more relaxed approach to the enforcement of compliance with rules, practice directions and orders. In our view, once it is well understood that the courts will adopt a firm line on enforcement, litigation will be conducted in a more disciplined way and there should be fewer applications under CPR 3.9. In other words, once the new culture becomes accepted, there should be less satellite litigation, not more.

[49] The other decision to which we wish to refer is that of Andrew Smith J in *Raayan Al Iraq Co Ltd v Trans Victory Marine Inc* [2013] EWHC 2696 (Comm). The claimant applied for an extension of two days for the service of its particulars of claim. In substance, the application was for relief from sanctions under CPR 3.9. The judge acknowledged that the list of circumstances that was itemised in the earlier version of the rule had gone. Nevertheless, he proceeded "somewhat reluctantly" to apply the old checklist of factors. We accept that, depending on the facts of the case, it will be appropriate to consider some or even all of these factors as part of "all the circumstances of the case". But, as we have already said, the most important factors are the need for litigation to be conducted efficiently and at proportionate cost and to enforce compliance with rules, practice directions and orders.

[50] Having examined the case by reference to the old checklist of factors, Andrew Smith J concluded at para 18 that the "overriding objective demands that relief be granted and I grant it". But it seems to us that he may not have recognised the particular importance of the two elements of the overriding objective that are mentioned in the revised version of CPR 3.9. It is true that at para 15 the judge referred to the culture of delay and non-compliance and what Sir Rupert Jackson had said about that in his Final Report. As to the effect of the revision to CPR 3.9, he said:

"Nor do I accept that the change in the Rule or a change in the attitude or approach of the courts to applications of this kind means that relief from sanctions will be refused even where injustice would result."

[51] It seems to us that, in making this observation, the judge was focusing exclusively on doing justice between the parties in the individual case and not applying the new approach which seeks to have regard to a wide range of interests.

The application for relief in the present case

[52] We start by re-iterating a point that has been made before, namely that this court will not lightly interfere with a case management decision. In *Mannion v Ginty* [2012] EWCA Civ 1667 at para 18, Lewison LJ said:

> "It has been said more than once in this court, it is vital for the Court of Appeal to uphold robust fair case management decisions made by first instance judges."

[53] We have set out the Master's reasoning at paras 16 to 18 above. Mr Browne makes a number of detailed criticisms of her reasoning. First, he says that she was wrong to state at para 35 that it was only as a result of being chased by her that the claimant's solicitors filed the budget at the last minute. In our judgment, this was a reasonable view for the Master to hold. She did not know that, during the days before 18 June, the defendant's solicitors were chasing the claimant's solicitors for their costs budget and that their filing of the budget was probably in response to pressure from them rather than the court.

[54] Secondly, Mr Browne criticises the finding at para 38 of the judgment that the defendant's solicitors sought to engage the claimant's solicitors in discussion of budget assumptions. We accept that there was no specific evidence before the Master to support this finding. But as early as 11 June, the defendant's solicitors had been chasing the claimant's solicitors for their costs budget with a view to exchange. It is true that the defendant's solicitors did not spell out that, following exchange, they wished to discuss the budget assumptions. It can, however, properly be said that, until there had been an exchange, a discussion on assumptions would have been impossible.

[55] Thirdly, Mr Browne criticises para 62. The aim of ensuring that the parties are on an equal footing is not only mentioned in PD 51D para 1.3, but also generally as part of the overriding objective. Mr Browne submits, therefore, that the Master erred in saying that this aim related to decisions made as part of cost budgeting, rather than sanctions for failure to engage with the process at all. There is some force in this criticism, but the Master correctly stated at para 62 that the new versions of the overriding objective and CPR 3.9 "highlight the emphasis to be placed, now, on rule compliance and one has to give effect to that".

[56] In our view, even if there is some force in all three of these criticisms, they do not go to the heart of the Master's reasoning. Her main finding was that the claimant's solicitors had been in breach of two provisions of PD 51D and that,

in the light of the new approach mandated by the *Jackson* reforms, the case for granting relief from the CPR 3.14 sanction was not established.

[57] Finally, Mr Browne submits that the decision to refuse relief did not give effect to the overriding objective. His main points are the same as those summarised at para 31 above. It is not suggested that the Master failed to have regard to any of these points in her comprehensive judgment. They would have carried considerable weight if the application had been considered under the earlier version of CPR 3.9. The Master was right to recognise that the emphasis has now changed. In these circumstances, we consider that there is no proper basis for interfering with her decision. On the question of prejudice, we wish to highlight the fact that there was no evidence to show what prejudice (if any) the claimant would suffer as a result of a refusal to grant relief.

[58] A central feature of Mr Browne's submission was that, whenever a sanction is imposed, the court must have regard to considerations of proportionality. In this case, he says that a more proportionate response would have been to grant partial relief from the sanction, for example, by making an order that the costs budget should be 50% of the actual estimated figure or should not include the costs connected with the budget itself. We accept that the Master had the power to make such an order. But we do not consider that the grant of partial relief from CPR 3.14 will often be appropriate. The merit of the rule is that it sets out a stark and simple default sanction. The expectation is that the sanction will usually apply unless (i) the breach is trivial or (ii) there is a good reason for it. It is true that the court has the power to grant relief, but the expectation is that, unless (i) or (ii) is satisfied, the two factors mentioned in the rule will usually trump other circumstances. If partial relief were to be encouraged, that would give rise to uncertainty and complexity and stimulate satellite litigation.

Conclusion

[59] We therefore dismiss the appeals against both orders. The Master did not misdirect herself in any material respect or reach a conclusion which was not open to her. We acknowledge that it was a robust decision. She was, however, right to focus on the essential elements of the post-Jackson regime. The defaults by the claimant's solicitors were not minor or trivial and there was no good excuse for them. They resulted in an abortive costs budgeting hearing and an adjournment which had serious consequences for other litigants. Although it seems harsh in the individual case of Mr Mitchell's claim, if we were to overturn the decision to refuse relief, it is inevitable that the attempt to achieve a change in culture would receive a major setback.

[60] In the result, we hope that our decision will send out a clear message. If it does, we are confident that, in time, legal representatives will become more efficient and will routinely comply with rules, practice directions and orders. If

this happens, then we would expect that satellite litigation of this kind, which is so expensive and damaging to the civil justice system, will become a thing of the past.

Solicitors: *Atkins Thomson Solicitors* for the appellant
Simons Muirhead and *Burton Solicitors* for the respondent

INDEX

References are to paragraph numbers.

After the event (ATE) insurance	2.1
advice	2.3.15
qualified one-way costs shifting (QOCS) and	4.8
recovery of premium	2.3.1, 2.5.5.1
Alternative business structures (ABS)	1.1.3
Appeals	
1 April 2013 CFAs	2.3.3
detailed assessment	9.3
qualified one-way costs shifting (QOCS)	4.10
Arkin Principle	3.3
Assignment of CFAs	2.4.1
burden of contract cannot be assigned	2.4.1.2
death	2.4.1.3
dissatisfied clients	2.4.1.3
minors	2.4.1.3
patients	2.4.1.3
personal contracts	2.4.1.1
Before the event (BTE) insurance	2.3.6
discounted CFA	2.3.12
instruction by insurer	2.3.9
satisfactory	2.3.7
no instruction from insurers	2.3.13
Bill of costs	
budget	6.2.9
form of	9.9
points of dispute	9.10
Budgeting	6.2
assumptions	6.2.4
cost management conferences	6.2.8
cost management orders	6.2.7, 6.2.9, 6.4
costs process	6.4
counsel	1.10
fast track, non-applicable	5.1.5
filing and service of budget	6.2.4
failure to file	6.2.6
form	6.2.4
completing	6.2.5
hearing preparation	6.2.9
pilots	6.5
planning	
the case	6.2.2
the firm	6.2.1
post issue	6.2.4

Budgeting—*continued*	
teamwork	6.2.3
variations	6.5
Burden of contract	
assignment	2.4.1.2
Cancellation of Contracts Made in a Consumer's Home or Place of Work etc Regulations 2008	1.7
Capping	5.1.1, 5.1.2, 6.3
application for	6.5
defendant's fast track costs	5.4.6
Children *see also* Minors	
fixed recoverable costs	
fast track	5.4.4
settlements	5.3.4
Civil Justice Council	
conditional fee agreements (CFAs)	3.1.3
Working Party	3.1.5, 3.6
Client care	1.2
outcomes	1.2, 1.3
'indicative behaviours' (IBs)	1.2
Principles	1.2
Client costs	1.9, 5.1.1
assessment	1.9
delivery of bill	1.9
fixed recoverable costs *see* Fixed recoverable costs	
Code of Conduct *see* Solicitors Regulation Authority (SRA)	
Conditional fee agreements (CFAs)	2.1
1 April 2013	2.3
appeals	2.3.3
calculating success fee	2.3.18
completing agreement	2.3.17
counsel	2.3.4
disbursements	2.3.16
form	2.3.5
legal expenses insurance *see* Legal expenses insurance (LEI)	
personal injury exceptions	2.3.1
qualifying date for regime	2.3.2
collective CFAs (CCFAs)	2.3.2
1 November 2005–31 March 2013	2.2
assignment *see* Assignment of CFAs	
counsel	1.10
defective *see* Defective CFAs	
development	2.1

Conditional fee agreements (CFAs)—*continued*	
signed pre-1 April 2013 – costs disclosure	9.17.1
Consumer Protection (Distance Selling) Regulations 2000	1.8
Contingency fee agreements *see* Damages-based agreements (DBAs)	
Counsel	1.10
budgeting	1.10
conditional fee agreement (CFA) 1 April 2013	2.3.4
fixed recoverable costs	5.7
formal legal contract	1.10
Court orders	6.6
Damages-based agreements (DBAs)	
adverse costs liability	3.3
CFA v DBA	3.5
Civil Justice Council	3.1.3
Working Party	3.1.5, 3.6
content	3.6
contingency fees	
Ontario model	3.1.2, 3.4
United Kingdom	3.1.1
United States	3.1.2
future of	3.7
Jackson review	3.1.4
Legal Aid, Sentencing and Punishment of Offenders Act 2012 (LASPO)	3.2.1
additional requirements for personal injury claims	3.2.1.5
compliant DBA is 'not unenforceable'	3.2.1.1
indemnity principle applicable	3.2.1.6
meaning of DBA	3.2.1.2
prescribed requirements	3.2.1.3, 3.2.1.4
operation	3.4
Death	
assignment of CFAs	2.4.1.3
Deductible benefits	
Part 36 offers	7.5.7
Deed of variation	2.5.2
Default costs certificate	9.12
Defective CFAs	2.5
deed of variation	2.5.2
notice	2.5.7
price increase clause	2.5.6
rectification	2.5.1
equitable, by court	2.5.3
retrospectively	2.5.5
retrospectivity	
recoverability of ATE	2.5.5.1
termination of existing CFA and starting again	2.5.4
Detailed assessment	9.1
agreed costs	9.11
appeal, effect of	9.3

Detailed assessment—*continued*	
assessment procedure	
party and party costs	9.8
time for	9.7
authorised court officer	9.4
bill of costs	
form of	9.9
points of dispute	9.10
budget	6.2.9
costs disclosure	9.5
CFAs signed pre-1 April 2013	9.17.1
court orders	6.6
default costs certificate	9.12
hearing	9.15
requesting	9.13
provisional assessment	9.14
tactics	9.16
time for	9.2
venue	9.6
Disbursements	2.3.16
fast track fixed recoverable costs	5.4.3
Disclosure *see* Detailed assessment	
Dissatisfied clients	
assignment of CFAs	2.4.1.3
Final hearing summary assessment	8.3
Fixed recoverable costs	5.1.1
'between the parties' costs	5.1.1
budgets	5.1.5
counsel	5.7
CPR format	5.1.4
fast track	5.1.2, 5.1.3, 5.4
children	5.4.4
costs of interim applications	5.4.7
defendant's costs	5.4.6
disbursements	5.4.3
escape	5.4.5
fixed trial costs	5.2.2
offers	5.4.8
claimant's	5.4.8.2
defendant's	5.4.8.1
stages	5.4.2
tables	5.4.1
fixed costs	5.1.1, 5.1.2
future of	5.9
London weighting	5.5
multiple claimants	5.6
RTA claims	
first portal (notifications 30 April 2010–29 April 2013)	5.2.4
MIB schemes	
uninsured drivers	5.2.5.1
untraced drivers	5.2.5.2
'predictive costs' regime for low value claims	5.1.2
accidents 6 October 2003–31 July 2013	5.2.3
second portal	5.3
post-31 July 2013 accidents	5.3.2
road traffic cases	5.3.1
second portal	5.3
cases falling out of protocol	5.3.6

Index

Fixed recoverable costs—*continued*
  second portal—*continued*
    failure to follow protocol   5.3.5
    offers within portal   5.3.3
    post-31 July 2013 accidents   5.3.2
    road traffic cases   5.3.1
    settlements for children   5.3.4
  small claims track   5.2.1
  summary of applicable schemes   5.10
  swings and roundabouts of regimes   5.1.3
  working with   5.8

Hodgson immunity   3.3

'Indicative behaviours' (IBs)   1.1.1, 1.4
  client care and outcomes   1.2
  funding information to client   1.4.1
Interim applications   5.4.7
Interim payments
  multitrack trial   8.4

Jackson review
  pros and cons of contingency fee agreements   3.1.4
  qualified one-way costs shifting (QOCS)   4.2

Legal Aid, Sentencing and Punishment of Offenders Act 2012 (LASPO)
  damages-based agreements (DBAs)   3.2.1
    additional requirements for personal injury claims   3.2.1.5
    compliant DBA is 'not unenforceable'   3.2.1.1
    indemnity principle applicable   3.2.1.6
    meaning of DBA   3.2.1.2
    prescribed requirements   3.2.1.3, 3.2.1.4
  referral fee ban   1.5
Legal expenses insurance (LEI)   2.3.6
  advice   2.3.15
  before the event (BTE) insurance   2.3.6
    satisfactory   2.3.7
    no instruction from insurers   2.3.13
  freedom of choice   2.3.8
  instruction by BTE insurer   2.3.9
  retainer   2.3.10
    discounted CFA   2.3.12
    terms and conditions of business   2.3.11
  self insurance   2.3.14
London weighting
  fixed recoverable costs   5.5

Minors *see also* Children
  assignment of CFAs   2.4.1.3
Mixed claims   4.7

Multiple claimants
  fixed recoverable costs   5.6
Multitrack trial   8.4

'New claims process'
  road traffic accidents   5.1.2
Non-portal offers
  acceptance   7.5.3
    procedure following   7.5.10, 7.5.11
    when permission is needed   7.5.4
  amount
    as single sum, periodic payment, etc   7.5.5
    interest   7.5.6
  costs following trial on liability or preliminary issue   7.5.12
  deductible benefits   7.5.7
  defendant failing to make offer   7.5.15
  formalities   7.5.1
  period for acceptance
    cost consequences of accepting offer within   7.5.8
    late acceptance outside   7.5.9
  tactical offers   7.5.14
  timing and clarification   7.5.2
  withdrawal   7.5.13

Offers to settle claims *see* Part 36 offers to settle

'Outcomes-focused regulation' (OFR)   1.1

Part 36 offers to settle
  CPR, rr 36.1–36.15 claims   7.4
  CPR, rr 36.16–36.22 portal claims   7.4
  dealing with   7.3
  fixed recoverable costs   5.4.8
    claimant's offers   5.4.8.2
    defendant's offers   5.4.8.1
  history   7.1
  Jackson reforms   7.2
  non-portal offers *see* Non-portal offers
  portal offers   7.6
  qualified one-way costs shifting (QOCS)   4.4
Patients
  assignment of CFAs   2.4.1.3
Personal contracts
  assignment   2.4.1.1
Personal injury claims
  ATE insurance   4.8
  CFA exceptions   2.3.1
  fixed recoverable costs
    fast track, tables   5.4.1
    small claims track   5.2.1
  qualified one-way costs shifting (QOCS)   4.7
  statutory requirements   3.2.1.5

'Predictive costs' regime
  low value RTA claims   5.1.2
    accidents 6 October 2003–31 July
      2013   5.2.3
Proportionality   6.1
  achieving   6.4
  'and at proportionate cost'   6.1.1
  post-1 April 2013   6.1.1
  principles   6.2
  transitional provisions   6.1.2

Qualified one-way costs shifting
    (QOCS)   4.1
  appeals   4.10
  application of regime   4.3
  CPR and   4.3
    Part 36 offers   4.4
  definition   4.3
  discontinued claims   4.9
  'fundamental dishonesty'   4.6
  Jackson review   4.2
  mixed claims   4.7
  strike out applications   4.5

Referral arrangements   1.5
  joint or shared marketing
    arrangements   1.5
  referral fee ban   1.5
    breach of   1.5
Retainer   1.6
  costs part   1.6
  legal expenses insurance (LEI)   2.3.10
    discounted CFA   2.3.12
    terms and conditions of
      business   2.3.11
  non-costs parts   1.6
  termination   1.6
  types   1.6
Risk management and compliance
  Compliance Officer for Finance and
    Administration (COFA)   1.1.2
  Compliance Officer for Legal
    Practice (COLP)   1.1.2
  Suitability Test   1.1.2
Road traffic accident (RTA) claims
  first portal (notifications 30 April
    2010–29 April 2013)   5.2.4

Road traffic accident (RTA)
    claims—*continued*
  MIB schemes
    uninsured drivers   5.2.5.1
    untraced drivers   5.2.5.2
  'new claims process'   5.1.2
  'predictive costs' regime   5.1.2
    accidents 6 October 2003–31 July
      2013   5.2.3
  second portal   5.3
    post-31 July 2013 accidents   5.3.2
    road traffic cases   5.3.1

Self insurance   2.3.14
Small claims track
  personal injury cases   5.2.1
Solicitors Regulation Authority (SRA)   1.1
  alternative business structures
    (ABS)   1.1.3
  breach of Principles   1.1.1
  client care and costs   1.2
    outcomes   1.2, 1.3
    'indicative behaviours' (IBs)   1.2
  Handbook   1.1
  'indicative behaviours' (IBs)   1.1.1, 1.4
    funding information to client   1.4.1
  'outcomes-focused regulation'
    (OFR)   1.1
  referral arrangements   1.5
  retainer   1.6
  risk management and compliance
    Compliance Officer for Finance
      and Administration
      (COFA)   1.1.2
    Compliance Officer for Legal
      Practice (COLP)   1.1.2
    Suitability Test   1.1.2
  ten mandatory Principles   1.1.1
Success fee
  calculation   2.3.18
Summary assessment   6.7, 8.2
  budget   6.2.9
  final hearing   8.3

Trial   8.1
  multitrack   8.4
  summary assessment   8.2
    final hearing   8.3